Simplifies

Installation,

Optimization, and

Troubleshooting

Building Local Windows for Workgroups

Simplifies

Installation,

Optimization, and

Troubleshooting

Building Local Area Networks with
Windows for Workgroups

James Queen

M&T Books
A Division of M&T Publishing, Inc.
411 Borel Avenue, Suite 100
San Mateo, CA 94402

© 1993 by M&T Publishing, Inc.

Printed in the United States of America

All rights reserved. No part of this book may be reproduced or transmitted in any form or by any means, electronic or mechanical, including photocopying, recording, or by any information storage and retrieval system, without prior written permission from the Publisher. Contact the Publisher for information on foreign rights.

Limits of Liability and Disclaimer of Warranty
The Author and Publisher of this book have used their best efforts in preparing the book and the programs contained in it. These efforts include the development, research, and testing of the theories and programs to determine their effectiveness.

The Author and Publisher make no warranty of any kind, expressed or implied, with regard to these programs or the documentation contained in this book. The Author and Publisher shall not be liable in any event for incidental or consequential damages in connection with, or arising out of, the furnishing, performance, or use of these programs.

All brand names, trademarks, and registered trademarks are the property of their respective holders.

Library of Congress Cataloging-in-Publication Data

Queen, Jim
    Building local area networks with windows for workgroups / Jim Queen
      p. cm.
    Includes index.
    ISBN 1-55851-299-3

96   95   94   93   4 3 2 1

Developmental Editor: Tom Maremaa
Copy Editor: Peter Weverka
Cover Design: Lauren Smith Design

Table of Contents

Why This Book Is for You 1

Introduction 3
    Chapter-by-Chapter Summary 3
    Windows—Past, Present, and Future 5
        Windows for Workgroups Features 6
    A Proviso 8

Chapter 1: Hardware and Operating System Requirements 9
    Designing the Network 9
    Windows Operating Modes 10
    Workstation Requirements 11
        CPU Requirements 11
        Memory Requirements 12
        Hard Disk Requirements 12
        Video Requirements 13
        Mouse Requirements 13
        DOS Requirements 14
    Choosing Network Components 14

Chapter 2: Designing the Physical Network 21
Cabling the Network...21
    Star Wiring Systems 22
    Ring Cabling 25
    Bus Cabling 25
    Comparing Cable Designs...26
Selecting a LAN Architecture...27
    Ethernet..28
    ArcNet...29
    Token-Ring 30
    Comparing LAN Architectures 31
Summary..31

Chapter 3: Installing Windows for Workgroups 33
Creating a "Master" Windows Installation Server 33
    Choosing EXPRESS or CUSTOM Installation 35
    Registering and Adding Protocols to Windows..................36
    The CONFIG.SYS and AUTOEXEC.BAT Files 37
Starting Windows for Workgroups 38
Publishing the Master Windows Directory...............................41

Chapter 4: Using Workgroup Connection 45
What is Workgroup Connection?...45
Installing Workgroup Connection...46
Accessing Directories and Printers 53
Installing Windows from the Network......................................54

Chapter 5: Optimizing Server Performance.......................57
Starting Windows and Logging On 57
Customizing Windows for Each Workstation 58
    What to Do about Lost Passwords..59
    Making Network Modifications with the Control Panel.....60
    Sharing Resources vs. Local Application Performance........61
    Network Settings: Adapters, Logon, Networks, Passwords 62
    Effective 386 Enhanced Mode Settings 68

Table of Contents

    Scheduling and Virtual Memory 69
    Further Suggestions for Better Server Performance 70

Chapter 6: Using Windows for Workgroups 73
  Accessing Network Resources with UNCs 73
  Sharing Directories with the File Manager 76
  Printer Sharing on the Network 80
    Handling Print Jobs with the Print Manager 80
    Adding Separator Pages 81
    Background Printing 82
  The Common Dialog Library 83

Chapter 7: Windows for Workgroups Accessories 85
  ClipBook Viewer: A Clipboard for the Network 86
    Accessing a Shared ClipBook Page 88
  WinMeter: Tracking CPU Usage 89
  NetWatcher: Monitoring Connections to Your Workstation ... 92
  Chat: Talking with Other Users 93

Chapter 8: The Network Administrator 97
  Mail Administration 97
  Sharing Programs and Data Files 98
  Software Licensing Requirements 100
  Preventing and Controlling Viral Infections 101
  Network Backup and Recovery 102
  The Role of the Network Administrator 105

Chapter 9: Microsoft Mail 107
  How Mail Works 107
    Differences with Mail for PC LANs 108
  Creating a Post Office 109
  The Post Office Manager 112
  Using Mail 114
    Creating and Sending a Message 116
    Reading Messages 120

Storing Messages..120
Importing and Exporting Folders......................................122
Customizing Mail..123

Chapter 10: Schedule+ **125**
Setting Up Schedule+...126
An Overview of Schedule+..126
Scheduling Appointments..127
The Planner...130
Maintaining a Task List...131
Sending and Receiving Meeting Invitations.....................132
Schedule+ and the Network..134
Accessing Workgroup Schedules..135
Tracking Workgroup Resources..137
Allowing Others to Update Your Schedule.....................138
Merging Off-Line and Network Schedules.....................138
Schedule+: A Solid Performer..140

Chapter 11: Windows INI Files..**141**
Working with INI Files..141
WIN.INI...144
SYSTEM.INI..146
PROGMAN.INI..148
Summary...152

Chapter 12: DOS Applications in a Windows Environment **153**
Windows and the PIF File...154
DOS Applications in Windows' Standard and
Enhanced Modes..154
Working with PIF Files..155
Creating or Modifying a PIF...157
Enhanced Mode PIF Settings—Standard Options...........160
Enhanced Mode PIF Settings—Advanced Options.........164

Table of Contents

Standard Mode PIF Settings 168
Selecting Applications for the Network 169

Chapter 13: Troubleshooting Windows for Workgroups 171
Common Problems with Using Windows for Workgroups ... 171
    The Setup Program Fails to Work 171
    The Setup Program for the Network Fails 172
    The Video Display Goes Blank or Is Incorrect................ 172
    Windows Does Not Work in Enhanced Mode................ 173
    Windows Does Not Start in Enhanced Mode 174
    A Disk Error Is Reported when Accessing
        the Local Hard Drive 174
    The Workstation Can't Access the Network 175
    One Workstation Can't Attach to Another 175
    The Workstation Can't Print a Document 176
    An Error Message Appears when Printing
        to the Network Printer 176
    The Mouse Doesn't Work in Windows Applications 176
    The Mouse Doesn't Work in DOS Applications 177
    The DOS Application Crashes or Reports
        Insufficient Memory 177
    The DOS Communications Program Is
        Performing Poorly 178
    Specific DOS and Network Applications Are
        Experiencing Problems 179
    The Mail Program Cannot Access the Mail Directory ... 179
    NetWare Users Cannot See the Workgroup 180
    Users Can't Connect to a CD-ROM Drive
        on a Workstation 180
    Difficulties with TrueType Fonts 181
    System Integrity Violations 181
    General Protection Faults 182
Getting Additional Help 182
Microsoft Resource Kits 183

Building Local Area Networks with Windows for Workgroups

Appendix A: Windows Shortcut Keys 185

Appendix B: Windows for Workgroups Files 187
    WIN.COM 188
    The Core Files 188
    System Driver and Font Driver Files 188
        Mouse Driver Files 190
        Display Driver Files 190
        Other Driver Files 191
        Printer Driver Files 191
        Network Driver Files 194
        Multimedia Driver Files 195
        Font Files 196
        Vector Font Files 198
        TrueType Font Files 198
        Font Files for MS-DOS 198
        International Support Files 199
    MS-DOS Support Files for Windows for Workgroups 200
        MS-DOS Driver Files 200
        NDIS Network Adapter Card Drivers 201
        WinOldAp and the Grabber Files 202
        Files for Standard Mode Operation 202
        Files for Enhanced Mode Operation 203
    Files for Windows for Workgroups Applications 204
    Setup Files 208
    Other Files 209
        Custom Support Files 209
        Miscellaneous Files 209
    Deleting Files 209

Appendix C: Network Cabling Specifications 211
    Token-Ring Cable Specifications 211
        Basic Specifications 212
    ArcNet Cable Specifications 214
        Basic Specifications 215

Table of Contents

    Ethernet Cable Specifications 217
        10BaseT 218
        Basic Specifications 219
        10Base5 220
        Basic Specifications 220
        10Base2 221
        Basic Specifications 222

Glossary **225**

Index **235**

Why This Book Is for You

If you are responsible for installing or managing a Windows for Workgroups LAN, *Building Local Area Networks with Windows for Workgroups* is for you.

- For the novice, this book introduces local area networking technology and the Windows for Workgroups operating system. You will learn LAN basics, including hardware selection, cabling, installation, backup strategies, as well as how to share resources and use DOS applications on the network

- Experienced installers, resellers, consultants, and system administrators will benefit from the detailed troubleshooting advice, customization techniques, and insider tips for making the network run smoothly and increase user productivity.

From LAN fundamentals to advanced Windows for Workgroups topics, *Building Local Area Networks with Windows for Workgroups* presents a wealth of valuable information in a clear and practical manner that will help you make effective LAN planning and operating decisions.

Introduction

This book is intended for Windows for Workgroups network installers, administrators, and end-users. It provides a step-by-step guide both for installing the Windows network environment and using each network feature. Rather than delve into the fundamentals of the Windows operating system itself, this book focuses on the elements of Windows for Workgroups that set it apart from its cousin, Windows 3.1.

CHAPTER-BY-CHAPTER SUMMARY

Building Local Area Networks with Windows for Workgroups follows the natural progression of a network installation.

- Chapter 1 Describes the hardware and software requirements for a successful installation.
- Chapter 2 Discusses the physical design of the network cable plant.
- Chapter 3 Explains an installation method that can drastically reduce the amount of time it takes to install and update workstation copies of Windows for Workgroups. This installation method requires a companion product to Windows for Workgroups called Workgroup Connection.

Building Local Area Networks with Windows for Workgroups

Chapter 4	Provides detailed information on using Workgroup Connection both to install Windows and to provide DOS access to the network.
Chapter 5	Provides detailed instructions on configuring the network features of Windows for Workgroups via the Control Panel.
Chapter 6	Describes the network features of Windows for Workgroups and how to use them.
Chapter 7	Discusses new or updated Windows accessories that support the network.
Chapter 8	Discusses the role of the network administrator and the typical functions required for network maintenance.
Chapter 9	Provides detailed instructions on using Microsoft Mail with Windows for Workgroups.
Chapter 10	Shows you how to use Schedule+ with Windows for Workgroups.
Chapter 11	Discusses the functions of the initialization (INI) files used by Windows for Workgroups, and offers some undocumented settings you can use to manage the network.
Chapter 12	Looks at the form and function of DOS PIFs (program information files). While PIF settings are not specific to Windows for Workgroups, the potential difficulties in running DOS applications in a Windows environment warrant this information.
Chapter 13	Looks at common problems you could encounter with Windows for Workgroups. Each example includes a discussion of the various causes and recommends ways to identify and resolve the problem.
Appendix A	Provides information on Windows keyboard shortcuts.
Appendix B	Provides a complete listing of all the Windows for Workgroups files.
Appendix C	Provides cabling design specifications.
Glossary	Supplied definitions to commonly used terms.

Introduction

As you can see, there is something for everyone here. DOS users who wish to access network resources via Workgroup Connection will be interested in Chapter 4. Mail and Schedule+ users can go to Chapters 9 and 10 for a complete guide to these programs. The remaining chapters are geared more for the network installer and administrator.

WINDOWS—PAST, PRESENT, AND FUTURE

Microsoft Windows is arguably the first graphical interface standard to gain widespread user acceptance in the MS-DOS arena. While other products, notably Quarterdeck's DesqView, provided multitasking capabilities for Intel-based CPUs, the ability to run off-the-shelf applications concurrently coupled with the ease of use of the graphical interface virtually made Windows 3.0 an overnight success. Still, Windows 3.0 had enough problems to prevent its widespread use in the corporate environment. It did not provide for memory protection between applications, which resulted in frequent crashes and the dreaded unrecoverable applications error (UAE). Windows applications tended to be quite specific about what other applications could run concurrently. Windows 3.0 also suffered from performance problems, especially in printing. The largest obstacle to corporate acceptance, however, was the lack of network support. Microsoft initially left network interfacing to vendors such as Novell. Typically, this resulted in patches and network driver updates being distributed almost every month from a variety of sources.

Microsoft responded to the criticisms of Windows 3.0 by releasing Windows 3.1 and outlining its strategy for the continued development of the Windows product line, a strategy that includes the refinement of Windows, the addition of native network support through Windows for Workgroups, and Windows NT. Windows and Windows for Workgroups still operate under MS-DOS, but Windows NT will function both as the operating system and the user interface. It will be able to function in both standalone and networked modes. Windows NT builds on the graphical interface and ease of use of the Windows environment, while delivering Microsoft's first true 32-bit multitasking operating system. As a network server, Windows NT should provide services identical to those of a Windows for Workgroups server, but provide substantial performance improvements as well.

Understanding Microsoft's strategy helps us understand its motivation for developing Windows for Workgroups. Windows 3.1 is a robust product that can operate under a variety of LAN operating systems, but Microsoft would undoubtedly prefer your network operating system to be Windows NT. The network interface in Windows for Workgroups provides a taste of what we can expect from NT. Microsoft took the basic Windows 3.1 environment, added features for the sharing of resources between clients, and bundled them with typical workgroup communication software packages such as e-mail and calendaring. The message here is that users who develop a networked PC environment under Windows for Workgroups will be able to step up to Windows NT seamlessly. Servers that require the performance gains of Windows NT can be upgraded selectively, while users can continue to operate under Windows 3.1. Even without the potential for Windows NT, however, Windows for Workgroups is a powerful and robust peer-to-peer local area network. For environments that prefer the Windows interface, it is a viable alternative to other workgroup solutions.

Windows for Workgroups Features

The major enhancements to Windows for Workgroups include:

- An updated File Manager that allows you to make your floppy, hard disk, or CDROM drive directories shared workgroup resources and assign local drive letters to other workstation resources.

- An enhanced Print Manager for sharing workgroup printers. The Print Manager has been upgraded to support banner pages that separate user print jobs.

Introduction

- Microsoft Mail and Schedule+, which provide electronic mail services and the ability to schedule meetings with other workgroup members.

- NetWatcher and WinMeter, two accessories for monitoring the utilization of system resources.

- Chat, an interactive accessory that allows workgroup members to "type" messages to one another.

- The ClipBook, an update to the Windows Clipboard that uses object linking and embedding (OLE) and allows pasted objects to be updated automatically when the source object is modified.

- Built-in support for the Novell NetWare IPX/SPX protocol stack. Workgroup users can use both workgroup resources and NetWare resources concurrently.

- Control Panel support for the allocation of CPU resources between local applications and network requests.

- Workgroup Connection, which allows workgroup PCs to access shared resources directly from DOS. Workstations that do not meet the minimum requirements for Windows, such as XT class systems, can also use Workgroup Connection. Included with Workgroup Connection is a DOS-based Mail program that communicates with Windows Mail. Workgroup Connection can make Windows installation a lot easier. Rather than carry floppy disks to each workgroup PC, you can install Windows from a central location with Workgroup Connection.

Building Local Area Networks with Windows for Workgroups

A PROVISO

Somewhere out there is a network manager who will attempt to network hundreds of workstations with Windows for Workgroups. Realistically, however, you should consider several factors when building a WfW network.

Windows for Workgroups connections use a communications protocol called NETBEUI, an extension of IBM's NETBIOS protocol. NETBIOS's name scheme requires the network manager to assign unique network names to every device on the network. In an environment with 20 to 30 users, this can easily result in a name table in excess of one hundred names. In larger networks, the number of users on a single segment or server can cause serious performance delays. With other networks, savvy network managers can segment the network by adding additional network adapters to a server, by installing additional servers, and by using routers to segment traffic. NETBIOS, however, is not a routable protocol. Traffic on a segment must be bridged to all other segments when communicating across the network, so segmenting is not possible.

In reality, Windows for Workgroups is designed for networks of 2 to 25 users. The software itself is not limited to a specific number of users, but the administrative overhead and performance penalties associated with a larger number of users becomes prohibitive. Windows for Workgroups' native support for Novell's NetWare and Microsoft LAN Manager, however, will allow you to incorporate a WfW environment into a larger network and still maintain virtually autonomous networks for smaller workgroups within a corporation. Windows for Workgroups is much more at home, however, in smaller companies who neither need nor can afford the expense of a complex network operating system.

1 CHAPTER

Hardware and Operating System Requirements

This chapter offers brief design tips for setting up a network, information about Windows operating modes, a description of hardware and software requirements for running a workstation, and some advice on choosing network components.

DESIGNING THE NETWORK

The one thing most likely to change in any network design is its size. As a consultant and network administrator with over ten years' experience, I have never in hundreds of network installations seen a network that did not expand, usually at the request of the same users who saw no reason for the LAN to begin with! As you design your system, consider its growth requirements for at least the next twelve months. While you may end up replacing some portions of your system sooner, a design that supports your growth requirements for at least a year will probably be worth what you paid for your LAN.

You don't want to reinstall your LAN wiring frequently. Unless you plan to redesign your office layout down the road, consider installing wiring in every location where you might eventually install a workstation. Do this at the same time that you wire for existing systems. By preparing for growth when you install your cable, you'll be able to add workstations with a minimum of disruption and in a simple, building-block fashion.

If you are using existing wiring, have a qualified installer check the wiring to verify that it meets the specifications for your network topology. Have the installer pay particular attention to cable lengths. If your cable installer is unfamiliar with the cable specifications for your network topology or suggests that the cable specifications are too rigid, get another installer!

Windows for Workgroups is a *peer-to-peer* operating system. This means that virtually any PC on the network can function as both a workstation and a server. As the network manager, you have to decide which systems will provide network disk directory and printer sharing. You can make every workstation on the network a shared device, but the costs will be high in terms of greater administrative complexity, additional user training and support, and the performance penalties inherent in providing shared resources. Because of these concerns, most peer networks evolve into a design remarkably similar to higher-end networks—one or more servers are selected as "dedicated" servers. Rather than upgrading all the systems in your environment, this design allows you to spend more money on a few selected systems but provide performance benefits to everyone on the LAN.

A network with more than 20 to 25 users likely has a greater number of shared printers, a fairly large number of user mailboxes to maintain, and possibly a significant number of shared network directories, as well as the user NETBIOS names themselves. About now is when you should start considering the selection of a full-time network administrator. While Windows for Workgroups builds on the ease-of-use of the Windows 3.1 environment, someone in your organization will need to be very familiar with the inner workings of WfW. A part-time administrator would ultimately be unable to support the system in the event of a problem.

WINDOWS OPERATING MODES

Since Windows for Workgroups is an extension of the basic Windows 3.1 platform, the basic requirements are identical. Windows sup-

Hardware and Operating System Requirements

ports Intel 80286, 80386, and 80486 processor based systems; however, some WWG features are not supported on 80286 systems.

Windows 3.1 supports two operating modes, *standard* and *enhanced*. Standard mode provides multitasking support for Windows applications and the ability to address up to 16Mb of extended memory. This is the only mode available to 80286 workstations. In standard mode, you can connect to shared directories and printers in your workgroup. You cannot, however, share your own directories or printers with other users. Although you can run DOS applications in standard mode, the DOS application will suspend all Windows programs when active, and Windows will suspend the DOS application when Windows applications are running.

Windows enhanced mode operations require an 80386SX or higher CPU. This mode takes advantage of the built-in memory management capabilities of these processors to provide multitasking support for both Windows and DOS applications. In enhanced mode, you can share your resources with others, even when running DOS applications.

WORKSTATION REQUIREMENTS

The CPU, memory, hard disk, video, mouse, and DOS requirements for running Windows for Workgroups on a workstation are described below.

CPU Requirements

Windows will select the appropriate operating mode on startup, based on the hardware it detects in your system.

- If you have an 80286 CPU with at least 1Mb of RAM or an 80386/80486 system with less than 3Mb of RAM, Windows will start in standard mode.

- If you have an 80386/80486 system with at least 3Mb of RAM, Windows will start in enhanced mode.

It is also possible to override these settings by using command line parameters when starting Windows. The command WIN/S will force your system to operate in standard mode. In some cases, you can use WIN/3 to force enhanced mode operations on 80386/80486 systems that have defaulted to standard mode (usually because of a lack of memory). Forcing your system to use enhanced mode is not generally recommended, however, since many operations may fail due to memory constraints.

Memory Requirements

Although 3Mb of RAM is sufficient to allow a workstation to load Windows in enhanced mode, Windows' performance will suffer. When Windows does not have sufficient memory to load an application, it attempts to swap other programs to disk to free up memory. While this may be acceptable for a standalone workstation, you don't want a server system to swap to disk because network access comes to a standstill during the swap operation. Windows will access up to 16Mb of RAM, so consider installing as much memory as you can afford to for server systems that will be used heavily. For optimum performance, allocate as much memory as necessary to load and run the applications on your server, and give the remaining memory to SmartDrive, the disk-caching software. At a minimum, I would install 8Mb of RAM in a server and allocate 6Mb to Windows and 2Mb to SmartDrive.

Hard Disk Requirements

A complete installation of Windows for Workgroups requires slightly over 15Mb of hard disk space. During installation, you may choose not to install certain portions of Windows for Workgroups; the minimum installation will take approximately 9.5Mb. The portions of Windows you can choose not to install include the on-line help files, e-mail, and workgroup scheduling, but not the ability to act as a server. A "dedicated" server that doesn't require these files would actually require less disk space for Windows than a user PC. In addition to Windows itself, most users will want to set up a swap file so that Windows can open more applications concurrently (Windows will swap unused applications to

Hardware and Operating System Requirements

disk, depending on available memory). A swap file can be as large as a hard disk, but typically would be between 2Mb and 4Mb in size.

Video Requirements

Windows' graphical interface requires a video adapter and monitor that supports high-resolution graphics. The minimum video requirement is a Hercules-compatible monochrome display, but a VGA color monitor and adapter is recommended. While most VGA monitors and adapters are supported by the generic VGA driver included with Windows, you should check with your computer dealer to verify that your video hardware will work with Windows. In some cases, you need to install special drivers for your hardware.

Windows for Workgroups includes drivers for the following:

- Compaq Portable Plasma Display
- ET 4000 adapters (512K or 1Mb)
- Hercules-compatible monochrome adapters and monitors
- IBM EGA-compatible displays and adapters
- IBM XGA-compatible displays and adapters
- IBM 8415/a display
- Olivetti/AT&T Monochrome or PVC display
- Standard VGA (color or monochrome)
- Super VGA-compatible (800×600) adapters
- TIGA video adapters
- Video 7 (512K or 1Mb)

Mouse Requirements

Windows for Workgroups supports the following mice:

- Genius Serial Mouse
- Hewlett-Packard Mouse
- IBM PS/2 Mouse
- Logitech Mice
- Microsoft Mouse (Serial or Bus)
- Mouse Systems Mouse (Serial or Bus)

Even if your mouse is not listed, it may work with one of these drivers. If not, contact the manufacturer or your dealer. Windows allows other drivers to be added during installation.

DOS Requirements

Since Windows is itself an extension to the MS-DOS operating system, you will also need a current DOS version. While any DOS 3.3 or higher version will work, for maximum benefit you should use DOS 5.0. DOS 5.0 can load a portion of itself into upper memory blocks that are not normally used, thereby allowing more memory for DOS applications running under Windows.

Many computer manufacturers, such as Compaq and AST, provide modified versions of MS-DOS that have been customized for their hardware. These companies recommend using their versions of MS-DOS on their hardware, but you shouldn't attempt to use their DOS on other computer brands because the modifications are likely to cause problems for Windows.

Since MS-DOS is limited to addressing 640K of memory, a memory manager is also required. During installation, if Windows detects a third-party memory manager, such as QuarterDeck's QEMM, it will attempt to use this manager; otherwise it will install its own manager.

If your system is an 80286 or you do not expect to run DOS applications with significant memory requirements, the HIMEM memory manager and DOS 5.0 should provide you with sufficient DOS resources. Third-party memory managers, however, can often provide as much as 50K to 75K of additional memory for DOS applications.

CHOOSING NETWORK COMPONENTS

One of the most confusing choices you may be faced with when you install Windows for Workgroups is the selection of the network hardware. Windows for Workgroups supports a wide variety of network adapters. Table 1-1 lists the network adapter drivers included with WfW. If you already have a network and your card isn't listed in the table, contact your dealer or the card manufacturer to see it they provide drivers for Windows for Workgroups.

Hardware and Operating System Requirements

Table 1-1. Network Adapters Supported by Windows for Workgroups

3Com EtherLink
3Com EtherLink 16
3Com EtherLink II or IIP
3Com EtherLink III
3Com EtherLink/MC
3Com EtherLink Plus
3Com TokenLink
Advanced Micro Devices AM2100/PCNet
Amplicard AC 210/AT
Amplicard AC 210/XT
ARCNET compatible
Artisoft AE-1, AE-2, or AE-3
Artisoft AE-2 (MCA) or AE-3 (MCA)
Cabletron E2000 Series DNI
Cabletron E2100 Series DNI
DCA 10 Mb
DCA 10 Mb Fiber Optic
DCA 10 Mb MCA
DCA 10 Mb Twisted Pair
DEC DEPCA
DEC EE101 (built-in)
DEC Ethernet (All types)
DEC EtherWorks LC
DEC EtherWorks LC/TP
DEC EtherWorks LC/TP_BNC
DEC EtherWorks MC
DEC EtherWorks MC/TP
DEC EtherWorks MC/TP_BNC
DEC EtherWorks Turbo
DEC EtherWorks Turbo/TP
DEC EtherWorks Turbo/TP_BNC
DECpc 433 WS (built-in)
IBM Token Ring (all typ
Intel EtherExpress 16, 16/4, or 16TPes)
Intel TokenExpress EISA 16/4
Intel TokenExpress MCA 16/4
National Semiconductor AT/LANTIC 16-AT3
National Semiconductor Ethernode *16AT
NCR Token-Ring 4 Mbs ISA
NCR Token-Ring 16Mbs ISA
NCR Token-Ring 16Mbs MCA
NE1000 compatible

Building Local Area Networks with Windows for Workgroups

NE2000 compatible
Novell/Anthem NE1000
Novell/Anthem NE1500T
Novell/Anthem NE2000
Novell/Anthem NE2100
Novell/Anthem NE/2
Olicom 16/4 Token-Ring
Proteon ISA Token-Ring(1340)
Proteon ISA Token-Ring(1342)
Proteon ISA Token-Ring(1346)
Proteon ISA Token-Ring(1347)
Proteon MCA Token-Ring(1840)
Proteon Token-Ring (P1390)
Proteon Token-Ring (P1392)
Pure Data PDI508+ (ArcNet)
Pure Data PDI516+ (ArcNet)
Pure Data PDI9025-32 (Token Ring)
Pure Data PDuC9025 (Token Ring)
Racal NI6510
RadiSys EXM-10
SMC ARCNETPC
SMC ARCNET PC100, PC200
SMC ARCNET PC110, PC210, PS110, PS210, PC250
SMC ARCNET PC130/E
SMC ARCNET PC120, PC220, PC260
SMC ARCNET PC 270/E
SMC ARCNET PC600W, PC650W
SMC (WD) EtherCard (All types except 8013/A)
SMC (WD) EtherCard Plus (WD8003E)
SMC (WD) EtherCard Plus 10T/A (MCA) (WD8003W/A)
SMC (WD) EtherCard Plus w/boot socket (WD8003EB)
SMC (WD) EtherCard Plus w/boot socket (WD8003EBT)
SMC (WD) EtherCard Plus 10T (WD8003W)
SMC (WD) EtherCard Plus16 w/boot socket (WD8013EBT)
SMC (WD) EtherCard Plus/A (MCA) (WD8003E/A or 8003ET/A)
SMC (WD) EtherCard Plus Elite 16 Combo (WD8013EW)
SMC (WD) EtherCard Plus Elite 16 (WD8013EP)
SMC (WD) EtherCard Plus Elite 16T (WD8013W)
SMC (WD) EtherCard Plus Elite (WD8003EP)
SMC (WD) EtherCard Plus TP (WD8003WT)
SMC (WD) StarCard PLUS (WD8003S)
SMC (WD) StarCard PLUS/A (MCA) (WD8003ST/A)
SMC (WD) StarCard PLUS with onboard Hub (WD8003SH)
Zenith Z-Note

Hardware and Operating System Requirements

Most of the network adapters listed in Table 1-1 can be broken into one of three common types: Ethernet, ArcNet, or Token-Ring (4Mb or 16Mb). Cards from different vendors can be installed in the same network if they support the same protocol. A 16Mb Intel Token-Express, for example, will communicate with workstations using 16Mb IBM Token-Ring adapters. The only functional difference between all these network drivers is in NetWare support. All the drivers listed in Table 1-1 can support both Windows and NetWare protocols concurrently, *except* for the ArcNet drivers.

Selecting the correct network topology can be confusing, since there aren't any guidelines to suggest one design over another. As a general rule, ArcNet and 4Mb Token-Ring networks will perform slower than Ethernet or 16Mb networks. Ethernet, however, has a slight edge in performance over 16Mb Token-Ring, at least initially. Under heavy traffic loads, 16Mb Token-Ring networks suffer less degradation and will provide an overall higher throughput. Finally, from a price perspective, Ethernet is considerably less expensive than Token-Ring.

While I do not know what network topology you will choose, if we assume your Windows for Workgroups network doesn't exceed the 25 user self-imposed limit, Ethernet would probably provide the best performance for your dollar. Microsoft apparently agrees with this assessment, since they sell a version of Windows for Workgroups bundled with Intel EtherExpress adapters. These cards feature switchless setup via software, and, during installation, Windows for Workgroups detects their presence and configures itself automatically.

When you install the network adapter, be sure to record the switch settings, or setup parameters, as appropriate. All EISA and MCA cards (as well as some ISA adapters) use software to configure the board. These settings determine the *interrupt* used by the card, as well as other settings, such as RAM addresses and DMA channels.

As a general rule, these settings must not conflict with any other device in your system, such as modems, CD-ROM drives, or the mouse. The most common conflicts are with interrupts. A system with two serial ports or a serial port and an internal modem will use interrupts 3 and 4. The recommended interrupt for most network adapters is either 2 or 5, although these may also be in use. Many newer adapters now also support the use of higher interrupt numbers (9–15).

If you are unsure about the available interrupts and addresses in your system, have a qualified technician or consultant help you out. Windows for Workgroups will most likely crash during installation if there is a hardware conflict. Table 1-2 lists interrupts for 80286 or higher systems. If your system lacks a device, such as a COMM port, you may be able to use that interrupt for your network adapter.

Table 1-2. Interrupts for 80286 or Higher Systems

IRQ Number	Used by
2	EGA/VGA video adapter
3	Serial port-COMM 2
4	Serial port-COMM 1
5	Available (unless used by parallel port LPT2
6	Floppy-disk controller
7	Parallel port LPT1
8	Real-time clock
9	Cascades to 2 (may be available)
10	Available
11	Available
12	Mouse (on PS/2 and EISA machines with mouse port)
13	Math co-processor
14	Hard-disk controller
15	Available

In addition to the network adapter, you will have to select a cable plant. The cabling decision should be made at the same time you select a network adapter because your cable layout may determine what type of network card you can support.

The most common cable types include coaxial (similar to cable TV cable), shielded twisted pair, and unshielded twisted pair. Coax-

Hardware and Operating System Requirements

ial cable is typically run in a daisy-chain fashion, from workstation to workstation. Twisted pair cabling is typically run from each workstation back to a central patch panel, where it is patched into a *multistation access unit*, or MSAU.

With the advent of unshielded twisted-pair network adapters, more companies are opting to run LANs from existing telephone-grade wire. While this may be a viable option, consider having a qualified installation company evaluate the quality and cable lengths of the installed wiring.

If you are running new cable, particularly in an Ethernet environment, you may be considering coaxial (ThinNet) cable. Coaxial cable is easy to run, inexpensive, and requires no central wiring hub. ThinNet installations may be susceptible to greater downtime, however, since a cable disconnect or break will shut down the entire segment. If you choose ThinNet, be sure your installer uses crimp-on connectors, and instruct your users not to stress the cable by inadvertently pulling on it.

Many Ethernet cards now provide support for 10BaseT (twisted-pair) wiring. Since each workstation wire travels to a central hub, a cable disconnect will only affect that station. (Of course, if the station is a server your users might notice a problem!)

Additional information on cable layout, and specifications for Token-Ring, ArcNet, and Ethernet, is available in Appendix C.

CHAPTER 2

Designing the Physical Network

In Chapter 1, we discussed some of the physical requirements in Windows for Workgroups for network adapters and cabling. This chapter focuses on how to select an appropriate network topology and cable plant. It also explains the comparative strengths and weaknesses of the different wiring topologies and LAN architectures.

The three most common network platforms available today are Ethernet, Token-Ring, and ArcNet. While Ethernet still has an edge in installed systems, Token-Ring networks are increasingly becoming the network topology of choice. ArcNet, on the other hand, has a large installed base, but fewer new ArcNet installations are made every year. We'll discuss the reasons for ArcNet's decline in popularity later in this chapter.

CABLING THE NETWORK

The first step in installing the physical network is the selection and installation of the cable. While estimates vary, it's generally agreed that between 70 and 90 percent of all network outages are caused by cable problems. Depending on the size of your network, you may choose to install the wiring yourself, particularly if only a few systems in close proximity are involved. The Windows for Workgroups kit that comes with Intel EtherExpress adapters includes preassembled cables for just such an environment.

Building Local Area Networks with Windows for Workgroups

On the other hand, in an environment with a large number of users, or where the systems are not conveniently located, installing your cable may require professional help. If you select a contractor to provide the cable and installation, make sure the company is familiar with network cabling, including distance limits and the specific limitations of the network topology. Many companies are familiar with installing telephone and security system wiring, but these types of equipment are far more forgiving in terms of cable than your average network adapter. Ask the installer for references, not only for network installations but for installations using the same topology you've selected for your environment.

Cabling between workstations is done in one of three methods: with star topology, ring topology, or bus topology. Each method is explained below.

Star Wiring Systems

Figure 2-1 shows an example of a *star topology*. With star topology, each workstation has its own cable segment connecting it back to a central *hub*. Hubs typically support 4, 8, or 12 connectors. Star topology is increasingly becoming the design of choice because it provides for central management of the wiring and faster fault isolation.

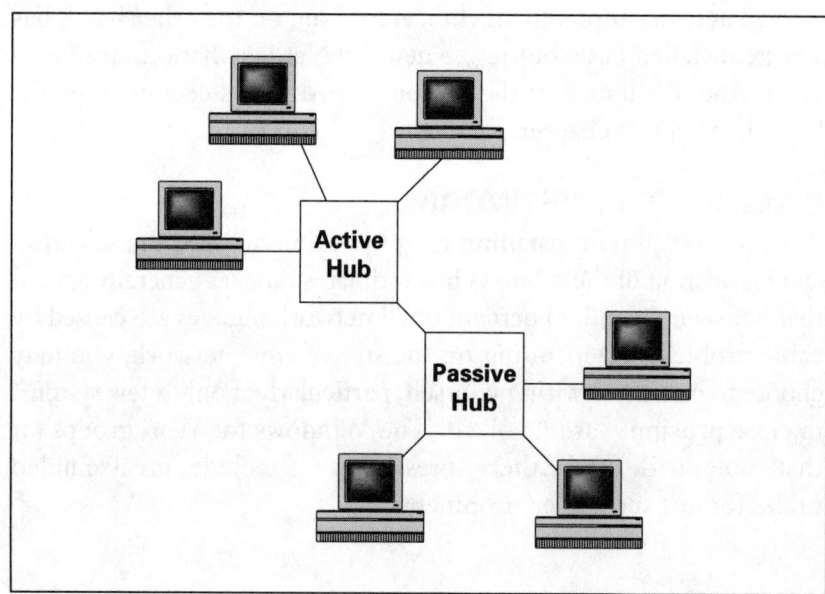

Figure 2-1. Star topology. Each workstation on the LAN connects to a hub. Hubs typically support 4, 8, or 12 connectors. Each link to another hub uses one of the available connections.

Designing the Physical Network

Telephone wiring is typically run in a star fashion, so it's often possible to use existing telephone wire to install the network. You should be aware, however, that telephone wire is unshielded. Using telephone wire reduces the acceptable length of a cable run from the wiring closet to the desktop.

Most ArcNet networks use the star topology with coaxial cable connecting the workstations to the hubs and the hubs to one another. Coaxial cable allows for longer cable runs than twisted-pair wiring. Active hubs in the star environment are usually powered devices and can be chained either to another active hub or to an unpowered passive hub. Passive hubs cannot be used to chain additional hubs.

The primary advantage of star topology is that a segment from a hub to a workstation can be lost without affecting all the users on the network. In a peer environment such as Windows for Workgroups, a segment failure is more likely to affect a great number of users. The centralized hub environment allows for improved central monitoring and management.

Although its name implies a ring topology, Token-Ring is actually a type of star environment. Instead of active and passive hubs, the workstation wiring is connected to a *media access unit* (MAU). The MAU has two special ports called *ring-in* and *ring-out* that cannot be used to connect workstations. Ring-in and ring-out ports connect MAU units to each other:

- The ring-out port in a MAU is connected to the ring-in port on the next MAU.

- The last MAU ring-out port is connected to the ring-in port on the first MAU.

This creates a logical ring for the "token," or data packet, as shown in Figure 2-2.

Figure 2-2. Token-Ring cabling. The typical MAU has eight workstation ports in addition to the ring-in and ring-out ports. Always "close" the ring by connecting the last MAU ring-out to the first MAU ring-in port.

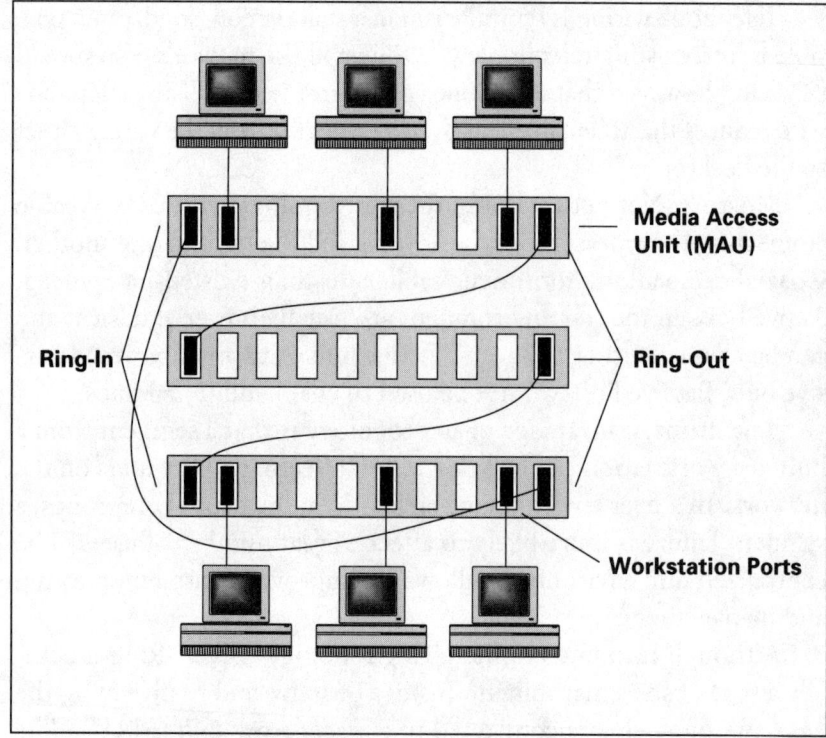

Unlike ArcNet, Token-Ring uses dual twisted-pair cabling to connect workstations and MAUs. This requires the cable run to have at least four wires available. Only two wires are used, one for transmitting and one for receiving, and the additional pair acts as a backup path if the "ring" detects a wire or MAU fault. In the event of a cable break between MAUs, the MAU above the fault will "wrap" data onto the unused pair, and no workstation will be affected. In addition to this hardware protection, the specification for Token-Ring includes a number of fault-monitoring capabilities that a technician can access for tuning and verifying the performance of the ring.

Designing the Physical Network

Ethernet, traditionally a bus topology, can also be wired in a star topology by using a wiring specification designated as 10BaseT. This specification uses unshielded twisted-pair wires and so-called *concentrators* (hubs). Concentrators are typically 12-port boxes and can be chained to each other via the twisted-pair port or by coaxial cable.

Ring Cabling

Very few network systems use a true physical *ring topology* in which the cable travels from station to station in a circle. The notable exception is a *fiber distributed data interface* (FDDI). This is a high-speed (100 Mb/sec) network design typically used in a corporate *backbone* (a high-speed link between file servers), or where data security is a primary concern. (The fiber-optic medium used in this technology makes it difficult to intercept data on the "wire.")

Bus Cabling

A *bus topology* connects workstations in daisy-chain fashion, either by connecting the cable directly to the station, as shown in Figure 2-3, or via drop cables from the bus to the workstation, as in Figure 2-4.

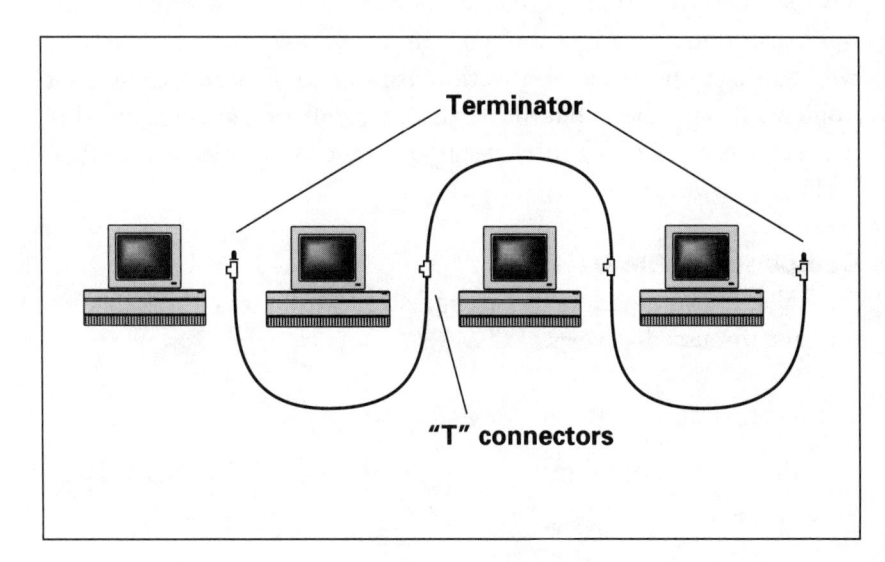

Figure 2-3. Local bus network. The "T" connectors must be connected directly to the workstation network adapter; no drop cable can be used.

Figure 2-4. Bus network. The backbone cable is typically a thick coaxial segment; it allows for considerably longer runs than the local bus cable.

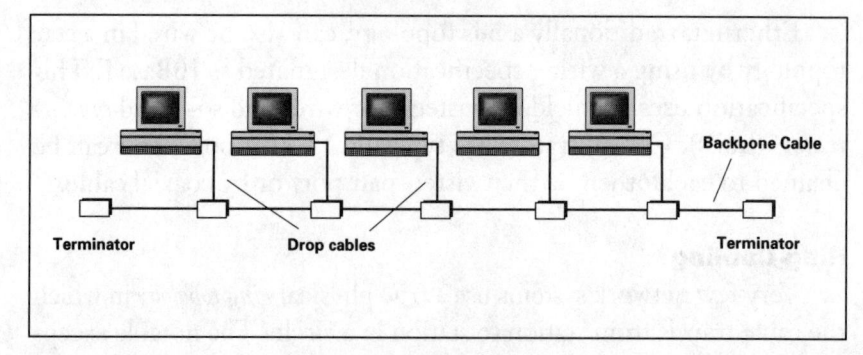

Bus and local bus networks are primarily used for Ethernet environments. For local bus Ethernet cable, the specification is RG-58 A/U coaxial cable, commonly known as Thinnet. This topology is probably the easiest and least expensive method of connecting workstations, but it is also the most prone to failure because a break or disconnect anywhere on the cable will shut down the entire segment. If you elect to use Thinnet, be sure to use crimp-type, not screw-on, BNC connectors. Explain to your network users the importance of maintaining the wire connections to the "T" connectors. If you move a workstation, you can disconnect the "T" from the network card without disrupting operations, but you cannot remove the terminator or wire connections. A bus connection using thick Ethernet cable does not have this problem, but the cable and installation are considerably more expensive. Thick Ethernet supports much longer cable runs than Thinnet, however.

Comparing Cable Designs

Table 2-1 summarizes the strengths and weaknesses of the topologies just discussed.

Designing the Physical Network

Table 2-1. Comparison of Wiring Topologies

Topology	Advantages	Disadvantages
Star: coaxial	LAN faults are isolated. Central monitoring.	Requires purchase of hubs, additional cable runs.
Star: twisted pair	Same as above. May be able to use existing wire.	Same as above. Requires skilled installation and certification of wire.
Token-Ring	Highly fault-tolerant. Maintains performance under high traffic.	Expensive. Requires skilled installers. Can be difficult to troubleshoot without the proper tools.
Ring	Fault-tolerant, dual ring design. FDDI rings support extremely high-traffic densities.	Generally used for corporate or education system backbone. Expensive and difficult to install.
Local Bus	Inexpensive, easy to install and to troubleshoot.	Single point of failure. User can disconnect LAN.
Bus	Long cable runs for the backbone. Supports drop cable to station.	Requires special taps into backbone. Cable specifications are exact.

SELECTING A LAN ARCHITECTURE

Before you make a final determination on a cable plant, you'll need to select a network adapter. While the sheer number of network cards supported by Windows for Workgroups precludes a discussion of every card, most of the cards fall into one of the three network architectures mentioned earlier in this chapter—Ethernet, ArcNet, and Token-Ring. Token-Ring comes in two flavors, 4 Mb/sec and 16 Mb/sec. While ArcNet is rated at 2.5 Mb/sec and Ethernet at 10 Mb/sec, there are other factors that affect the actual throughput of all these cards. By the time this book is printed, several vendors expect to have a new "fast" Ethernet rated at 100 Mb/sec. DataPoint Corporation, the developer of ArcNet, also has a 20 Mb/sec version of ArcNet that will operate on the same network with standard ArcNet.

Ethernet

Ethernet was developed by the Xerox Corporation, which released its first product in 1975. This version differed widely from the Ethernet used today, but it did use a communications method called carrier-sense multiple access with collision detection (CSMA/CD). Carrier sense means that the workstation listens for a quiet period (the carrier) before transmitting. Multiple access means multiple computers can use the same network cable. Collision detection means that two stations that do transmit at the same instance will recognize that the data packets were destroyed, and they will retransmit the lost data packet.

Ethernet now supports three popular cabling specifications:

- **10BaseT—Unshielded twisted-pair (UTP)**
  This is a star topology, connecting workstations via a network cable concentrator. The twisted-pair drop can be up to 100 meters (approximately 328 feet) long.

- **10Base2—Thinnet**
  Thinnet cable runs can extend for 185 meters (approximately 607 feet) without repeaters.

- **10Base5—Thick Ethernet**
  This is the bus topology discussed earlier. A single Thicknet cable can be 500 meters (1640 feet) long without using a repeater.

In addition to these specifications, some manufacturers, such as 3Com and SMC, have developed network cards that support cable lengths that exceed the Ethernet specification. Normally you can mix Ethernet cards from different vendors, but if you use the extended length features of these cards and exceed the cable spec-

Designing the Physical Network

ification for Ethernet, all your network cards should be from the same manufacturer.

Regardless of the topology, you should not expect any performance differences between Ethernet networks that run on any of these cable types, since the transmission rate is the same.

Ethernet is considered a fast network, and typically will perform much better than ArcNet. With only a few workstations on a segment, Ethernet performs on a par with 16Mb Token-Ring networks. However, as traffic loads increase, the number of collisions and retransmissions will cause Ethernet to slow down. Given the bursty nature of network traffic, a 20-station network will perform quite well using Ethernet.

Ethernet prices have declined considerably over the past year, with network adapters now selling in the $100 to $150 range. If you purchase the Windows for Workstations Starter Kit, you'll receive Intel EtherExpress network cards and Thinnet cable. With the ability to literally plug and play, this is the easiest way to get started with Windows for Workgroups.

ArcNet

DataPoint Corporation developed the Attached Resource Computer Network (ArcNet) in 1977. ArcNet uses a token-passing scheme similar to Token-Ring, but it supports either bus or star wiring topology.

Every network card requires a unique address. While Ethernet and Token-Ring cards are assigned an address by the manufacturer, ArcNet adapters have a set of switches that you must set to assign an address (from 1–255).

ArcNet is easy to install, and the boards and hubs are very inexpensive. Typically, an ArcNet card sells for well under $100, whereas a Token-Ring card can cost $400 or more. ArcNet's active hubs regenerate the signal, while the passive hubs do not. When cabling hubs together, you can connect an active or passive hub to another active hub, but you cannot chain a second hub off a passive hub. The maximum cable length varies from 120 meters (393 feet) to 606 meters (1988 feet), depending on the cable and hub connection.

ArcNet only recently gained Institute of Electrical and Electronic Engineers (IEEE) certification however, so its acceptance in the corporate environment has been limited.

ArcNet's token-passing scheme means that performance under a heavy load does not degrade as quickly as Ethernet, but its overall performance is not impressive.

Windows for Workgroups supports several different ArcNet boards, but you cannot run both Windows NETBEUI drivers and NetWare drivers concurrently, due to a design limitation in the ArcNet protocol.

Token-Ring

The first token-ring design, in 1969, is attributed to E.E. Newhall. In 1984, IBM announced a token-ring product and submitted a design to the IEEE that was later adopted. This design called for a simple dual twisted-pair connection from the workstation to a wall socket, with a central patch panel to a series of multistation access units (MAUs).

The physical ring is capable of handling data at 4 Mb/sec or 16 Mb/sec, but all devices must be set for the same speed. Attempting to activate a device at the wrong speed can cause the entire ring to fail.

Each ring can theoretically support up to 260 workstations. In practice, it's not uncommon for a 16Mb ring to have over 100 active workstations, given its high performance under heavy loads.

Token-Ring network problems, given the dual data path described earlier in this chapter, can be more difficult to isolate and resolve.

Token-Ring is considerably more expensive than ArcNet and Ethernet. The MAUs can cost several hundred dollars each (for eight stations) and vendors have artificially maintained a high price on the network adapters (although recently prices have begun to drop). Additionally, special data connectors and wall plates are used to install the cable.

Designing the Physical Network

Comparing LAN Architectures

Table 2-2 summarizes the advantages and disadvantages of Ethernet, ArcNet, and Token-Ring LAN architectures.

Table 2-2. Comparison of LAN Architectures

LAN Architecture	Advantages	Disadvantages
Ethernet	Relatively inexpensive, easy to install and maintain.	Bus cable systems are fragile. Under heavy loads, Ethernet performance suffers.
ArcNet	Very inexpensive. Robust and not as sensitive to flaws.	Poor performance. Does not support dual protocol stacks.
Token-Ring	16Mb supports high-traffic volumes. Ring has backup data path for fault-tolerance.	Difficult to install and troubleshoot. Very expensive.

SUMMARY

No one cable topology and network protocol is right for every installation. Nevertheless, Windows for Workgroups' design limitations would suggest that for most new installations a network based on Ethernet is probably your best bet. The performance in a 2–25 node environment will be as high or higher than Token-Ring, and the cost difference between Ethernet and ArcNet is not significant. On the other hand, if you have an existing network that uses these topologies, or you need to connect to a corporate environment that dictates a specific topology, Windows for Workgroups should be able to accommodate that as well. Microsoft apparently agrees with this evaluation, since it choose to bundle Ethernet adapters with its Starter Kit.

A final caveat when choosing a network adapter: make sure the adapter supports the cable plant you have chosen. Some Ethernet cards, for example, only support 10Base2 or 10Base5 connections. You'll need special converters if you want to connect one of these cards to a network designed for 10BaseT. It's easier to purchase an adapter that already supports the 10BaseT connector.

3 CHAPTER

Installing Windows for Workgroups

This chapter explains the first-time procedure for installing Windows for Workgroups. Before running the Windows Setup installation program, you should have completed cabling your system, installed the network cards in the workgroup computers, and performed some basic testing of the network hardware.

Most network cards provide diagnostic software to test connectivity to other systems. The Intel EtherExpress SETUP program, for example, allows you to perform both internal diagnostics and network diagnostics by attempting to establish a link with another EtherExpress card. If you are upgrading DOS as part of the installation, complete the DOS upgrade before you install Windows.

CREATING A "MASTER" WINDOWS INSTALLATION SERVER

The installation method outlined in this chapter and in Chapter 4 is done with a product called Workgroup Connection, a $79 add-on to Windows for Workgroups developed by Microsoft in conjunction with WfW. With Workgroup Connection, workstations that can't run Windows (such as 8088-based systems) can access shared directories and printers on the LAN.

Building Local Area Networks with Windows for Workgroups

Workgroup Connection allows us to install Windows on each workstation from the network, saving ten to fifteen minutes per installation, as well as a lot of disk swaps. The network-based installation requires a single workstation running Windows for Workgroups with the entire set of Windows files in a shared master directory.

Since a shared server must be running in Windows enhanced mode, the minimum configuration for a shared server is an 80386sx with 3Mb of RAM. The master Windows directory requires 20Mb of disk space, and an additional 9.5Mb of disk space is required for the local copy of Windows.

Creating the "master" copy of Windows on the network is as simple as inserting Disk 1 of the Windows for Workgroups program in the floppy drive (A: or B:), switching to that drive letter, and entering the following command:

```
SETUP /A
```

The /A parameter instructs Windows Setup to install *all* Windows files to the local hard drive, in the directory you specify, such as C:\WGMASTER. Setup will prompt you to insert each additional disk until all the Windows files have been installed.

> **NOTE:** It is *not* necessary or even desirable to install the full set of Windows files on more than one workstation in your group. Using Workgroup Connection, you'll be able to install Windows on your other computers directly from a single master location.

Individual files on the Windows disks are compressed to reduce the number of disks required, so you can't simply copy the files directly. Setup decompresses them as part of the installation procedure. Once all the Windows files are installed, Setup returns you to the DOS prompt. At this point, you are ready to install a custom version of Windows for this workstation, using the master directory as the source.

Installing Windows for Workgroups

At the workstation containing the master Windows directory, switch to the C:\WGMASTER directory (or the directory name you used), and run the

    SETUP

command. Setup will execute a second time, but this time it will install the actual Windows files and drivers required for this system. You must select a different location for this copy of Windows, such as C:\WINDOWS. Since all the necessary Windows files are located in the master directory, this installation will run much faster than the previous one.

CHOOSING EXPRESS OR CUSTOM INSTALLATION

You will be given the option to run either an EXPRESS or CUSTOM installation at this point.

- The EXPRESS version automatically installs Windows, searches your local path for applications, and attempts to install the correct drivers for your network adapter.

- The CUSTOM installation requires you to select the network adapter, specify the location of various Windows files, and choose whether you want to install the MSMail and Schedule+ applications bundled with Windows.

Even for experienced installers, the EXPRESS method is preferred, since it requires little intervention on your part. If disk space may be a problem, you can use CUSTOM and tell Windows not to install optional programs. Even if you don't install MSMail and Schedule+ on this system, you can later elect to run these applications from another workstation.

Building Local Area Networks with Windows for Workgroups

Registering and Adding Protocols to Windows

During this installation, you will be prompted for your full name, your system name, and the workgroup name, as shown in Figure 3-1.

- The Name you enter here is how you will appear in the Mail directory; the system name is how others will view your PC resources.

- The Computer Name you enter here establishes your NETBIOS name (how others in your workgroup identify you).

- The Workgroup Name defines the default workgroup you wish to be part of. The Workgroup Name is important: when you are installing other systems, you *must* use the same workgroup name, or you will be unable to share resources with these systems.

Figure 3-1. Registering Windows. The Computer Name entered here establishes your NETBIOS name (how others identify you). The Workgroup name defines the default workgroup you wish to be part of.

```
┌─────────────────────────────────────────────┐
│              Windows  Setup                  │
│                                              │
│  Please type your full name in the box below.│
│  You may also specify the name of your       │
│  company if Windows will be used for         │
│  business purposes.                          │
│                                              │
│  Name:    [                              ]   │
│                                              │
│  Company: [                              ]   │
│                                              │
│  Type a name for your computer.  This name   │
│  identifies your computer to others in your  │
│  workgroup.                                  │
│                                              │
│  Computer Name: [                        ]   │
│                                              │
│  Enter the name of the workgroup you want    │
│  your computer to belong to.                 │
│                                              │
│  Workgroup:  [                           ]   │
│                                              │
│  Then choose Continue or press ENTER.        │
│                                              │
│   [ Continue ]    [ Exit Setup ]   [ Help ]  │
└─────────────────────────────────────────────┘
```

Installing Windows for Workgroups

3

If your system is also connecting to another network, such as Novell's NetWare or Microsoft's LAN Manager, Setup will provide you with the option to load additional drivers so that Windows can communicate with these networks. Figure 3-2 shows the Compatible Networks screen. This screen allows you to add additional protocols, such as Novell's IPX/SPX. Windows for Workgroups uses NETBIOS for workgroup connectivity.

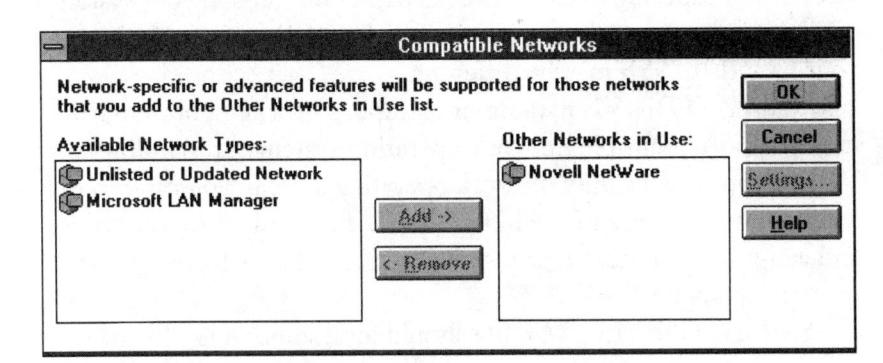

Figure 3-2. Adding protocols to Windows. This screen allows you to add additional protocols, such as Novell's IPX/SPX.

When Setup completes, you will have the option to restart the system or return to DOS. If you exit to DOS, be sure and reboot your system before attempting to run Windows for the first time.

The CONFIG.SYS and AUTOEXEC.BAT Files

In addition to configuring Windows, Setup will create new AUTOEXEC.BAT and CONFIG.SYS files on your local boot drive. NOTE: Setup does not save or append to old copies of these files. If they exist, Setup will overwrite them with its own files. Rename these files or make a backup copy before running the Setup installation.

Your CONFIG.SYS file should now look something like this:

```
FILES=30
BUFFERS=30
device=C:\WINDOWS\protman.dos /i:C:\WINDOWS
device=C:\WINDOWS\elnkii.dos
device=C:\WINDOWS\msipx.sys
```

```
device=C:\WINDOWS\workgrp.sys
LASTDRIVE=G
DEVICE=C:\WINDOWS\HIMEM.SYS
DEVICE=C:\WINDOWS\SMARTDRV.EXE /DOUBLE_BUFFER
STACKS=9,256
```

The four lines pointing to device drivers in the C:\WINDOWS directory are specific to the network adapter installed in your system. The elnkii.dos driver is specific to the 3COM Etherlink II adapter; your CONFIG.SYS may be different.

The LASTDRIVE parameter is important when your environment supports multiple network operating systems. If Windows for Workgroups is your only network operating system, you can modify this parameter to read LASTDRIVE=Z. This will allow you to use and assign drive letters *H* through *Z* to shared directories on other workgroup systems.

Your AUTOEXEC.BAT file should look something like this:

```
C:\WINDOWS\SMARTDRV.EXE /L
C:\WINDOWS\net start
C:\WINDOWS\msipx
C:\WINDOWS\netx
PATH C:\WINDOWS;C:\NET;c:\dos
SET TEMP=C:\WINDOWS\TEMP
```

The msipx and netx commands are specific to environments with both Windows and NetWare. If you didn't tell Windows to install NetWare (or Microsoft LAN Manager) drivers, you shouldn't see these lines.

STARTING WINDOWS FOR WORKGROUPS

When you reboot the system, the Windows for Workgroups drivers should load and you should see a DOS prompt. You can either type **WIN** at this point or place the WIN command at the end of your AUTOEXEC.BAT file.

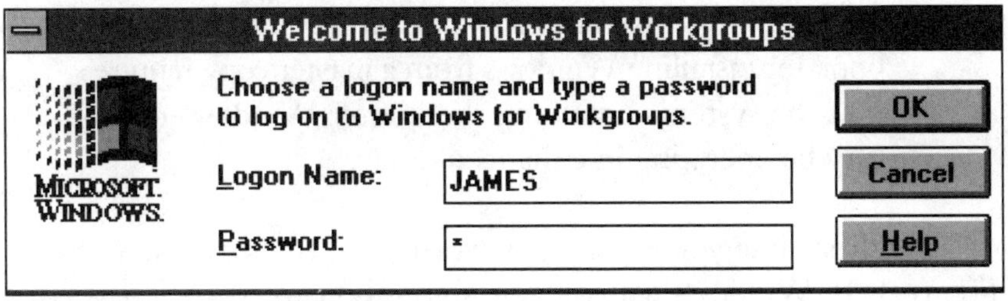

Installing Windows for Workgroups

Figure 3-3.
The "Welcome" Logon screen. If you don't enter a password here, Windows will ask you to create a password table every time it starts.

When Windows loads, you should be presented with a "Welcome" logon screen, as shown in Figure 3-3. This display appears when you start Windows for Workgroups. If, however, Windows was unable to start in enhanced mode, you will receive the error message shown in Figure 3-4. Typically, this message is generated when running Windows on an 80286 system or on an 80386/80486 system with less than 3Mb of RAM.

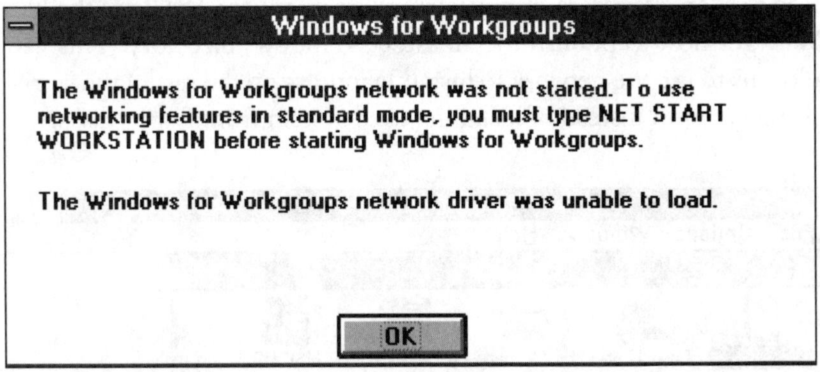

Figure 3-4.
This error message appears if Windows is unable to start in enhanced mode.

If you want to operate in standard mode in this instance, exit to DOS and add the command NET START WORKSTATION prior to running Windows. This will allow you to access shared resources on systems running Windows in enhanced mode. However, you will not be able to share your directories or printers with others.

Building Local Area Networks with Windows for Workgroups

NOTE: The installation procedure described in this book for installing Windows from a master copy requires that the system containing the master Windows directory be operating in enhanced mode.

The first time you enter a password from the logon screen (see Figure 3-3), Windows will ask you if you want to create a password file. If you don't enter a password here, Windows will ask you to create a password table every time it starts. Although the password file is saved on the local drive, it is encrypted to prevent others from using your password. If more than one user will work at this workstation, the new user can backspace over the Logon Name and enter a new name. Windows will create a new user automatically.

After logging on, your screen should look similar to the one in Figure 3-5. Notice the File Manager icon in the Main program group. The File Manager and the Print Manager are the two primary programs used to share resources among workgroup members. We'll use the File Manager now to publish the "master" Windows directory. This will allow us to use the network to install Windows on the rest of the workgroup systems, instead of installing each system from floppy disks.

Figure 3-5. Program Manager with the Main program group open. Double-click on a group to open it, or click on the down-arrow at the top of a group title bar to close it.

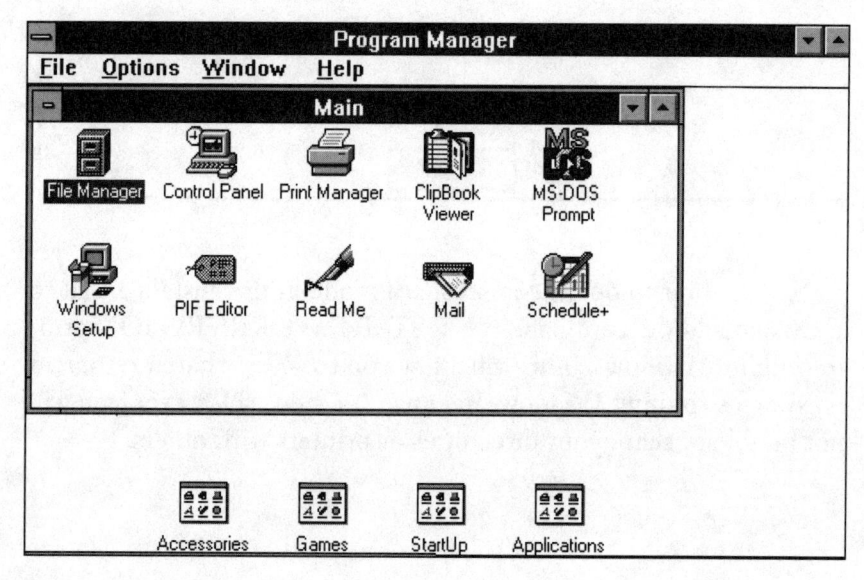

Installing Windows for Workgroups

PUBLISHING THE MASTER WINDOWS DIRECTORY

If the Main group is not open, double-click on the Main icon at the bottom of the screen. If another window is blocking your view of the Main group, try clicking once on the down-arrow at the upper-right corner of that window.

With the Main program group open,

1. Start the File Manager by placing the cursor on the File Manager icon and clicking the left mouse button twice. You can also select the File Manager by clicking on its icon once and pressing Enter on the keyboard.

    Another way to open the File Manager is to select its icon with the mouse, move the cursor to the **File** command on the top menu bar, and press and hold the left mouse button. You will see a list of menu options. Still holding the mouse button down, move the cursor to the **Open** command, and release the mouse button.

2. At first glance, the Windows for Workgroups File Manager looks just like the Windows 3.1 File Manager. However, when you select the Disk command at the top of the screen, you'll find options for connecting and disconnecting to network drives, and for sharing your system with others. Select the **Disk** command.

3. We want to publish the master Windows directory, so select **Share As...** from the Disk menu, as shown in Figure 3-6.

Building Local Area Networks with Windows for Workgroups

**Figure 3-6.
Directory sharing with the File Manager. The Share As... command allows you to create shared network directories. To share an entire drive, enter the drive letter and a backslash (\) at the prompt.**

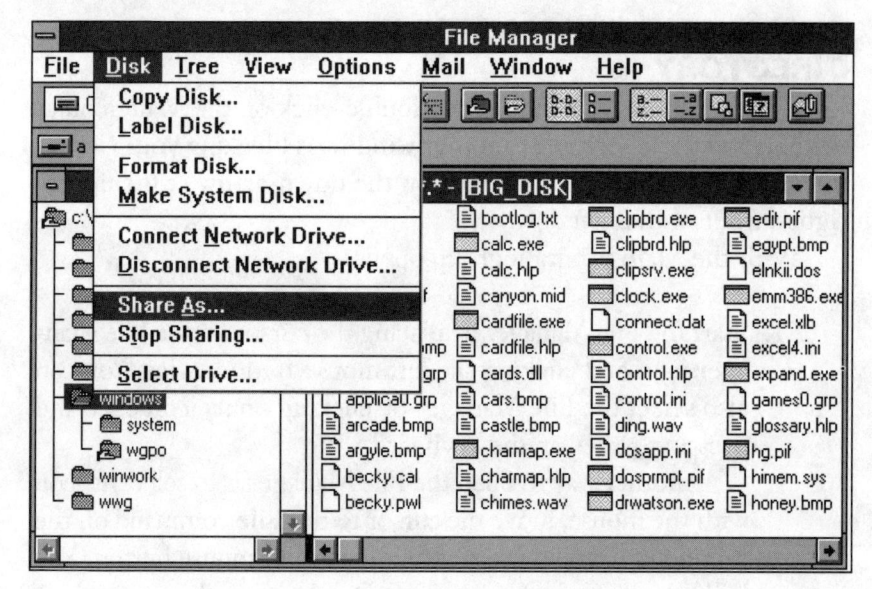

4. The Share Directory box appears, as in Figure 3-7. Here, you fill in the Share Name and path for our local drive and directory. The Share Name is how others will see this directory on our system. The Share Name and Path are explained below.

**Figure 3-7.
Sharing the Windows Master Directory. To prevent users from accidentally deleting or modifying files in this directory, the Access Type has been set to Read-Only.**

Installing Windows for Workgroups 3

In the example in Figure 3-7, the Share Name is Win‑Master and it points to C:\WGMASTER, the location of the master Windows directory. If, during installation, we had named this personal computer CHRIS, other users who wanted to access this directory would select \\CHRIS\WIN‑MASTER as their path.

Notice that WINMASTER is not limited to the eight-character name limit imposed by DOS. The Share Name field will allow up to twelve characters.

5. You can enter a Comment up to 45 characters long on this screen. Users who attempt to access this directory from their File Manager will see this comment next to the Share Name.

6. Check the **Re-share at Startup box** if you want this directory to be available automatically to others whenever you start Windows.

7. Check an Access Type radio button to set the directory as read-only (our choice for the master Windows directory), full (read/write), or password-based. The buttons are explained below.

   If you select *Depends on Password*, Windows will present a dialog box to enter the password for Read-Only, and for Full. Each user would have to enter the correct password for the level of access you want them to have.

   The *Read-Only* password is optional. If you enter a password here, the directory is read-only, but users will still have to provide the correct password to access it.

   Full gives users complete read/write access.

8. Click on the **OK** button on the Share Directory screen. Users can now access this directory as if it was on their local drive.

Chapter 4 will discuss Microsoft's Workgroup Connection and how it can be used to install Windows for Workgroups on the rest of your workgroup systems.

CHAPTER 4

Using Workgroup Connection

This chapter explains what Workgroup Connection is, how to install and use Workgroup Connection, and finally how to install Windows from the network.

WHAT IS WORKGROUP CONNECTION?

Unlike other peer-to-peer networks, Windows for Workgroups does not include native support for client or server workstations running on DOS alone. Microsoft developed Workgroup Connection to provide DOS client access to the Windows for Workgroups directory and print services. Workgroup Connection even includes a DOS-based Mail program so that DOS users can exchange electronic mail with Windows workgroup members. The ability to access the network from DOS clients allows you to setup devices such as centralized backup stations or fax and e-mail gateways without spending money to update PCs to support the Windows environment.

You may have DOS users who are not ready to give up their C:\ prompt just yet, so Workgroup Connection allows them to access the network without making the switch to Windows. Since older systems typically require video and memory upgrades just to run Windows in standard mode, the cost savings from Workgroup Connection can be significant. Still, the largest benefit I found when using Workgroup Connection was the time saved doing the network installation of Windows.

The installation procedure described in Chapter 3 and here in Chapter 4 assumes you are using Workgroup Connection. You can elect to run Windows Setup from the floppy drive on each and every workstation, and then hunt for the diskettes the next time you need to change a workstation driver, or you can use Workgroup Connection. Using the network to install Windows will reduce the installation time for each workstation from approximately thirty minutes to perhaps ten minutes, depending on your familiarity with the Windows Setup program. Later, you can make changes or update drivers from a central location, thereby easing the task of administering Windows.

INSTALLING WORKGROUP CONNECTION

Workgroup Connection consists of a single diskette with the installation and driver files to support DOS workstation access to shared Windows for Workgroups directories and printers. Workgroup Connection requires 1Mb of disk space, or about 1.3Mb if you install the optional DOS Mail software. Using Workgroup Connection and the master Windows directory as outlined in Chapter 3, you can install additional workgroup copies of Windows without resorting to shuffling floppy diskettes for each installation. You can also use this method to update a workstation at a later date.

Installing Workgroup Connection is straightforward. Insert the Workgroup Connection diskette in either the A: or B: drive, change to that drive letter, and enter the following command:

```
SETUP
```

You'll be presented with the screen shown in Figure 4-1. To proceed, press Enter.

The next screen, shown in Figure 4-2, allows you to choose the directory for Workgroup Connection. Installing Workgroup Connection to a separate directory allows you to switch between DOS and

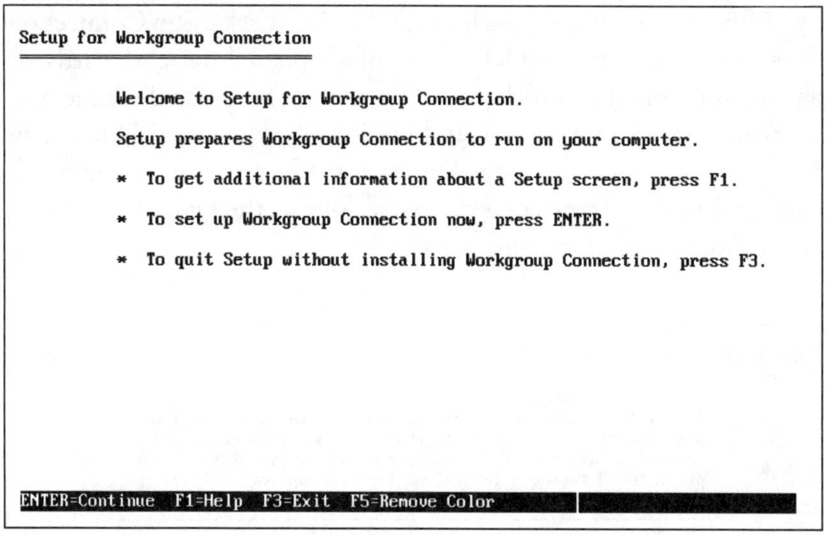

Using Workgroup Connection

4

```
Setup for Workgroup Connection

        Welcome to Setup for Workgroup Connection.

        Setup prepares Workgroup Connection to run on your computer.

        *  To get additional information about a Setup screen, press F1.

        *  To set up Workgroup Connection now, press ENTER.

        *  To quit Setup without installing Workgroup Connection, press F3.




ENTER=Continue   F1=Help   F3=Exit   F5=Remove Color
```

Figure 4-1. The opening Setup for Workgroup Connection screen. Press Enter to set up Workgroup connection.

Windows connectivity to the network, as necessary. Do *not* install Workgroup Connection in the same directory as Windows: the Workgroup Connection NET.EXE file for DOS access is different from the NET.EXE file used by Windows.

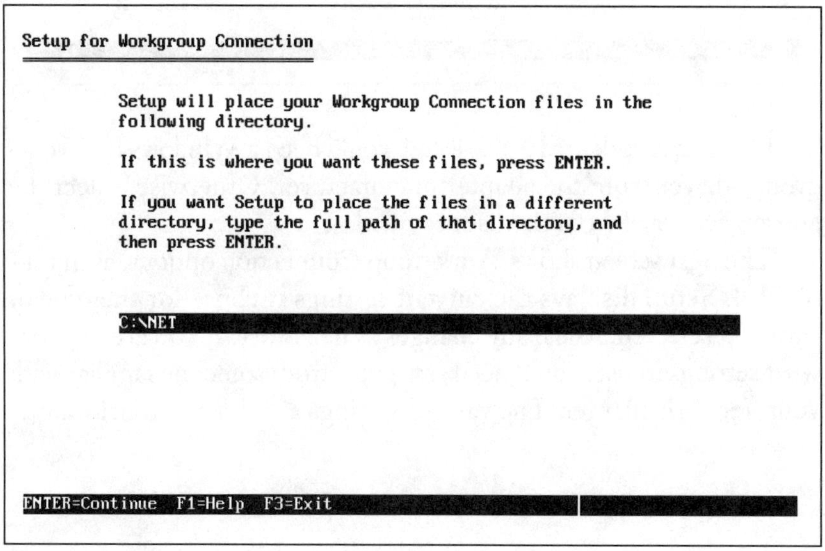

```
Setup for Workgroup Connection

        Setup will place your Workgroup Connection files in the
        following directory.

        If this is where you want these files, press ENTER.

        If you want Setup to place the files in a different
        directory, type the full path of that directory, and
        then press ENTER.


        C:\NET




ENTER=Continue   F1=Help   F3=Exit
```

Figure 4-2. Placing Your Workgroup Connection Files in a directory. Either press Enter to accept the listed directory or type in a new directory and then press Enter.

47

Building Local Area Networks with Windows for Workgroups

After you've selected the location for the Workgroup Connection files, you'll be presented with a list of supported network cards, as shown in Figure 4-3. Workgroup Connection supports the same network interface adapters as Windows for Workgroups. Table 1-1 in Chapter 1 lists these adapters. Different workstations on the network can use different brands of adapters, as long as the type of card (Ethernet, ArcNet, etc.) remains the same.

Figure 4-3. Selecting the network card installed in your computer. Press Enter after you've selected the card.

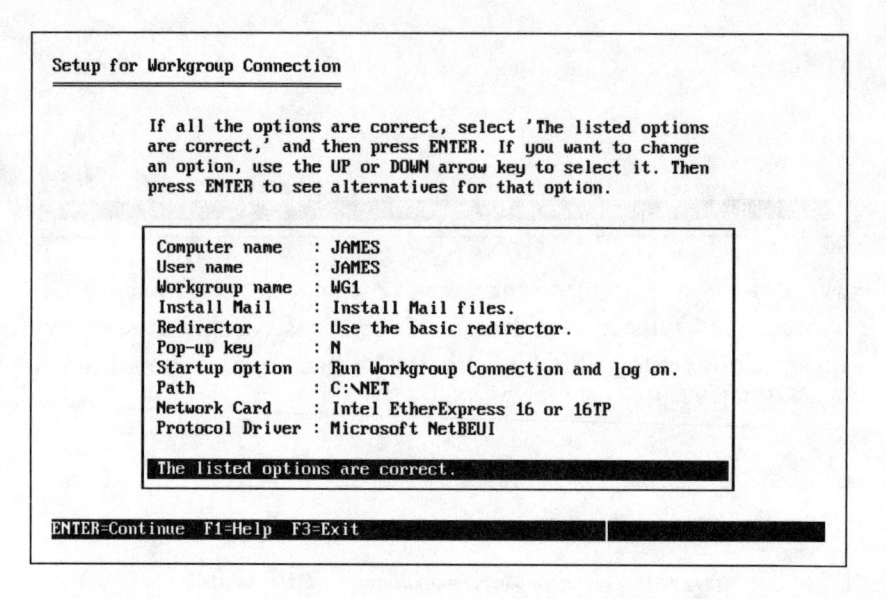

```
Setup for Workgroup Connection

        If all the options are correct, select 'The listed options
        are correct,' and then press ENTER. If you want to change
        an option, use the UP or DOWN arrow key to select it. Then
        press ENTER to see alternatives for that option.

        ┌─────────────────────────────────────────────────────────┐
        │ Computer name    : JAMES                                │
        │ User name        : JAMES                                │
        │ Workgroup name   : WG1                                  │
        │ Install Mail     : Install Mail files.                  │
        │ Redirector       : Use the basic redirector.            │
        │ Pop-up key       : N                                    │
        │ Startup option   : Run Workgroup Connection and log on. │
        │ Path             : C:\NET                               │
        │ Network Card     : Intel EtherExpress 16 or 16TP        │
        │ Protocol Driver  : Microsoft NetBEUI                    │
        ├─────────────────────────────────────────────────────────┤
        │ The listed options are correct.                         │
        └─────────────────────────────────────────────────────────┘

ENTER=Continue   F1=Help   F3=Exit
```

If your network card is not listed, you'll need a Windows for Workgroups driver from the adapter manufacturer. Otherwise, select the appropriate card from the list provided.

The next screen shows Workgroup Connection options, as in Figure 4-4. Setup displays the current settings it chose for the type of card you selected. Make any changes as necessary. If you are not sure what settings to use, you'll need assistance from someone familiar with your network adapter. The various settings are described below.

Using Workgroup Connection

4

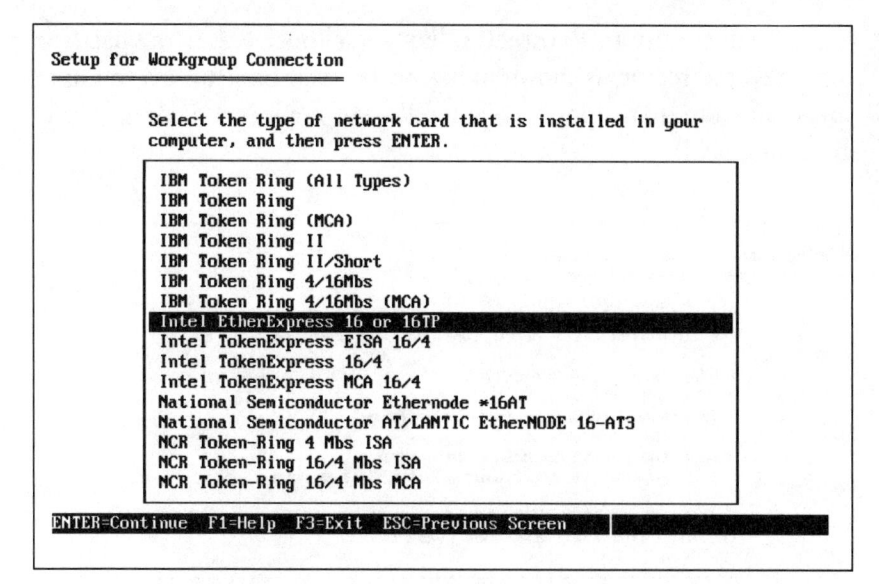

```
Setup for Workgroup Connection

     Select the type of network card that is installed in your
     computer, and then press ENTER.
     ┌─────────────────────────────────────────────────────────┐
     │ IBM Token Ring (All Types)                              │
     │ IBM Token Ring                                          │
     │ IBM Token Ring (MCA)                                    │
     │ IBM Token Ring II                                       │
     │ IBM Token Ring II/Short                                 │
     │ IBM Token Ring 4/16Mbs                                  │
     │ IBM Token Ring 4/16Mbs (MCA)                            │
     │ Intel EtherExpress 16 or 16TP                           │
     │ Intel TokenExpress EISA 16/4                            │
     │ Intel TokenExpress 16/4                                 │
     │ Intel TokenExpress MCA 16/4                             │
     │ National Semiconductor Ethernode *16AT                  │
     │ National Semiconductor AT/LANTIC EtherNODE 16-AT3       │
     │ NCR Token-Ring 4 Mbs ISA                                │
     │ NCR Token-Ring 16/4 Mbs ISA                             │
     │ NCR Token-Ring 16/4 Mbs MCA                             │
     └─────────────────────────────────────────────────────────┘
 ENTER=Continue    F1=Help   F3=Exit   ESC=Previous Screen
```

**Figure 4-4.
Workgroup Connection options. To change an option, press the Up or Down arrow key to select it.**

First you select a Computer name. Typically, both the Computer name and the User name are the same, but if your company moves people around frequently, you may wish to use job titles, room numbers, or even phone extensions for the Computer and User name. No two computers in a workgroup can have the same name, and if you connect to other networks, such as NetWare or LAN Manager, don't choose names already in use on those networks. For example, don't use a NetWare server named "Accounting" and a workgroup workstation named "Accounting."

After naming the system, you'll need to assign it to a workgroup. The Workgroup name *must* match the Workgroup name you used when installing the master copy of Windows. Setup will display a summary screen with the options you selected, as well as default choices for installing its DOS Mail software and startup sequence. Your screen should now look something like Figure 4-4.

Workgroup Connection's Mail program allows DOS users to communicate with Windows users. If you don't intend to use the DOS Mail, you can tell Workgroup Connection not to install it.

Building Local Area Networks with Windows for Workgroups

The next option, Redirector, lets you choose either the basic or advanced redirector, as shown in Figure 4-5. Use basic unless you have an application that supports Named Pipes (an advanced communications protocol).

Figure 4-5. Choosing a redirector. Unless you use programs that support Named Pipes, choose the basic director.

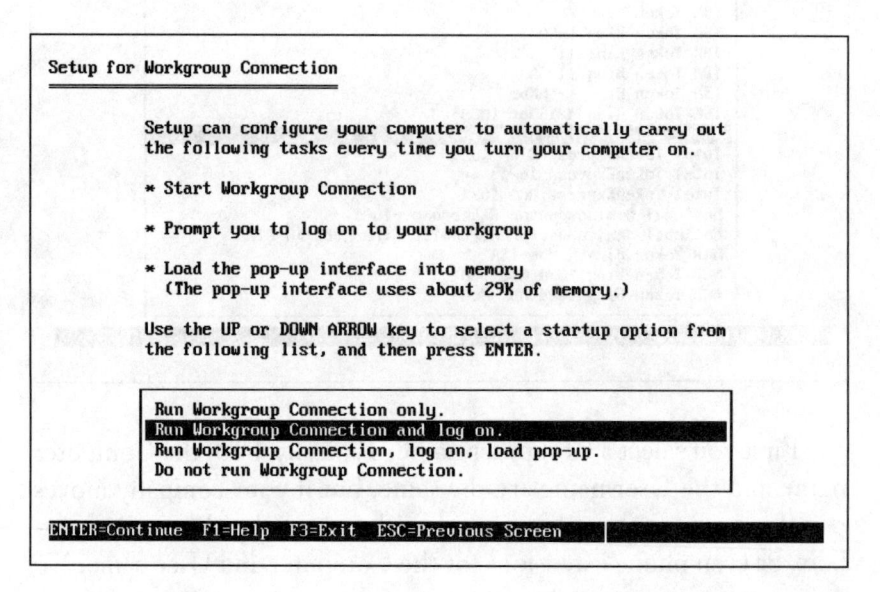

```
Setup for Workgroup Connection

    Setup can configure your computer to automatically carry out
    the following tasks every time you turn your computer on.

    * Start Workgroup Connection

    * Prompt you to log on to your workgroup

    * Load the pop-up interface into memory
      (The pop-up interface uses about 29K of memory.)

    Use the UP or DOWN ARROW key to select a startup option from
    the following list, and then press ENTER.

    ┌─────────────────────────────────────────────────────┐
    │ Run Workgroup Connection only.                      │
    │ Run Workgroup Connection and log on.                │
    │ Run Workgroup Connection, log on, load pop-up.      │
    │ Do not run Workgroup Connection.                    │
    └─────────────────────────────────────────────────────┘

ENTER=Continue   F1=Help   F3=Exit   ESC=Previous Screen
```

The Pop-up key allows the NET.EXE command to remain resident in memory so you can attach to network drives or printers from within DOS applications (keeping NET.EXE resident uses approximately 30K of memory).

There are four startup options for Workgroup Connection, as shown in Figure 4-6:

- Run Workgroup Connection only, which loads the network drivers.
- Run Workgroup Connection and log on, which logs in to the network.
- Run Workgroup Connection, log on, and pop-up, which loads NET.EXE.
- Do not run Workgroup Connection.

Using Workgroup Connection

4

Since we are installing Workgroup Connection so we can connect to the Windows "master" installation server, select the default option, number 2, to automatically log in to the network.

```
Setup for Workgroup Connection

        Workgroup Connection provides two redirector files:
        basic and full. You can specify which redirector you
        want to use.

        The basic redirector provides all standard workgroup
        functions, such as connecting, disconnecting, and
        browsing. It uses less memory and disk space than the
        full redirector.

        Use the full redirector only if you use programs that
        use advanced network functions, such as named pipes.

              ┌─────────────────────────────────────────┐
              │ Use the basic redirector.               │
              │ Use the full redirector.                │
              └─────────────────────────────────────────┘


 ENTER=Continue   F1=Help   F3=Exit   ESC=Previous Screen
```

**Figure 4-6.
Startup options
for Workgroup
Connection.
Choose an option
and press Enter.**

To verify the network adapter settings, move the cursor to the Network Card option and press Enter. From here, you can choose

- the Change driver for network card option to change to a different card; or
- the Edit settings for network card driver option to edit the settings for your selected adapter.

When you're done, press Enter.

After verifying the correct settings, press Enter twice to return to the main Setup screen. When you tell Setup to proceed, it will copy the necessary files to the installation directory, and create an AUTOEXEC.BAT and CONFIG.SYS file with the necessary commands to run your startup selection. If you have existing

Building Local Area Networks with Windows for Workgroups

AUTOEXEC.BAT and CONFIG.SYS files, they will be renamed with the extension .001 (or .002, etc., if .001 files exist).

A successful installation of Workgroup Connection will display the screen shown in Figure 4-7.

Figure 4-7. A successful installation of Workgroup Connection brings up this screen. You must reboot your system before you can use Workgroup Connection.

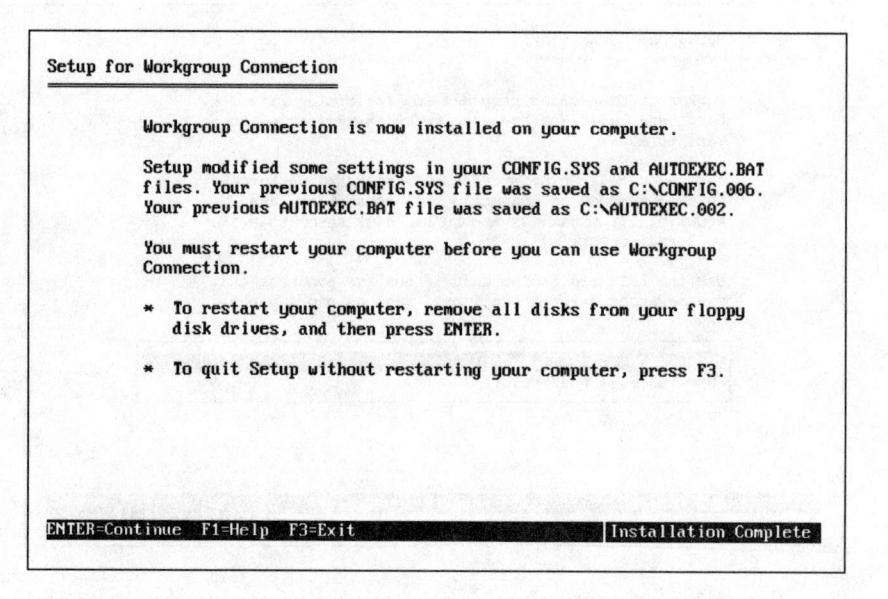

```
Setup for Workgroup Connection

    Workgroup Connection is now installed on your computer.

    Setup modified some settings in your CONFIG.SYS and AUTOEXEC.BAT
    files. Your previous CONFIG.SYS file was saved as C:\CONFIG.006.
    Your previous AUTOEXEC.BAT file was saved as C:\AUTOEXEC.002.

    You must restart your computer before you can use Workgroup
    Connection.

    *  To restart your computer, remove all disks from your floppy
       disk drives, and then press ENTER.

    *  To quit Setup without restarting your computer, press F3.




ENTER=Continue   F1=Help   F3=Exit                    Installation Complete
```

When you reboot your system, Workgroup Connection will load and execute the startup option you chose. If you did not elect to automatically log on to the network at startup, you'll need to change to the directory where Workgroup Connection is installed and run the

    NET

command. Enter your user name and a password. Since this is the first time you've logged in, Workgroup Connection will offer you the option of creating an encrypted password table for accessing the network.

Each workstation in the network maintains its own local password table, so it's up to the users to keep their passwords synchronized if they use multiple workstations. While it's not necessary to set up and

Using Workgroup Connection

use passwords, you may want to go ahead and choose one, since Workgroup Connection and Windows for Workgroups continue to ask you to create a password table every time they start.

The logon function in Workgroup Connection and Windows for Workgroups is more informational than functional. When you are accessing network resources, your logon name tells the server who is using the resource. The password file can be renamed or deleted, and then restored at a later date, so bypassing this "security" feature would be relatively easy.

After logging onto the network, the NET.EXE pop-up box will appear. At this point, you are ready to connect to the master server and install Windows from the network.

ACCESSING DIRECTORIES AND PRINTERS

In Chapter 3, we set up a Windows Workgroup server and made the master Windows directory a read-only shared resource on the network. If you forgot or neglected to write down the name of this server and the resource, use the Tab key to move the highlight bar to the Browse option. Workstations with a mouse and the appropriate DOS drivers loaded in AUTOEXEC.BAT or CONFIG.SYS can also use the mouse to select the menu items in the NET.EXE dialog box.

Browse will display all the workstations on your network that have Windows for Workgroups running. Select the workstation you want and the shared directories will appear in the lower box. Highlight the appropriate directory and press Enter. The popup menu should now show a drive letter associated with that directory. You can select other drive letters as necessary.

> **NOTE:** You can use any drive letter not already in use by a local device, up to the LASTDRIVE parameter defined in the CONFIG.SYS file. If you need additional drive letters, modify (or add) the following CONFIG.SYS statement:
>
> ```
> LASTDRIVE=Z
> ```

If you are using both Windows for Workgroups and NetWare, you'll need to balance the drive letters used by Windows against your NetWare requirements.

The NET.EXE popup menu also allows you to share printers on Windows servers. In Chapter 9 we'll look at printer sharing, but selecting a printer in Workgroup Connection is similar to selecting a directory. From the popup menu, use the Tab key to move to the Show Printers option on the topmost menu bar.

The highlighted character in each menu option acts as a shortcut. Hold down the Alt key and press the highlighted letter to jump directly to that option. If you make a mistake, use the Esc key to return to the previous screen.

From the Printer Connections screen, you can assign LPT1 through LPT9 to a shared printer. Additionally, you can view, pause, restart, and delete print jobs using the Show Queue option on the Printer Connections screen.

Finally, note the Reconnect at startup box on both the Disk Connections and Printer Connections screens. Using the Tab key, move the cursor to this box and press the spacebar. This toggles the box on and off. As you define connections to shared resources on the LAN, you can check this box.

The next time you start Workgroup Connection, these resources will automatically be connected, if they are available. If the resource is unavailable, Workgroup Connection will display an error message and ask you if you want to continue to attempt to connect to this device on subsequent logons.

INSTALLING WINDOWS FROM THE NETWORK

At this point, you should have the master Windows directory assigned to a local drive letter, typically D: or E:. To install Windows from the network,

1. Exit the NET.EXE popup by pressing the **Esc** key.

2. Switch to the correct drive letter.

Using Workgroup Connection

3. Execute a **DIR** command and see the Windows files on the remote server.

4. Execute the **SETUP** command and proceed with installing Windows for Workgroups on the local hard drive.

If you recall, in Chapter 3 we executed Setup twice. The first time, we used Setup to install all the Windows files in a master directory. The second time, we ran Setup to create a local set of Windows files for that workstation.

The Setup procedure we are running now should be virtually identical to the second procedure run on the master system: we are simply installing Windows from the network, instead of from the local drive.

The Windows installation will once again modify your AUTOEXEC.BAT and CONFIG.SYS files. As part of this change, it will tell AUTOEXEC.BAT to load the NET.EXE from the Windows directory. The NET.EXE configuration in the Windows directory and the NET.EXE configuration in the Workgroup Connection directory are not compatible. If you want to retain the Workgroup Connection AUTOEXEC.BAT file, rename this file before executing the SETUP command.

Once Setup is complete, you can rename the AUTOEXEC.BAT file created by Windows and switch between the two as necessary. Even if you won't be using Workgroup Connection, it's a good idea to preserve its AUTOEXEC.BAT file so you can rerun Windows Setup from the network.

When the Setup procedure completes, reboot the system. The AUTOEXEC.BAT assigns the Windows directory to the path, so simply typing WIN at the DOS prompt will load WINDOWS. Typically, you'll want to add this command to the end of your AUTOEXEC.BAT file.

As I mentioned earlier, the installation method described in this chapter is not found in the Windows for Workgroups installation manual. I stumbled on this method while trying to decide how to install

Building Local Area Networks with Windows for Workgroups

Windows on one of my test network stations—one with a single 5¼-inch drive. Although my copy of Workgroup Connection was also on a 3½-inch diskette, I simply copied all the files on this diskette onto a 1.2Mb diskette. Microsoft's technical manual, the *Windows for Workgroups Resource Kit*, does mention this method as a viable means of installing Windows for Workgroups. Still, for the "typical" network, Microsoft assumes the installer will take the complete set of Windows disks to each workstation on the network and install Windows via the floppy drive.

The server-based method, while requiring additional disk space on the "master" Windows server, drastically reduces the amount of time and work involved in setting up additional workstations. As hardware needs change, you can quickly connect the modified workstation to the master server and update the Windows settings, or even install an entirely new copy. This method will also allow you to install Windows on machines that don't support your Windows media (that is, 5¼-inch floppy drives with 3½-inch Windows diskettes). Finally, this method introduces the installer to Workgroup Connection itself.

While Windows for Workgroups is intended for offices running primarily Windows applications, Workgroup Connection offers a quick and easy method of accessing shared directories and printers from the DOS prompt. Users who dial into the network via remote control software such as PCAnywhere can upload and download files on shared directories and print to network printers without having to execute Windows.

CHAPTER 5

Optimizing Server Performance

With Windows for Workgroups, every Windows-enabled workstation running in enhanced mode can act as a directory and/or a print server. This chapter will discuss the network specific-features of the Windows Control Panel, as well as provide some tips for optimizing server performance.

STARTING WINDOWS AND LOGGING ON

In Chapter 3, we installed Windows for Workgroups on a master server, loaded Windows, and assigned a directory as a shared resource. To do this, the server had to be operating Windows in enhanced mode.

If you're not sure what operating mode you're using, select About Program Manager from the Help menu in the Program Manager. As shown in Figure 5-1, the About Program Manager screen tells you what mode you're using, as well as how much memory is available and your available system resources.

Building Local Area Networks with Windows for Workgroups

Figure 5-1. Select About Program Manager from the Help menu to determine Windows' operating mode, available memory, and available system resources. Available memory includes the amount of memory available using either the temporary or permanent swap file.

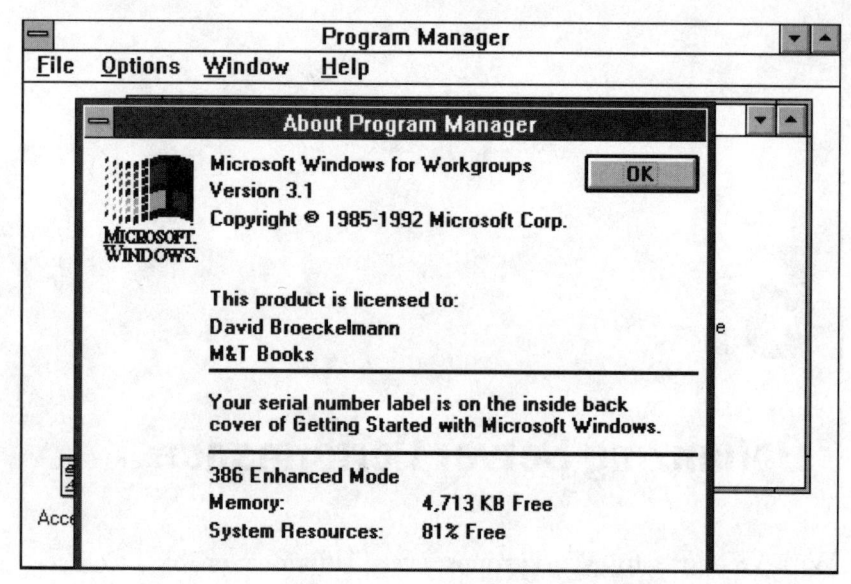

Since enhanced mode operation is required for allowing other workgroup members to access your local devices, this chapter will assume you are operating in enhanced mode. Users running Windows in standard mode can perform many of the functions discussed here, but they won't be able to share their drives or printers with others.

CUSTOMIZING WINDOWS FOR EACH WORKSTATION

Now we'll go into starting Windows for Workgroups in detail, and discuss customizing Windows for each workstation.

If you have not already started Windows, do so now. Unless the WIN command has been added to the AUTOEXEC.BAT file, in which case Windows loads itself, simply type

```
WIN
```

at the DOS prompt. This will load Windows and present the "Welcome" logon screen.

Optimizing Server Performance

Enter a name and (optional) password in the Logon Name and Password boxes. If the user name is new, you'll be asked if you want to create a password file for this user name.

If you select No, you'll be able to log in with this name, but each time you log in with this name you'll be asked if you want to create the password file. Since the password file is maintained in the local Windows directory, users who travel between workstations in the workgroup should consider using the same password on every PC they operate (Windows will *not* synchronize passwords between workstations).

What to Do about Lost Passwords

If a user forgets his or her password, you'll need to delete the password control file for his or her user name, like so:

1. Log in to Windows at the user's workstation.

2. Use the NotePad to open the SYSTEM.INI file.

3. Look in the [Password Lists] section of this file and find the user name and its associated password file name. Delete this file from the WINDOWS directory (it is not necessary to edit the SYSTEM.INI file).

    For example, if the SYSTEM.INI entry is

    ```
    [Password Lists]
    BECKY=C:\WINDOWS\BECKY.PWL
    ```

    delete the file BECKY.PWL from the Windows directory. The next time Becky attempts to log in, Windows for Workgroups will display an error telling her that the password file is missing or damaged, and allow her to create a new password file.

Building Local Area Networks with Windows for Workgroups

Making Network Modifications with the Control Panel

The most common Windows custom options are located in the Control Panel, a Windows utility in the Main program group, which is shown in Figure 5-2.

Figure 5-2. Windows Control Panel. The Network icon allows you to customize Windows performance as a server, as well as change network adapter settings.

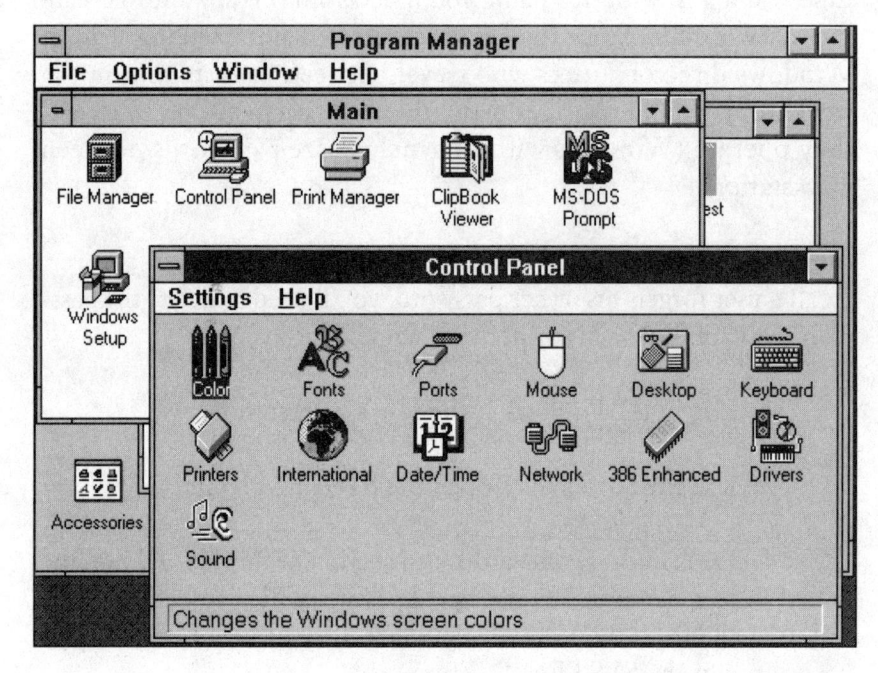

While most of the Control Panel options are identical to those in Windows 3.1, the Network icon is specific to Windows for Workgroups. It allows you to modify the computer name and workgroup used by a particular workstation.

Start the Network program by double-clinking its icon. You will be presented with a Network Settings screen similar to the one in Figure 5-3.

Optimizing Server Performance

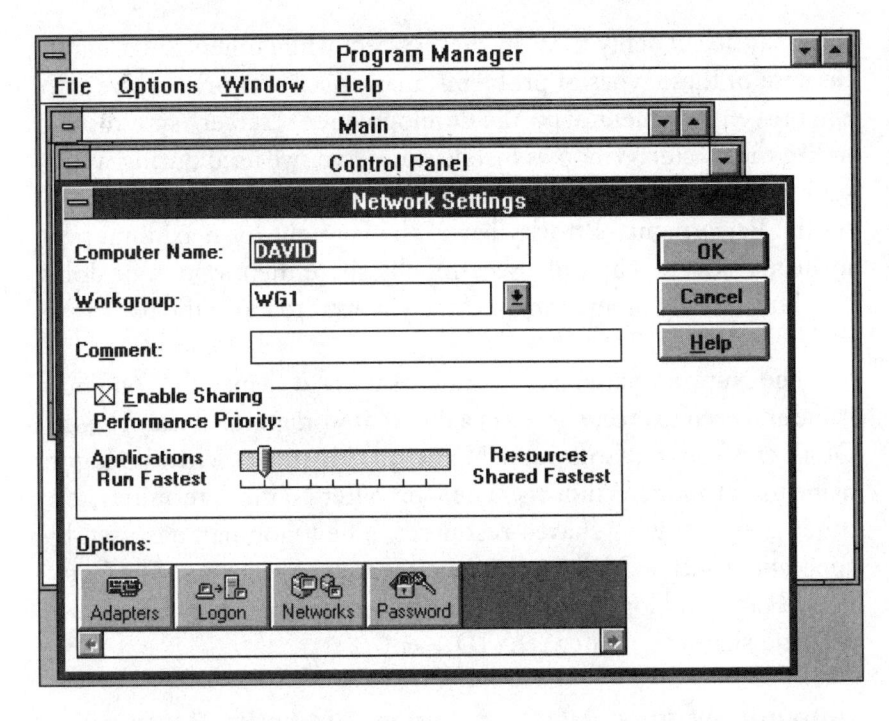

5

Figure 5-3. Network settings. The Computer Name is the NETBIOS name for your workstation—it does not have to be the same as your network logon name. This screen establishes your default workgroup connection, although you can switch to a different workgroup without using the Network Settings screen.

In order to share directories and printers from this workstation, the Enable Sharing button must be selected.

Sharing Resources vs. Local Application Performance

The Performance Priority sliding bar can be moved to allocate CPU time to local applications, in which case applications run faster, or to remote access, in which case resources are shared faster. Depending on the workstation, moving the bar too far to the right may make local users unhappy with the system performance of their applications.

Although Windows for Workgroups is designed as a peer network, with resources spread among many workstations, network management can become a nightmare. The ability to share a large number of disk drives can result in multiple copies of a single file, perhaps with subtle differences. Spreading data among multiple servers also increases the difficulty in maintaining proper system backups. Users may turn off network sharing when it affects their performance, or they may accidentally turn off their system while others are using it. Because of these types of problems, many peer networks evolve into a hybrid environment, with the development of "server" systems not unlike the master Windows installation server we used during workstation installation. If you do setup a "server" system, you'll want to set the Performance Priority bar to the far right for maximum performance. Users who only occasionally share their system or don't care how quickly others can access it will want to move the bar to the far left.

The Network Settings screen allows users to change the computer name and even to create or select a different workgroup, if they choose. Don't confuse the Computer Name on this screen with the logon name used to start Windows. The Computer Name determines how other users see your shared resources. The logon name is used by applications such as Mail for communicating between users. The Computer Name and logon name do not have to match—user FRED can use (and share) computer DAVID.

Network Settings: Adapters, Logon, Networks, Passwords

The Options buttons at the bottom of the Network Settings screen are:

- *Adapters*—for changing the network adapter configuration

- *Logon*—for changing logon information

- *Networks*—for adding or removing network drivers

- *Passwords*—for modifying passwords

Selecting the Adapters button brings up a Network Adapters screen similar to the one shown in Figure 5-4. From here you can remove the setting for this network adapter, add another network adapter, or configure the selected adapter from this screen.

Optimizing Server Performance

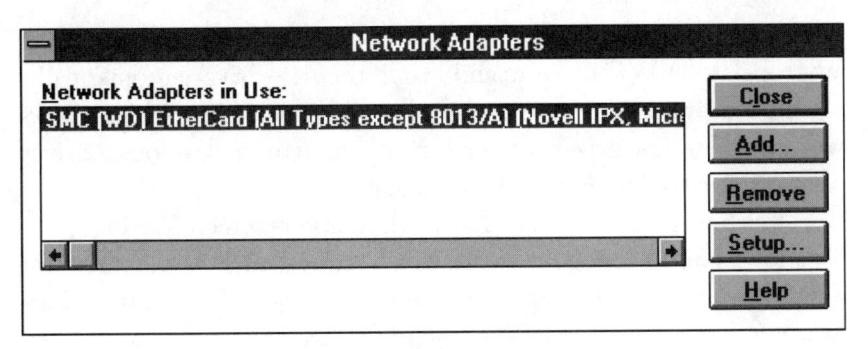

Figure 5-4. Network adapters. This dialog box allows you to view the current network adapter definition, change the adapter settings, or select a different adapter.

CAUTION: Unless you know what you are doing, do not make changes in the network adapter configuration. Improper settings can prevent Windows for Workgroups from loading properly.

Select the Add button to install a new adapter, which you choose from the same list used during Windows' initial installation (you will need the Windows diskettes to add drivers from this screen). Selecting Add will bring up the Install New Network Adapter screen shown in Figure 5-5.

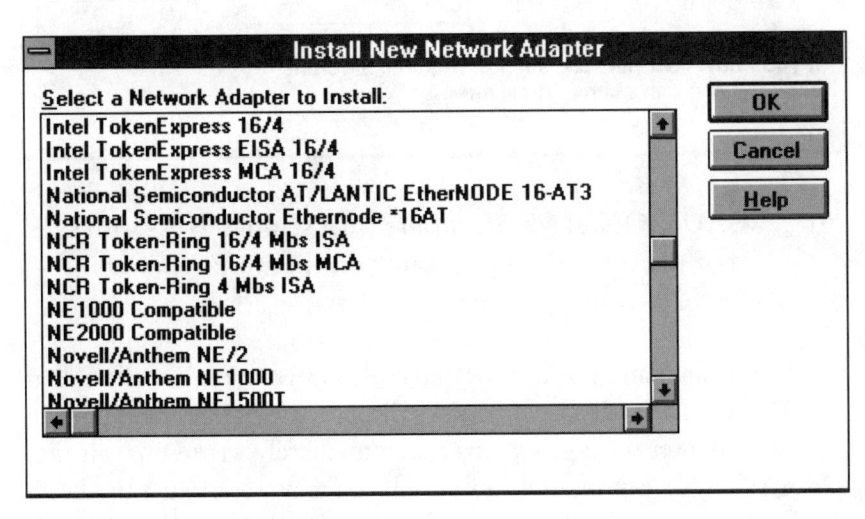

Figure 5-5. Supported adapters. This dialog box provides a scrollable list of the available network drivers in Windows for Workgroups.

Building Local Area Networks with Windows for Workgroups

Select the new adapter and press Enter. Windows will request the appropriate WWG diskette and install the new driver automatically. At the top of this list is the "unlisted adapter" selection, which allows you to add a new driver if your card manufacturer develops a driver that supports Windows for Workgroups.

The Setup button on the Network Adapters screen (see Figure 5-4) allows you to choose network card settings, such as the interrupt level, base memory address, and base input/output (I/O) address. Figure 5-6 shows an example for a system that uses a Standard MicroSystems Ethernet card. If you need to change the adapter settings at a later date in order to accommodate additional hardware, you'll need to manually change these settings.

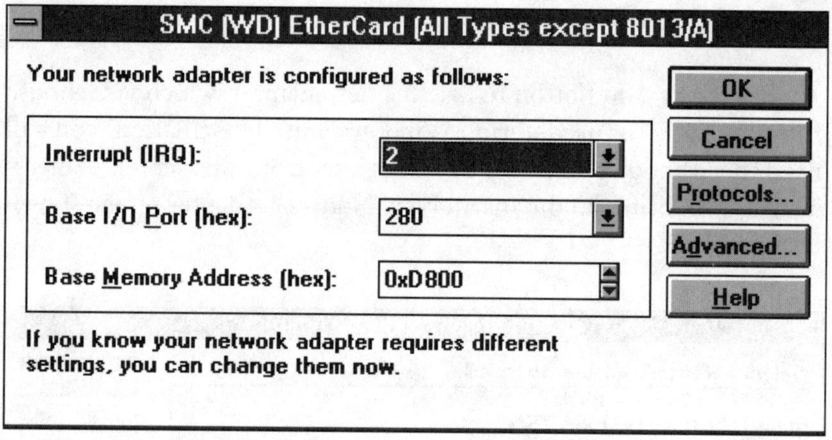

Figure 5-6. Configuring the network adapter. Windows for Workgroups can automatically detect and adjust these parameters on some cards, such as the Intel EtherExpress.

CAUTION: If you are unsure what settings to use with your network adapter, consult your network vendor or the adapter manufacturer.

Windows maintains network adapter information in a file called PROTOCOL.INI in the Windows directory. Changes made in the network adapter settings screens are immediately written to this file. Once Windows is properly configured, you may want to use the DOS ATTRIB command to mark this file as read-only.

Optimizing Server Performance

The Logon button allows you to choose a default logon name and whether or not you wish to log in immediately when you start Windows. When you choose Logon, the Logon Settings screen shown in Figure 5-7 appears.

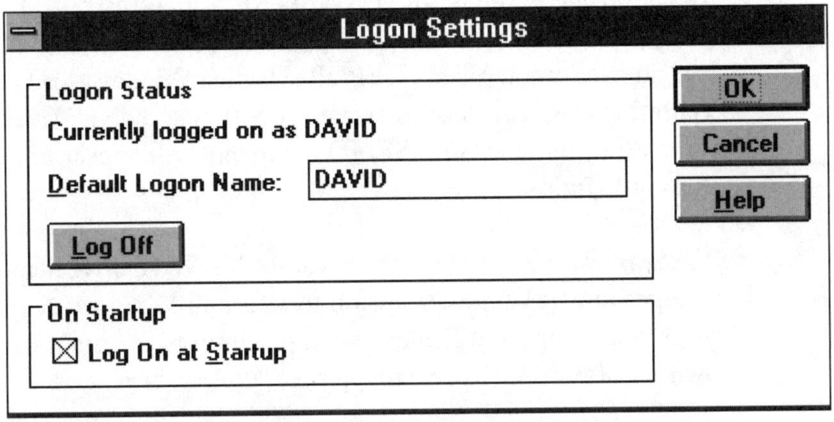

Figure 5-7.
The Logon Settings screen. Unlike most other networks, Windows for Workgroups requires a default logon name, even if several users share a single workstation.

If you want to automatically share your resources with others and automatically attach to other workgroup resources, you must log on at startup. However, if you will only occasionally use the network and other workgroup members don't need to access your directories or printers, you can click on the Log On at Startup box and remove the X. The next time you start Windows, it will skip the Logon screen. If later you choose to access the network, Windows will allow you to log in at that time.

The Networks button on the Networks Setting screen (see Figure 5-3) brings up the Compatible Networks screen (discussed in Chapter 3). This screen allows you to include support for other network operating systems, notably Microsoft's own LAN Manager and Novell's NetWare. Selecting either of these networks makes Windows modify the PROTOCOL.INI file to include the necessary drivers to communicate with devices on these networks.

Building Local Area Networks with Windows for Workgroups

For NetWare support, the Settings... button is included on the Compatible Networks screen. Choose this button and you will see a screen similar to the one in Figure 5-8. Following is a summary of the options on the NetWare Driver screen.

- *Messages enabled* refers to NetWare's SEND and BROADCAST commands. Selecting this button tells Windows to load an application called NWPOPUP when Windows loads. With this program, short messages sent to you by NetWare users using the NetWare SEND command will appear in a pop-up Window.

- *NWShare handles* when set to on, causes NetWare drive map changes in any Windows session to affect all Windows sessions; when turned off, allows each program to maintain its own set of NetWare drive mappings.

- *Restore drives* when set to ON, resets all NetWare drive mappings when the user exits Windows to the state they were in when the user started Windows.

- *Printing options* allow you to customize the number of print jobs displayed in the Print Manager, the buffer size, and how often the Print Manager is updated (for NetWare print jobs).

- *Network warnings* alerts you to problems with the NetWare shell when loading Windows. Problems arise because of a cable fault, a downed NetWare server, insufficient memory to load the network driver, or an incorrect version of the driver. On is the recommended setting for this box.

Optimizing Server Performance

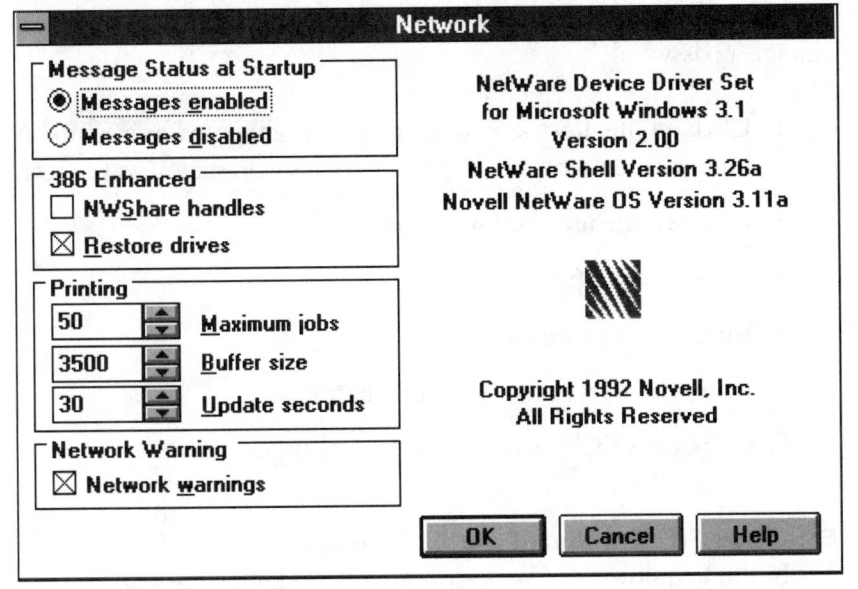

Figure 5-8.
The NetWare driver screen. The NetWare shell (NETX) Version 3.26a is the lowest shell version you can use with Windows for Workgroups.

Selecting the Password button on the Netware Settings screen (see Figure 5-3) brings up a Change Logon Password screen similar to the one shown in Figure 5-9. In the "What to Do about Lost Passwords" section of this chapter, you learned how to delete a password. This screen allows you to change a password from within Windows. However, you must know the user's current password.

Figure 5-9.
Changing your logon password. This updates the encrypted password file on the local drive. When entering the password, a series of asterisks will be displayed.

Building Local Area Networks with Windows for Workgroups

To find a user name on a workstation with multiple users and change a password:

1. Click on the down-arrow next to the highlighted user name. A list of all users who have logged in to this workstation will appear.

2. Click on the user you wish to modify.

3. Enter the old password.

4. Enter the new password.

5. Enter the new password confirmation.

6. Click the **OK** button to make the change.

Effective 386 Enhanced Mode Settings

In the Windows for Workgroups Control Panel (see Figure 5-2), the 386 Enhanced icon looks identical to its Windows 3.1 counterpart. It bears discussion in this chapter because of its influence on network performance. When you run this program, you'll see the 386 Enhanced screen shown in Figure 5-10.

Figure 5-10. 386 Enhanced mode settings. The Scheduling portion of this box refers to Windows and DOS inter-operability only. The time slices defined for Windows refer to all Windows applications when a DOS application is also running.

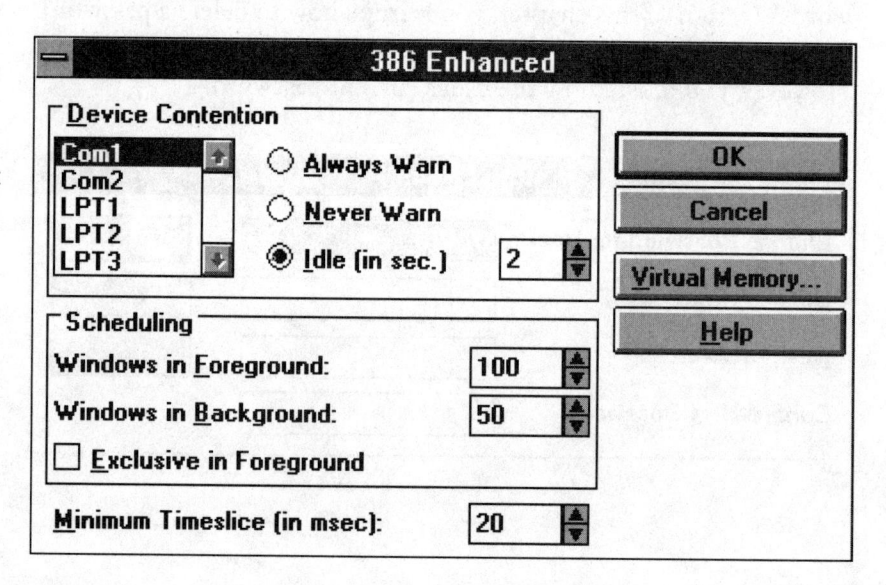

5

Optimizing Server Performance

Scheduling and Virtual Memory

The important settings for Windows for Workgroups are in Scheduling and Virtual Memory. Under Scheduling, the two values determine how many time slices to allocate to Windows when DOS applications are also running. Using the values in Figure 5-10, all Windows programs will run slower when a DOS application is active in the foreground than when Windows is in the foreground. Selecting the Exclusive in Foreground box tells Windows to suspend DOS programs when Windows is in the foreground.

Since sharing network devices is a function of Windows' enhanced mode, running DOS applications on a server and the settings you choose here can greatly affect remote access performance. If the workstation is running as the network mail server or performing other "server" style tasks that require frequent disk access, you should consider either *not* running DOS applications on this system or setting the time slice for Windows to high values.

Virtual memory refers to Windows' capability to swap portions of itself and Windows programs to disk, thereby freeing up memory for other Windows applications. Swapping can occur to either a permanent or a temporary swap file. While swapping to disk can provide you with the ability to use up to four times your actual memory, depending on disk space, it can also significantly affect both the performance of your system and other systems using your disk or printer.

Figure 5-11 shows a sample swap file setup screen. In this example, we already have an approximately 1Mb permanent swap file, and have the option to change this to a 1.5Mb temporary file. From a performance viewpoint, a permanent swap file is preferred, since the disk space used by a permanent file is not fragmented across the disk, whereas a temporary swap file can become quite scattered. The real reason for changing this value, however, results from Windows' automatic creation of temporary swap space if a permanent swap file does not exist.

Figure 5-11. Selecting a swap file. Most disk controllers that use or emulate the Western Digital disk controller chip set can provide faster swap performance if 32-bit disk access is selected. Don't use this setting if you are using a portable system with disk power-saving features.

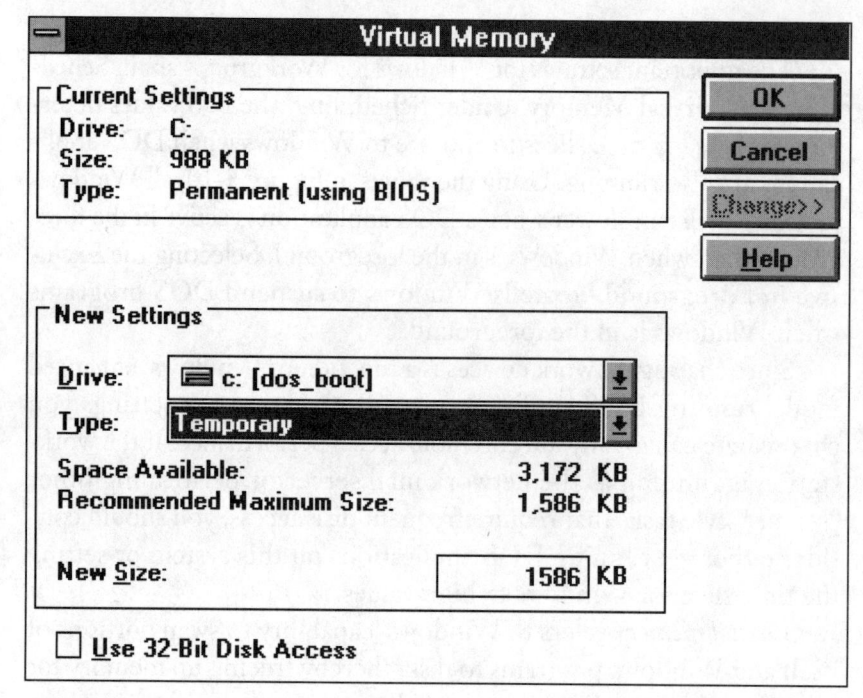

```
┌─ Virtual Memory ─────────────────────────────┐
│                                              │
│  ┌─ Current Settings ──────────────┐  [ OK ] │
│    Drive:  C:                                │
│    Size:   988 KB                   [Cancel] │
│    Type:   Permanent (using BIOS)            │
│                                     [Change>>]│
│                                              │
│                                     [ Help ] │
│  ┌─ New Settings ──────────────────┐         │
│    Drive:  [≡ c: [dos_boot]    ▼]            │
│    Type:   [Temporary          ▼]            │
│    Space Available:        3,172 KB          │
│    Recommended Maximum Size: 1,586 KB        │
│                                              │
│    New Size:               [ 1586 ] KB       │
│                                              │
│  □ Use 32-Bit Disk Access                    │
└──────────────────────────────────────────────┘
```

Under ideal circumstances, your system should be configured with sufficient memory to allow you to run all your Windows and DOS applications without swapping to disk at all. Try setting a permanent swap file of 0 bytes. If all your applications can still load and run, you're okay. If, however, you must use a swap file and will be sharing resources with other workgroup members, try to create a permanent swap file, and close out applications if they aren't needed.

In the example of our Mail server, disk swaps that occur during Mail access will virtually halt server network activity until the swap is complete.

FURTHER SUGGESTIONS FOR BETTER SERVER PERFORMANCE

Using a screen saver can degrade performance on a shared system. If the workstation will be left unattended, do not install a screen saver or use a screen saver such as Marquee, which is not CPU intensive.

Optimizing Server Performance

In standard mode, set the swap file to the fastest local hard drive, using the SWAPDISK= entry in the [NonWindowsApp] section of SYSTEM.INI. Systems running enhanced mode should use a permanent swap file on the fastest local hard drive (see the discussion of virtual memory in the previous section).

The ideal server does not use a swap file at all. Add enough memory to the server to allow all applications to run without swapping to disk.

In addition to allocating memory for applications, consider the size of the SmartDrive cache. Read requests serviced from the disk cache are considerably faster than read requests to disk, and CPU overhead is also much less.

If possible, do not run DOS applications on a server system. Even sitting at a DOS prompt, the DOS box uses an inordinate amount of CPU cycles, polling the keyboard for response. Windows applications will access the system CPU only on an as-needed basis.

Select the lowest resolution display to meet your needs. The standard VGA driver will provide better performance than higher resolution drivers. You may also want to consider a video adapter that provides its own video processor.

If the workstation will function as a dedicated server, use the Performance Priority slide bar to allocate maximum resources to sharing. However, since printer sharing requires the Print Manager program (a local application), you may need to adjust performance to provide sufficient CPU cycles for the Print Manager.

Use simple separator pages between print jobs on shared printers.

Don't use a network drive for temporary swap files (Windows does not support permanent swap files on a network drive).

Windows for Workgroups will work with many third-party disk compression programs. Even if you use a compression utility that supports Windows, do not install swap files to a compressed disk volume.

When setting up a Windows server, use as many of these recommendations as possible. A network with poor performance will result in annoyed users and very little management support. Use your fastest systems for directory sharing and slower systems for print sharing (print jobs are spooled to disk and are more a function of printer speed). Be aware, however, that a slightly slower system with a large amount of SmartDrive cache may perform much better than a faster system with insufficient RAM.

Consider the "server-centric" approach. Set up one or more fast systems with lots of memory and a fast hard drive, rather than distribute data and resources around the network, where they will be more difficult to manage. On the other hand, if your workstations are typically underused, you may see better performance by distributing the network load among several workstations. If this is the case, be sure and document the functions assigned to each workstation and make sure your users understand the network design.

CHAPTER 6

Using Windows for Workgroups

It is very unlikely that anyone comfortable with Windows 3.1 will have any trouble using Windows for Workgroups. If it weren't for the updated display screen and the logon options, they would probably not readily recognize the difference between the two when loading. From within an application, the only noticeable difference is when the application makes a call to what Microsoft calls the *common dialog dynamic link library* (DLL). The DLL provides a set of common functions for the File Open, File Save As, and Printer Setup commands.

Applications that access the common dialog link library can access network resources without resorting to the File Manager or Print Manager programs. The most noticeable differences between Windows 3.1 and Windows for Workgroups are in the File and Print Manager programs, however.

Before looking at the File Manager, Print Manager, and the common dialog link library, you should understand Windows for Workgroups' use of *universal naming conventions* (UNCs).

ACCESSING NETWORK RESOURCES WITH UNCS

The easiest method of accessing network resources in Windows is via UNCs. UNCs allow you to access any network device using the format

```
\\Servername\Sharename
```

The *servername* is the computer name you used when installing Windows at a specific workstation. When a directory or printer is made available for sharing, it is assigned a *sharename*. For example, if you wanted to print to a printer called LASER on a computer named RALPHS_PC, you could enter \\RALPHS_PC\LASER when selecting the network printer.

Although no two devices on a network can have the same servername, sharenames do not have to be unique. Both RALPHS_PC and DAVID can access a shared directory called ROOT, since each of these directories would be accessed using both the unique *servername* and the sharename.

Files can be accessed with UNCs using the following format:

```
\\Servername\Sharename\path\Filename
```

Let's assume David's PC also has a shared directory called BUDGET. This directory can be several levels deep, as in C:\EXCEL\SPREADS\BUDGET, but the remote user only has to know the servername (DAVID) and sharename (BUDGET) to access it via UNCs, as shown in Figure 6-1. Under the BUDGET directory, David has a file called JAN.XLS. To access this file from within Excel, we would select File Open, and enter the file name

```
\\DAVID\BUDGET\JAN.XLS
```

NOTE: Don't confuse the sharename with a subdirectory name. The BUDGET sharename used in this example could in fact be any subdirectory on DAVID. The path section of the UNC refers to any subdirectories below the shared directory.

6
Using Windows for Workgroups

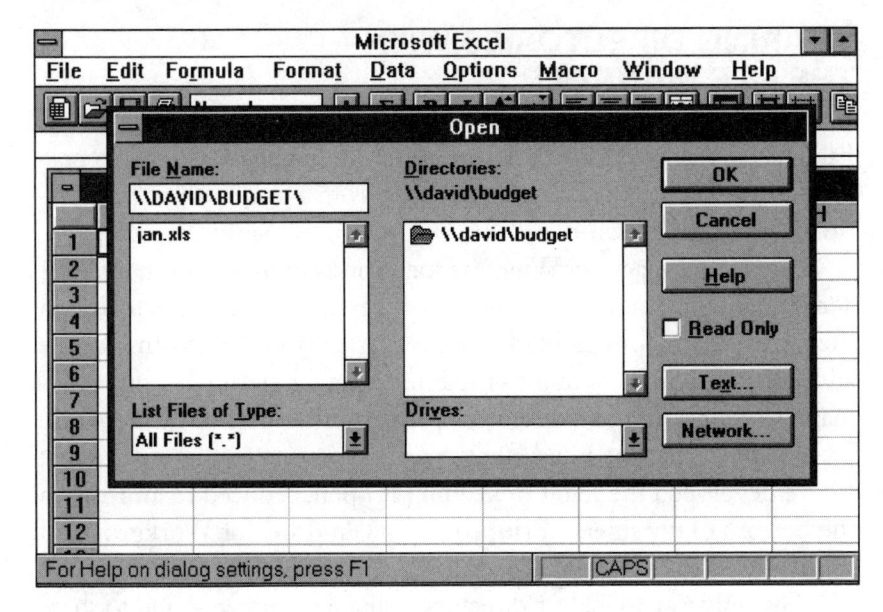

Figure 6-1. Excel spreadsheet using UNCs. Budget is the sharename David has assigned to a specific directory on his local workstation. Subdirectories of this directory would appear as folders under \\david\budget.

This method of accessing files or printers allows you to use network resources without establishing a permanent connection.

While not all Windows applications will support UNCs at present, if you keep server names and shared resource names short and simple, users will be able to access them quickly without having to use the File Manager, Print Manager, or the Network button within their application.

UNC supports NetWare servers by replacing the sharename with the NetWare volume name. A NetWare server named ACCOUNTING with a SYS volume would be accessed not as SYS:, but as

```
\\ACCOUNTING\SYS\
```

Finally, if the resource you are connecting to is password-protected, you will not be able to access it using its UNC name unless you have already established a connection via File Manager or Print Manager.

75

Building Local Area Networks with Windows for Workgroups

SHARING DIRECTORIES WITH THE FILE MANAGER

The File Manager program is located in the Main program group. Like its cousin in Windows 3.1, the File Manager allows you to perform a wide variety of DOS commands from a graphical representation of the disk directory.

The File Manager in Windows for Workgroups, however, includes additional command bar options for accessing shared directories on the network and for making local directories available to others. The additional functions built into the File Manager elevate it from a file-management utility to one of your primary interfaces to the network.

For me, using the File Manager has become so commonplace that I have developed the habit of keeping it open, reduced to an icon on the bottom of my screen. Prior to using Windows for Workgroups, I seldom used the File Manager.

The only way to make a directory available to others—and to share a directory—is via the Share As... menu option in the File Manager. Selecting this option brings up a Share Directory dialog box similar to the one displayed in Figure 6-2.

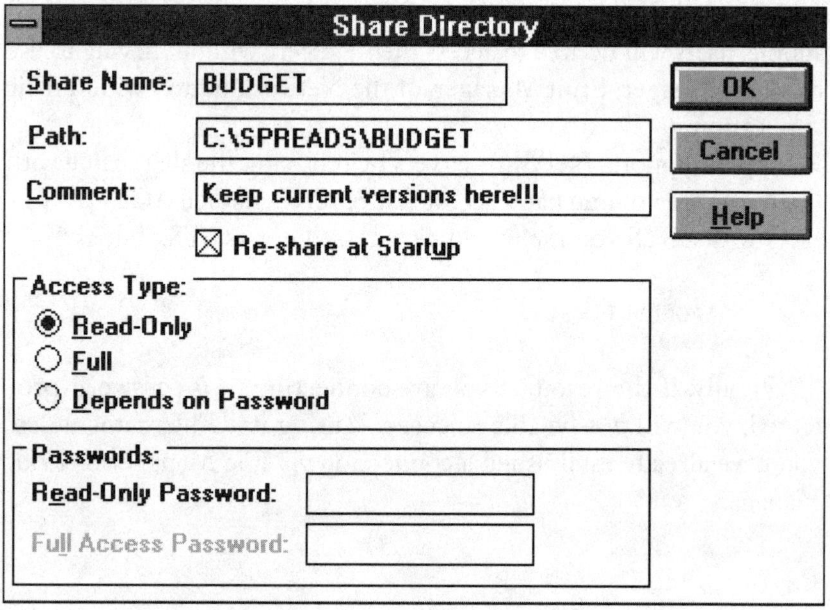

Figure 6-2. Creating a shared directory. Microsoft could have made this easier by adding a Browse button, but since they didn't, you need to know the full path when setting up a directory for sharing.

Using Windows for Workgroups

NOTE: You must be running Windows in enhanced mode to be able to share a directory with others.

To connect to a Network Drive, select the Connect Network Drive... option in the File Manager. This option allows you to assign a drive letter to a shared resource. In Figure 6-3, the user is connecting to a workstation named DAVID.

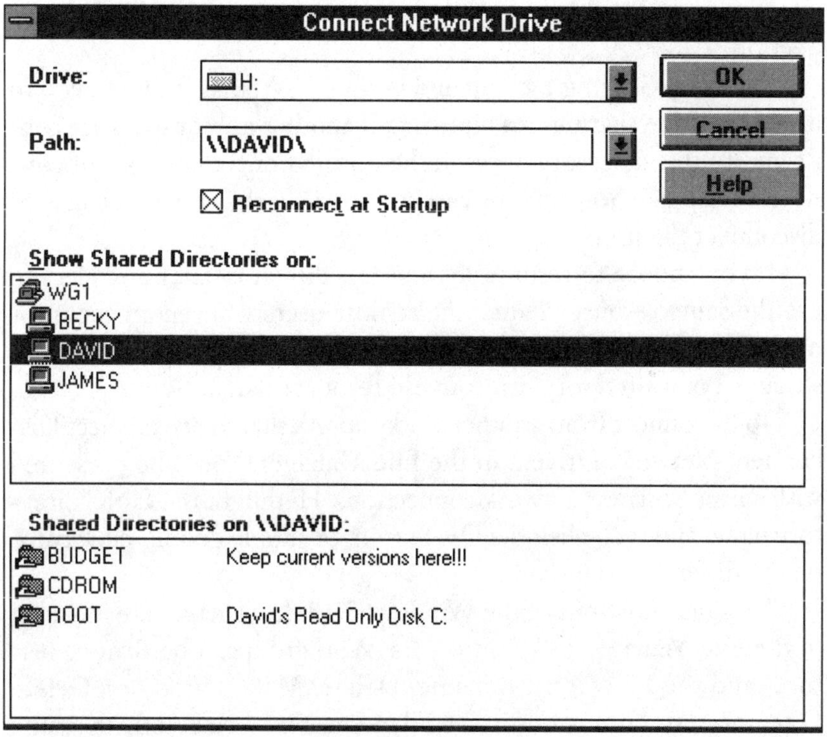

Figure 6-3. Connecting to a network drive. Notice the comment to the right of the shared directory BUDGET. This comment was created in the Share Directory dialog box in Figure 6-2.

The bottom portion of the Connect Network Drive dialog box displays the shared directories and their comments, exactly as David published them. In this example, BUDGET refers to a subdirectory under C:\SPREADS, while ROOT is the root directory (C:\).

David has published his entire drive for read-only access, but users with the correct password can write to the \SPREADS\BUDGET directory. David also has a CD-ROM drive that he is sharing with the network.

Select a drive letter to assign to a remote directory by pressing the down-arrow button to the right of the Drive box, then select the path either by typing the UNC name (\\DAVID\BUDGET) in the Path box or by highlighting the shared directory with the mouse.

The down-arrow button next to the Path box will display all previous network paths used by this workstation. You can also select this button and highlight one of the UNC names to establish a connection.

The Stop Sharing... command in the File Manager allows you to discontinue the sharing of a directory. If another user or users are connected to this directory, you will be notified of the number of connections in use. You can elect to continue sharing the directory, or disconnect the users.

If you choose to resume sharing this directory later and elect to use the same resource name, the remote users will reconnect automatically. The automatic reconnect can lead to confusion if you begin sharing a new directory using an old resource name!

To disconnect from another workstation's shared drive, select Disconnect Network Drive... in the File Manager. You'll be presented with a list of current network connections. Highlight the UNC directory name and then click the OK button, or simply double-click twice on the directory to disconnect.

All other functions of the Windows 3.1 File Manager are included in the File Manager in Windows for Workgroups. The Browse features and the File Copy, Rename, Delete, Make Directory, Delete Directory, etc. commands in the File Manager work exactly the same way in both versions. The Windows for Workgroups File Manager can perform these functions across the network, subject to the read-only and password restrictions set up by the network administrator.

File Manager has one other change to its menu bar—the Mail command.

Microsoft provides easy-to-use hooks so that users can access applications from within an application, and samples of these hooks can be

Using Windows for Workgroups

found in the File Manager. The Mail command allows you to create a mail message and send it without leaving your application.

Although the File Manager has close to sixty menu commands or options, users can learn how to create and share directories in a matter of minutes. The steps can be condensed to a short checklist, as follows:

To share a directory (enhanced mode only),

1. Open the File Manager.

2. Select **Share As...** from the Disk menu.

3. Assign a Share Name and enter the directory path.

4. Choose **Reshare at Startup** if this will be a permanent share setting.

5. Assign the access level and optional password.

6. Choose **OK**.

To access a shared directory (standard or enhanced mode),

1. Open the File Manager.

2. Select **Connect Network Drive...** from the Disk menu.

3. Choose a drive letter to assign the network directory to.

4. Select a workstation and the shared directory, or type the UNC name, if known.

5. Select **Reconnect at Startup** if this is a permanent connection.

6. Choose **OK**.

7. Enter the password, if necessary.

PRINTER SHARING ON THE NETWORK

Sharing printers is frequently one of the most difficult aspects of maintaining a network. Print jobs, particularly ones with graphics, can be extremely large and thus wind up putting a considerable amount of data on the network cable in a relatively short amount of time.

Networks that would normally support a larger number of users can become bogged down by excessive routing of print jobs.

When transmitting a print job to a print server, enough disk space must be available to accept the entire job. Since the printer is shared, no single print job will be sent until the entire file can be printed at once. In a nondedicated print server environment, such as Windows for Workgroups, you may also need to address a performance issue: the workstation receiving the print job will see performance degrading both when receiving the job and when printing it. Finally, in Windows for Workgroups, you have the added problem of driver configurations.

Each workstation that accesses a shared Windows printer must have the correct driver defined to LPT1, 2, or 3, and the user must connect the correct network printer to this port. Nonetheless, sharing print devices, especially expensive laser printers and plotters, has fast become a primary reason for installing small networks. The cost of a single PostScript-capable printer can easily pay for the entire network.

Handling Print Jobs with the Print Manager

The Print Manager in Windows for Workgroups provides options for sharing your printer with others, for connecting to other workstation-shared printers, for discontinuing sharing, and for disconnecting from a network printer. The status of print jobs sent from your workstation to another workstation can be viewed from within your Print Manager. However, once a job is transmitted for printing,

Using Windows for Workgroups

only the Print Manager at the printer host location can be used to cancel the job.

If you did not select a printer driver during Setup, you will need to do so before attaching to a remote network printer. Your copy of Windows will provide the necessary print driver information to your application and to the print queue, so it's important to select the proper printer driver at the workstation creating the print job. You may want to configure each workstation's printer setup with up to three different printer drivers, and then allow the user to connect to the appropriate network printer. Figure 6-4 shows the screen selecting a printer. You can add printers to the Print Manager via the Printer Program in the Control Panel.

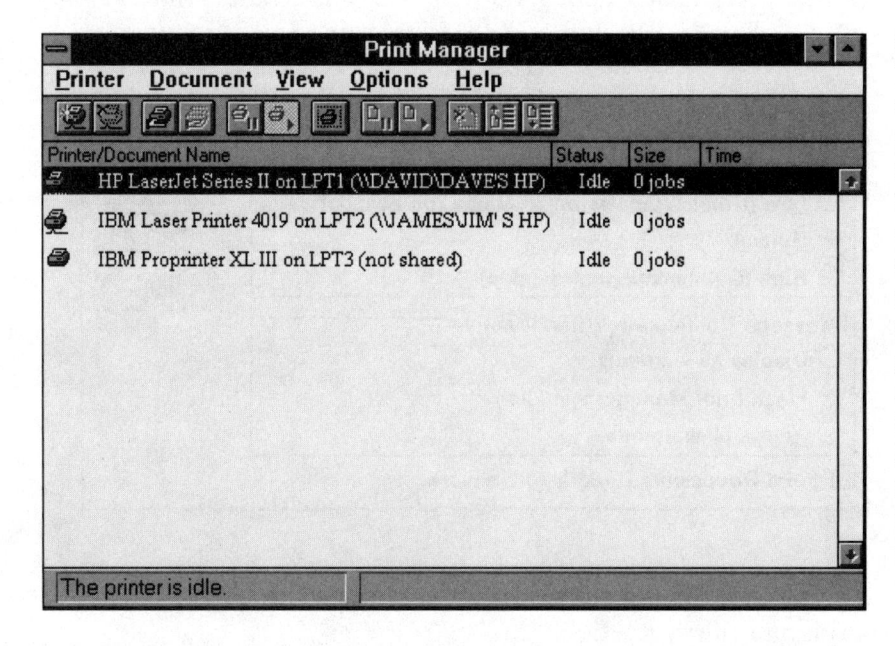

Figure 6-4. The Print Manager. Although you can connect up to ten printers (local or network) via the Print Manager, your application may not recognize some port names, such as com3 or com4. Printers are added to the Print Manager via the Control Panel's Printers program.

Adding Separator Pages

The Separator Pages command in the Print Manager Options menu supports four options for printing a separator page between print jobs on a networked printer (or even on your local printer, if you so desire). The options are:

- No separator page.

- A simple Courier font separator page, for slower or dot-matrix printers.

- A standard separator page, using the printer's standard fonts.

- A custom-designed separator page, using Windows' vector-base graphics metafiles.

Background Printing

Use the Background Printing command in the Print Manager for printer performance tuning, both for local and remote printing. Figure 6-5 shows the Background Printing dialog box.

Figure 6-5. Background printing. Check the Send Documents Directly to Network box if you are printing to a remote shared printer.

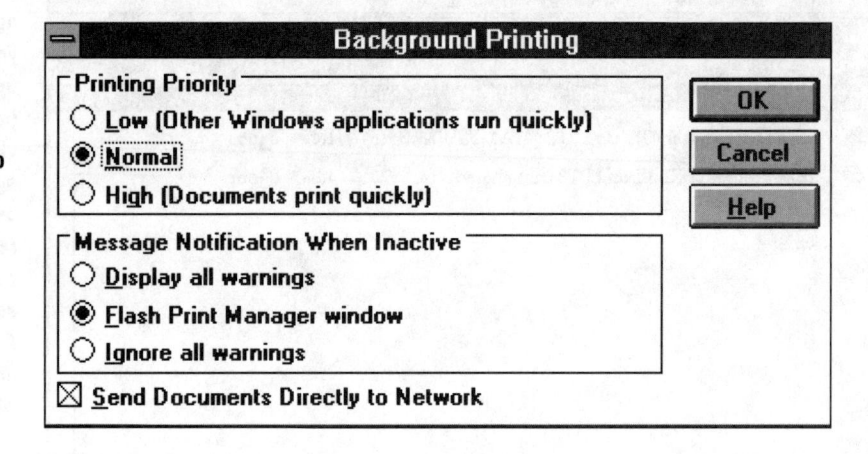

For network printer workstations, you will probably want to set Printing Priority to High.

The Send Documents Directly to Network box is for users printing to a remote printer. When this box is checked, the user can still view network queues and manage local printing, but print jobs sent to a network queue won't be routed through the local copy of Print Manager.

Using Windows for Workgroups

Although printer sharing with Windows for workgroups requires a little extra effort on your part—mostly to insure that the correct drivers are defined in each user copy of Windows—Print Manager makes it easy for network users to use and manage the network printers. In many instances, particularly when a workgroup is spread out, workgroup members use network printers as an informal (or formal) mail system—they print directly to their colleagues' printers.

THE COMMON DIALOG LIBRARY

By now you have probably become quite familiar with the Network button in the File Manager and Print Manager. Wouldn't it be nice if this button were available to you within Windows programs? As it turns out, Microsoft provides an updated common *dialog dynamic link library* (COMMDLG.DLL) file with Windows for Workgroups that provides the capability of the Network button.

Application programmers who access this library when performing File Open, File Save As, and Printer Setup commands within their programs can provide the Network access button with little or no extra programming effort.

Figure 6-6 shows the Network... button from the File Open command in Excel 4.0. Clicking on the Network... button allows the user to establish a network connection from within Excel. The Connect Network Drive box is identical to the connection box used in File Manager, shown in Figure 6-7.

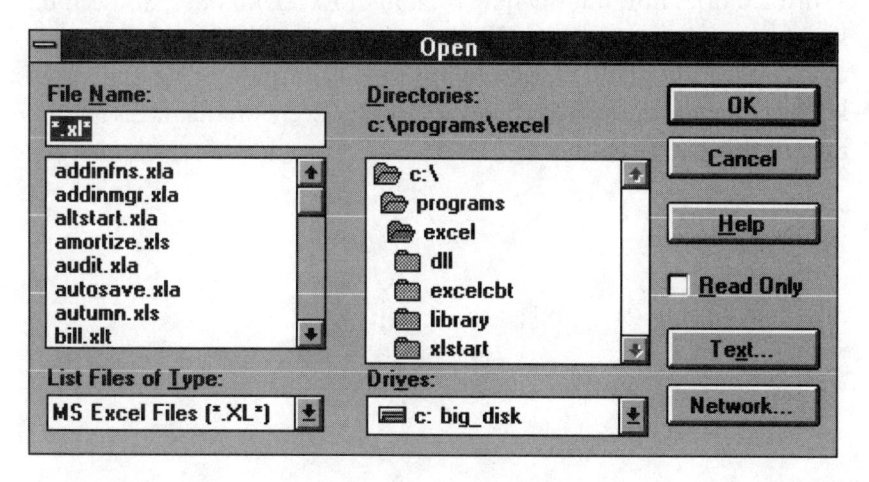

Figure 6-6. The Network... button. Applications that use the COMM-DIAG.DLL file in Windows for Workgroups will automatically be able to connect network directories or printers without leaving the program.

Building Local Area Networks with Windows for Workgroups

Figure 6-7. Connecting to a network drive. Programmers that use the common dialog library don't have to write additional code to access the network—this dialog box is shared by the application and the File Manager.

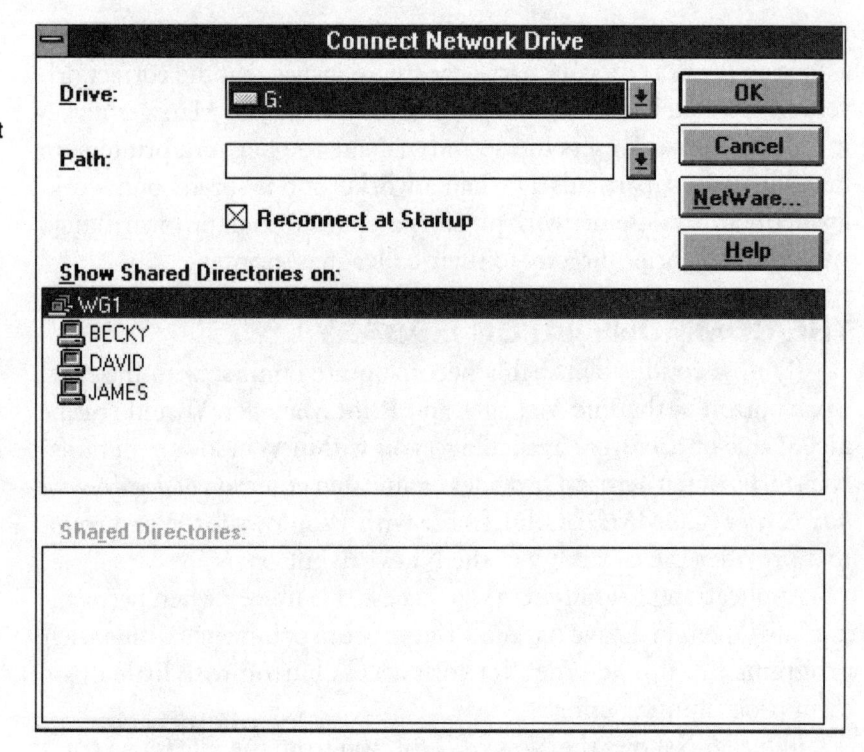

In some cases, workstations that connect to NetWare may not display the NetWare... button from within the application, due to the amount of memory stack space required to establish this connection.

Not all programs support the common dialog library just yet. My Word 2.0 does not, but my new version of Excel 4.0 does. You can be sure future versions of your Windows software will. If you have a specific application that you want to use with Windows for Workgroups, let the company know that you expect to see a version that takes advantage of this handy feature.

7 CHAPTER

Windows for Workgroups Accessories

Windows for Workgroups includes several new accessories, including the ClipBook Viewer, WinMeter, NetWatcher, Chat, and even a networked version of the Hearts card game.

- The ClipBook Viewer extends the Windows Clipboard across the network.

- WinMeter allows a user to determine the amount of CPU cycles in use for both local applications and server processing.

- NetWatcher indicates the number of remote connections to a Windows server.

- Chat allows you to establish a conversation, or "chat," with another user across the network.

Each accessory is described in this chapter.

CLIPBOOK VIEWER: A CLIPBOARD FOR THE NETWORK

Within Windows applications, a Cut or Copy command takes the highlighted information and places it in a temporary holding area known as the Clipboard. The ClipBook Viewer allows you to view the contents of the Clipboard, paste the Clipboard into individual pages in the ClipBook, and share these ClipBook pages with other members of your workgroup. If a remote user's application supports *dynamic data exchange* (DLE) or *object linking and embedding* (OLE), you can include ClipBook images directly in the application, while maintaining a link to the ClipBook. Subsequent changes made to the source ClipBook image will automatically update the remote application image.

Images can be placed in the Clipboard either through Cut or Copy commands from within an application, or by using the Print Screen key. While DOS uses the Print Screen key to send a copy of a text screen to the printer, Windows graphical screens cannot be handled in the same manner. Instead, pressing the Print Screen key takes the full Windows screen and places an image of it in the Clipboard. You can then paste the image into an application such as Paint or Word and use the print function in the application to print the screen.

Once you have captured an image into the Clipboard, follow these steps to make it accessible to the network:

1. Open the ClipBook Viewer program.

2. Select the **Paste** function. This will bring up the Paste dialog box shown in Figure 7-1.

3. Assign a name for the Pasted Image.

4. Click on the **Share Item now** button if you want remote users to be able to access the ClipBook image. This brings up the Share Clipboard Page dialog box, where you can allow users **Read-Only**, **Full**, or **Depends on Password** (password-pro-

Windows for Workgroups Accessories

tected) access to the image, as in Figure 7-2. Full access allows a remote user to modify and resave images in your ClipBook.

The **Start Application on Connect** box will automatically start the application that created the image whenever the shared image is accessed. If this option isn't checked, users will be able to access the image, but they will not be able to establish a dynamic link to the application unless the application is already running.

Click **OK** to leave this dialog box.

5. Click **OK** in the Paste box. A new ClipBook page will be created.

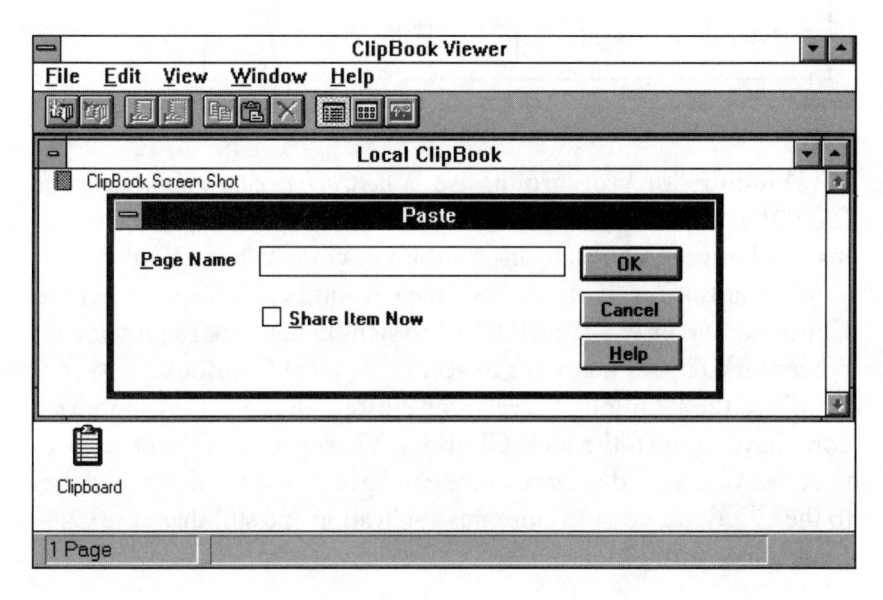

Figure 7-1.
Pasting to the ClipBook. Selecting Share Item Now allows other users to access images in your ClipBook.

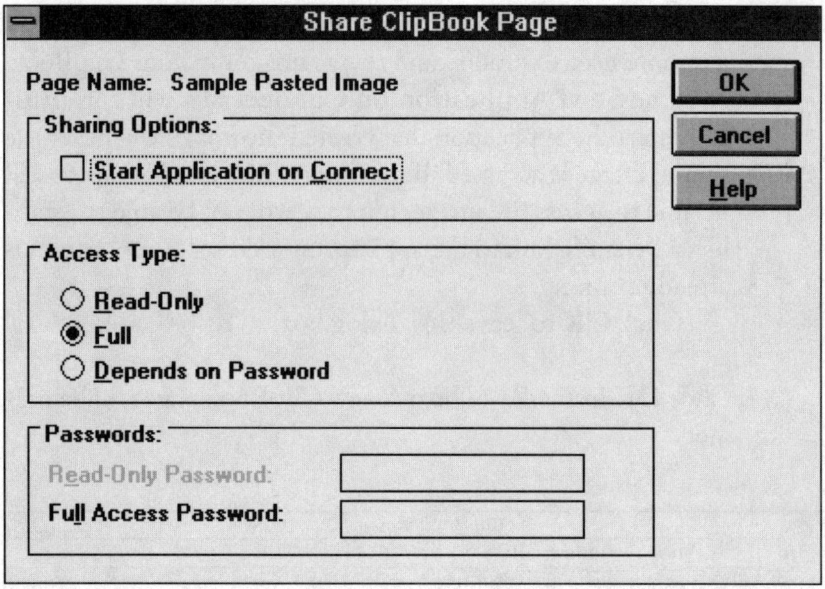

Figure 7-2.
Sharing a Clip-
Book page. Full
access allows a
remote user to
modify and
resave images in
your ClipBook.
Passwords can
be assigned both
read-only or full-
access by select-
ing the Depends
on Password but-
ton.

Windows for Workgroups uses a *network dynamic data exchange* (NDDE), an extension of Windows 3.1's DDE, to exchange information between workstations on the network. When Windows for Workgroups loads, it also loads a background application called the ClipBook Server (CLIPSRV.EXE) to handle network requests from other workstations that want to access the local ClipBook.

Since the ClipBook Server runs entirely in the background, you don't have to open the local ClipBook Viewer to allow remote users to access your stored images. Once you have pasted the desired images to the ClipBook, you can close this application and still share the ClipBook pages with others.

Accessing a Shared ClipBook Page

A user who wants to access a shared ClipBook page uses the ClipBook Viewer on the local workstation to connect to the remote ClipBook, as follows:

Windows for Workgroups Accessories

1. Select the **File** menu in the ClipBook Viewer.

2. Select the **Connect** option. This displays the Select Computer dialog box.

3. Choose the workstation, and the remote ClipBook will be displayed, as in Figure 7-3.

4. Simply double-click on the image to display it, or highlight the image and select the **Copy** command from the Edit menu. A copy of the image is pasted in the local Clipboard, where it can be pasted into the local ClipBook or directly into a Windows application.

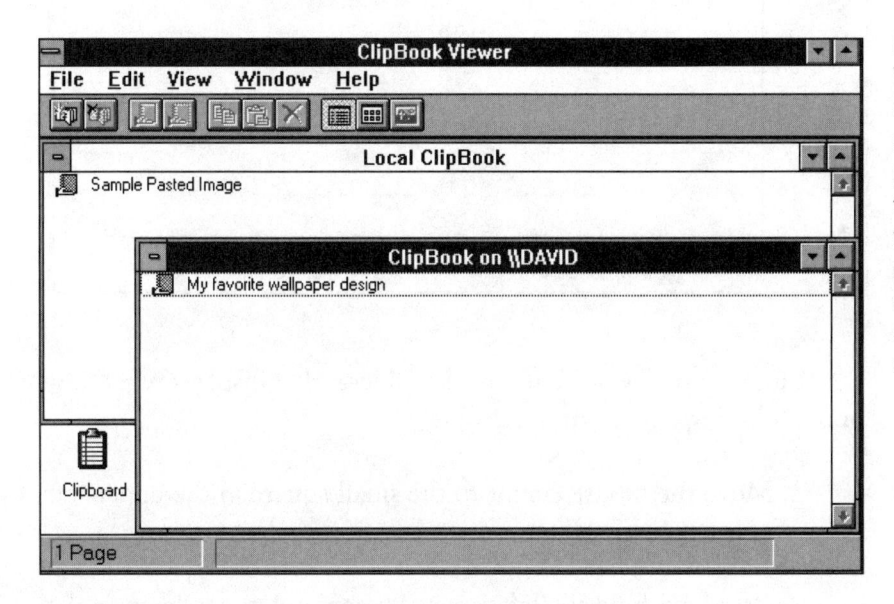

Figure 7-3. Viewing remote ClipBooks. You can access multiple ClipBooks at the same time. To view an image, simply double-click on the line containing the description.

WINMETER: TRACKING CPU USAGE

The WinMeter accessory allows you to track CPU usage at a workstation. WinMeter will not work on workstations running in standard mode or on workstations that have disabled sharing via the Networks option in the Control Panel.

WinMeter graphically displays the ratio between the amount of processor time in use for server and local processing. WinMeter can help the user determine how to adjust the slider bar in the Control Panel Networks option. It's also kind of neat just to watch. A sample WinMeter display is shown in Figure 7-4.

Figure 7-4. WinMeter provides a graphical comparison between total CPU utilization, local applications usage, and server usage.

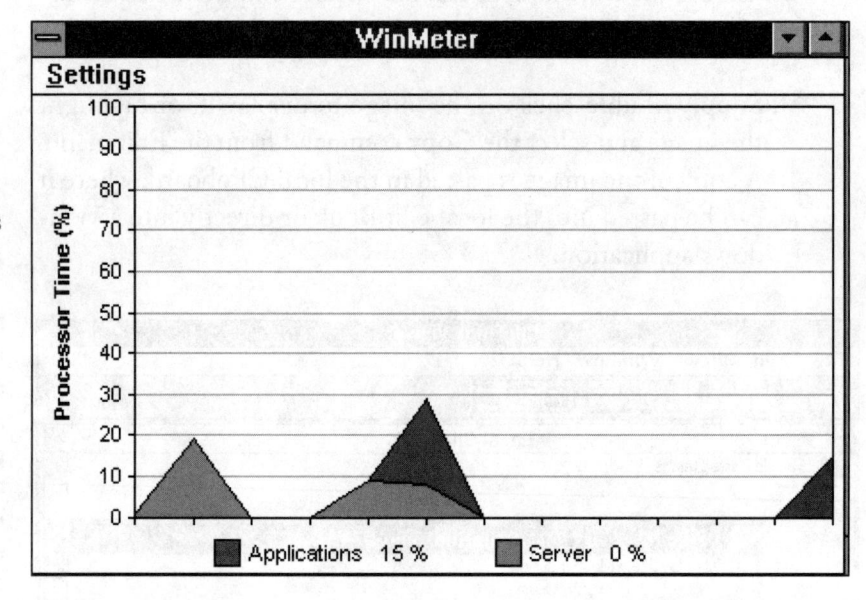

You can install WinMeter as a small icon that displays regardless of the Windows application running.

1. Move the mouse cursor to the small square in the upper-left corner of WinMeter.

2. Press and hold the left mouse button and move down to the **Always on Top** option. It is shown in Figure 7-5.

3. Use the down-button in the top-right corner of WinMeter to reduce the application to an icon.

Windows for Workgroups Accessories   7

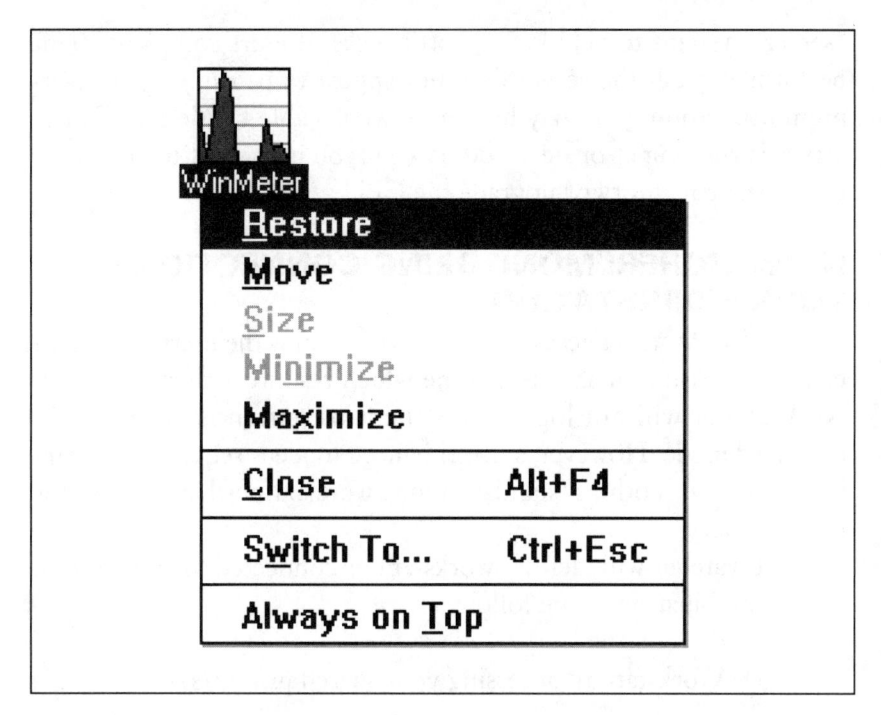

Figure 7-5. WinMeter's Always on Top option. Regardless of the size of the WinMeter window, selecting Always on Top tells WinMeter to remain on-screen regardless of the Windows applications running. You'll probably want to reduce WinMeter to an icon before selecting this command.

WinMeter will continue to run and display the CPU usage, and will remain on-screen regardless of the Windows program running. You can use the mouse to move the icon as necessary by clicking and holding the left mouse button while moving the icon.

To undo the Always on Top option, click once on the icon, and reselect the command.

Systems that have *advanced power management* (APM) enabled will not accurately display local application processing time with WinMeter. APM is typically used on notebook computers to conserve battery life. On workstations with APM enabled, WinMeter will display application utilization as 100 percent at all times. However, server utilization will display correctly on these machines. Disabling AMP when connected to the network allows WinMeter to correctly display applications usage.

For the average user, WinMeter is more interesting to look at than it is informational; however, you may want to use WinMeter on your "server" systems to help locate bottlenecks. If users complain about performance but the server does not appear to be running at maximum utilization, you may have a network cable bottleneck. If the server is running at or near 100 percent you may want to add additional cache memory or upgrade the CPU.

NETWATCHER: MONITORING CONNECTIONS TO YOUR WORKSTATION

The NetWatcher accessory allows you to view the users connected to your workstation and determine which resources they are using. NetWatcher will not load unless the workstation is operating in enhanced mode. However, since enhanced mode is required for sharing devices with others, standard mode workstations have no use for this accessory.

NetWatcher will identify workstations connected to your system in any combination of the following:

- Workstations accessing your shared printer(s)

- Workstations accessing your shared directories

- Workstations using Network DDE to talk to your system

Select the Connection option on Netwatcher's menu to see who you're connected to. In Figure 7-6, workstation BECKY has two remote connections. Workstation JAMES, the highlighted connection, is connected to both the POSTOFFICE directory and the ROOT directory, and is also connected to a shared printer on BECKY.

NetWatcher's Connection menu can also be used to disconnect a user. Highlight either the user or the specific user connection, and then choose Disconnect. Since this option will close any open files or applications the user has on your system, and can result in loss of data, do not use this option unless you know the user can be disconnected safely.

Windows for Workgroups Accessories

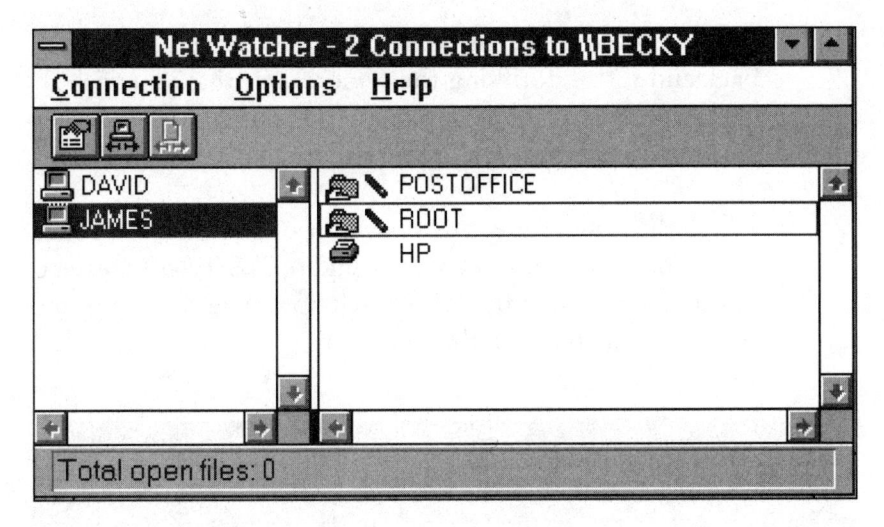

Figure 7-6.
NetWatcher allows you to monitor the connections to your workstation.

When would you use NetWatcher? If you attempt to unload Windows at a workstation that is sharing its disk or printer, or stop sharing a specific resource, Windows will tell you how many connections are active and ask you if you really want to disconnect them, but Windows doesn't tell you *who* these users are. NetWatcher allows you to determine who is using the system so you can disconnect them gracefully.

CHAT: TALKING WITH OTHER USERS

The Windows for Workgroups Chat option is an easy-to-use method of "chatting" with members of your workgroup, and it includes an amusing method of notifying you when others want to chat. To use Chat,

1. Select the **Dial** command from the Conversation menu. You'll see the familiar Select Computer list.

2. Choose another workstation. A telephone icon will appear on the remote workstation Program Manager screen, and the workstation speaker will beep approximately once every five seconds.

Building Local Area Networks with Windows for Workgroups

With each beep, the handset on the telephone will rock back and forth, notifying the remote user that you wish to chat. The "phone" will continue to ring until the remote user clicks on the phone icon or you choose to disconnect.

3. When the remote user answers, a set of conversation boxes appear on each user screen, as in Figure 7-7. Type a message in the upper box in the CHAT window. The remote user's response will appear in the lower box.

Figure 7-7. Windows' Chat function. The icon button bar allows you to quickly select commands for Dialing, Pick-Up, and Hang-Up.

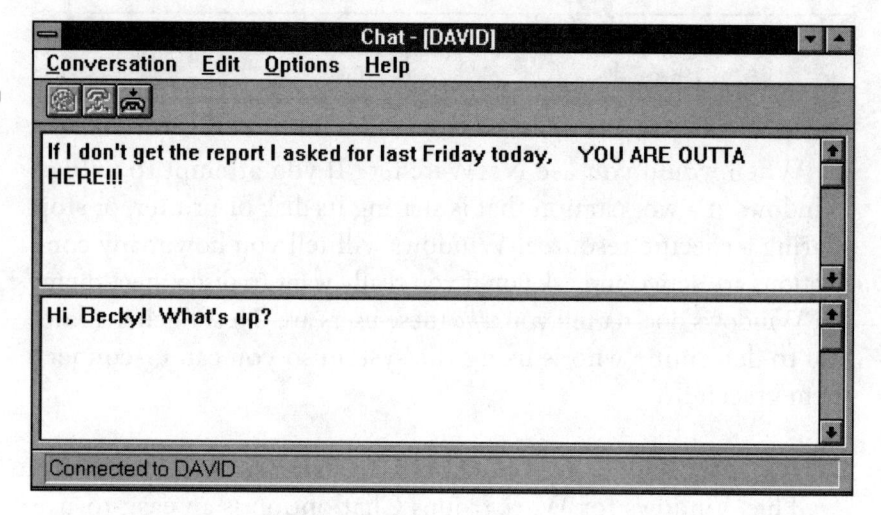

```
┌─────────────────────── Chat - [DAVID] ───────────────▼▲─┐
│ Conversation   Edit   Options   Help                     │
│ [icons]                                                  │
│ ┌──────────────────────────────────────────────────────┐ │
│ │ If I don't get the report I asked for last Friday    │ │
│ │ today,    YOU ARE OUTTA HERE!!!                      │ │
│ │                                                      │ │
│ └──────────────────────────────────────────────────────┘ │
│ ┌──────────────────────────────────────────────────────┐ │
│ │ Hi, Becky!  What's up?                               │ │
│ │                                                      │ │
│ └──────────────────────────────────────────────────────┘ │
│ Connected to DAVID                                       │
└──────────────────────────────────────────────────────────┘
```

The CHAT program does not support the transfer of graphic screens. The Cut, Copy, and Paste commands under the Edit menu only support the text boxes in Chat. You cannot paste from Paint into Chat, for example.

4. To disconnect at the end of the conversation, select **Disconnect** or click once on the Disconnect button below the menu bar.

7

Windows for Workgroups Accessories

As a long-time network administrator, I have always been on the lookout for features such as Chat. While DOS-based Chat programs have existed for NetWare and Netbios networks for some time now, they have generally been developed by third-party companies or individuals for their own use, or for distribution via shareware. Chat is a well-designed Windows tool that offers an easy method of communicating with other workgroup users in your office, even when they're on the "real" phone.

CHAPTER 8

The Network Administrator

In the previous chapters, we looked at the physical installation of the network components and the Windows software, and we examined the functions associated with using Windows for Workgroups in a shared environment. Using the network to its fullest entails considerably more than this, however. As the network administrator, you'll need to determine what network resources need to be shared, ensure that the users working on the PCs understand their role in the network, and assume responsibility for backing up and restoring data as necessary. Additional responsibilities include maintaining the correct number of software licenses for the number of active (concurrent) users on the network. In this chapter, we'll discuss these functions and the role of the network administrator.

MAIL ADMINISTRATION

I recommend making the network administrator the Microsoft Mail administrator as well. In larger environments, it is not uncommon to assign someone the role of dedicated mail administrator, but unless you will be connecting your mail system to others, the amount of time required to maintain the mail system is minimal. Since Windows for Workgroups Mail allows the user to maintain his or her own profile, most of your administrative duties will be limited to maintaining shared folders and periodically compressing the mail folders.

SHARING PROGRAMS AND DATA FILES

Like any peer network, Windows for Workgroups allows virtually any networked PC to provide file services to other network users. The only restriction is that the server PC be able to run Windows in enhanced mode, since file sharing occurs as a background Windows task. The security mechanisms in Windows for Workgroups lack the sophistication of larger server-centric networks, but users can still share a read-only directory with other users and, in so doing, they can share applications with others as well. Likewise, data directories can be shared in both read-only and read-write modes, as necessary.

Unlike most DOS applications, virtually all Windows programs are designed to be run on networks. A single copy of Microsoft Word for Windows, for example, can be installed on a single workstation. Once installed, the WORD directory can be defined as a shared resource and all workstations on the network can access Microsoft Word.

Whether you choose to install and provide access to some or all your programs in this manner depends on a variety of factors, including

- the disk space capacity on each workstation,

- how hard or easy it is to upgrade applications,

- software licensing restrictions,

- performance considerations.

Because a single Windows application can consume megabytes of disk space, installing software on a single workstation or just a few workstations in the group can significantly reduce the overall disk space requirements for the other workstations. Likewise, by limiting

The Network Administrator

the number of PCs containing application code, upgrading to a new version is considerably easier.

When you consider sharing applications from a single workstation, you should be aware of software licensing restrictions and the possible impact on performance. Some software licenses expressly prohibit the use of the program in a network environment or require the purchase of a special version of the software. These special versions typically provide network functions not available in the stand-alone version of the program.

On the performance side, sharing applications from a central workstation will impact the performance at that workstation. Depending on the number and complexity of the programs running at the "server," performance impact may run from negligible to serious. In addition, the amount of time required to load an application across the network in a peer environment is generally slower than the time it takes to access the program from a local hard drive.

In many cases, however, the advantages of installing an application from a central workstation outweigh the disadvantages. For example, I followed Microsoft's recommended installation for Windows and placed a copy of Windows on each workstation in my network. However, I could have placed a second copy of the Windows files in a different directory on a "server" and accessed that directory using Workgroup Connection. This would have allowed me to run Windows on a workstation that lacked a hard drive. Loading the network drivers (via Workgroup Connection) outside of Windows reduces the available memory for DOS applications, but it does allow you to run Windows on a system without its own local hard drive. Running applications from a read-only network directory also prevents users from inadvertently deleting application files.

If you decide to centralize some or all of your programs, place them in subdirectories under a common directory. Disk sharing in Windows for Workgroups is based on the directory structure: sharing a directory allows you to share all the directories below it. Thus, by placing all your shared applications in directories under a single directory called APPS, for example, you can assign APPS as the shared directory and make all the subdirectory programs immediately accessible. Figure 8-1 shows the APPS assigned as a shared directory, with Read-Only defined as the Access Type. Since the rights granted to APPS (read-only or read-write) are granted to all directories below it, you may want to set up one shared directory for applications that require a full read-write and another for applications that are read-only.

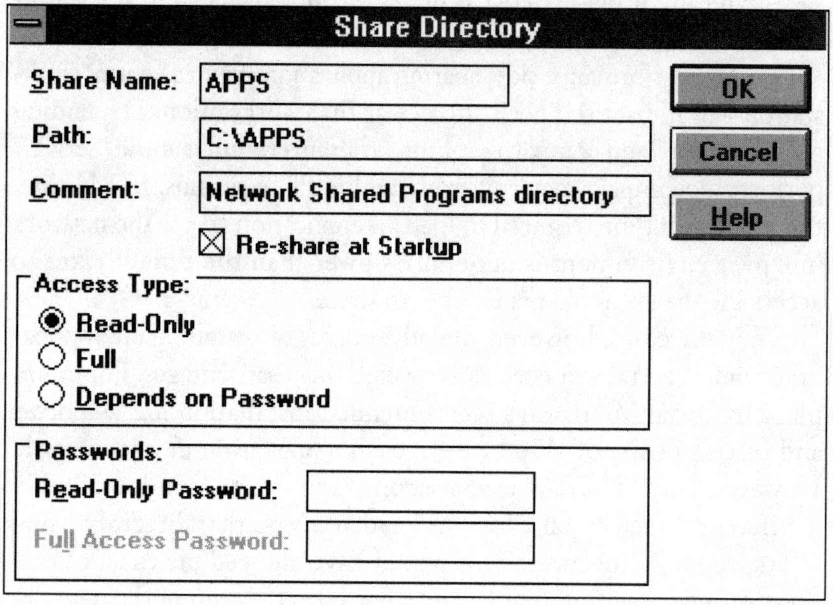

Figure 8-1. APPS as the shared directory. The read-only access assigned to APPS is granted to all subdirectories below APPS.

Very few applications require write-capability to the program directory, so use read-only access whenever possible, and use read-write sharing for data files only. Whenever possible, maintain data files, such as spreadsheets and database files, in separate directories from applications, both for sharing purposes and to eliminate confusion when updating the application.

SOFTWARE LICENSING REQUIREMENTS

As the network administrator, you are responsible for verifying that your company does not exceed the license restrictions for shared

The Network Administrator

applications. License restrictions vary, but as a general rule you need to purchase one license for every concurrent user—that is, one license for every user at present using the software. It is not unusual in a Windows environment for users to launch several applications and reduce the window for each application to an icon to make it easier to switch between applications. Most software vendors require you to count these applications as active.

Numerous third-party applications are available to assist you in maintaining records of applications usage. Most monitor the network by building a database with the number of users accessing each program and time-stamps for each instance in which an application is loaded and unloaded. Users who reboot their workstation without exiting applications can prevent you from obtaining an accurate usage count, however, so make sure users understand the need to exit programs in an orderly fashion.

PREVENTING AND CONTROLLING VIRAL INFECTIONS

Every network administrator's disaster recovery plan must take into account the possibility of a computer virus attack. Computer virus attacks can take many forms, from the relatively benign screen message all the way to total destruction of disk contents. No virus is capable of physical damage to your equipment, however, so a little bit of planning and common sense will go a long way to preventing virus damage.

A virus attack, by using the network to spread to other workstations, does most of its damage to your data, but a properly configured LAN can actually reduce the possibility of losing data. A virus contains program code that must be executed for the virus to be triggered, so infections cannot spread via data files; they can only infect executable programs or their overlay files. Programs executed from a read-only shared directory are therefore safe from virus attacks. In a peer environment such as Windows for Workgroups, you can access applications locally, bypassing the network, so additional precautions should be taken here, as outlined below.

Documented cases of viral infections from shrink-wrapped software are very rare. Most viral infections enter the PC via the floppy disk drive. A user, for example, brings an infected diskette from home or a technician loads PC diagnostics programs from an infected diskette. The other common method of infection is from software downloaded via the modem. The odds of infecting your network will be greatly reduced if you obtain virus-detection software and scan diskettes and downloaded programs before they enter the network.

Develop a schedule for scanning all the workstations on your network. Diskettes that are used to bring data files to and from work should be formatted without the /S parameter: the system files installed by this parameter are a common target of virus programs. Instruct users not to copy any executable programs on these diskettes. Periodically scanning all workstations and keeping diskettes formatted with the /S parameter out of the network can make it virtually impossible for a user to inadvertently infect your system.

Notice the word "inadvertently." The possibility always exists, however remote, that someone on your network will attempt to deliberately infect the network out of curiosity or malice. If this user is aware that virus-prevention methods are employed on the network, he or she will understand that the risk of detection is much higher. At any rate, if you do find yourself the victim of a virus attack, proper program and data backup procedures can reduce or even eliminate the damage.

NETWORK BACKUP AND RECOVERY

Several years ago, I was asked to install a new version of a network operating system on a company accounting server. My new customer wanted to save as much money as possible on the installation, so their administrator promised to back up the system before I arrived on-site. I was assured that the backup had been done and proceeded to reformat the server drive in preparation for the upgrade. After I completed the installation, I asked the administrator for the backup, and she handed me a single diskette. With a sinking feeling in the pit of my stomach, I asked her where the backup of the accounting program

8

The Network Administrator

was: the diskette contained their monthly backup of data files only. This network had been in operation for over a year, it used a highly customized accounting program, and not once had the administrator or the accounting software specialist made a backup of the actual accounting programs. The data files on the diskette were useless.

While the lesson I learned from this experience cost me a day's work, this company lost considerably more—far more than it would cost to implement a proper system backup and recovery plan.

The most common method of performing network backups is to tape drives. There are literally hundreds of drives on the market, ranging in size from 60Mb to several gigabytes (a *gigabyte* is 1000Mb). Tape drive prices have dropped rapidly in the last year as well, with 250Mb systems selling for under $300. While many network operating systems require special software for backing up the server, Windows for Workstations operates under DOS, so virtually any tape system will work.

With a Windows for Workgroups network, any workstation can be a server, and this adds to the complexity of developing a backup strategy. Programs and data can be distributed across the entire network. It is up to you to see that all of the necessary programs and data files are backed up properly. Backing up program files may seem unnecessary at first, but consider the amount of time it takes to install applications from diskettes and to customize them for your environment. In the case of a Windows word processor, macros are often developed, toolbars are customized, templates are developed, and dictionaries are updated. It is usually far simpler to restore the program from tape than to attempt to re-create all the steps involved in setting up the program initially.

The easiest method of backing up your network entails purchasing a tape drive large enough to hold, on a single tape, a full backup of all your programs and the data on each of your servers. In many cases this is not feasible, but if you are lucky enough to be able to do this, set up a rotation where you back up the entire network to tape every night. Select a tape rotation scheme that fits your business needs, but be sure to keep monthly or quarterly full backups, and even an annual backup, if necessary. Maintain a log of tape backups so that locating a file from a specific date is easy, and test the backup procedure by selecting a file or directory at random and performing a restore.

If your tape system cannot perform a full system backup to a single tape, perform a full backup to a set of tapes, and then perform incremental backups thereafter. Since incremental backups only back up modified files (and the same file can be modified several times over the course of a backup regime), a complete system restore typically requires, first, restoring the full backup, and second, restoring every single incremental backup made since then. For this reason, you'll want to periodically perform the full backup again.

Several tape vendors provide software that can help you develop a proper tape rotation scheme with a variety of methods. Some even track file versions for you and automatically maintain multiple copies of files across several tape volumes to insure data integrity. Tape-backup software comes at a price, however, and it may be less expensive to purchase a larger tape drive than to develop complex tape backup and restore procedures.

Whatever backup rotation you use, keep a complete set of relatively current backup tapes off-site. In the event of a disaster, you'll be able to restore network operations as quickly as you can get the equipment in place.

When you back up workstations and servers, be aware that programs and data files in use on the network cannot be properly backed up. One method of guaranteeing that files get backed up is to exit Windows and perform the backup from DOS. This effectively disconnects any user from the station while the backup is being performed.

On the other hand, you may want to back up a remote server to a local workstation tape drive by using the network. In this case the remote server must be running Windows, and you run the tape backup software on the local workstation from within Windows. You can use the NetWatcher utility to determine if any users have open files on the server. When performing a tape backup across the network, the local copy of Windows can negatively impact tape performance. You can avoid this by exiting Windows and using Workgroup Connection to access the remote server drive. For full backups, set a shared direc-

8
The Network Administrator

tory on the remote server to the root directory, that is, to C:\. Backing up a shared subdirectory on a remote server will typically back up its subdirectories as well, but files on the same level or higher levels are not backed up.

THE ROLE OF THE NETWORK ADMINISTRATOR

Like most peer networks, Windows for Workgroups can develop into network anarchy. Users can establish or delete shared directories and printers at will, and data files can be placed virtually anywhere on the network. It is up to you to develop network standards and training methods to insure that your users know how to use the network properly. Equally as important, you must document your work, including hardware configurations (network adapter switch settings, disk capacities, video configurations, etc.), application locations, key server configurations, and shutdown procedures. It is up to you to determine which servers, if any, require uninterruptible power supplies to prevent inadvertent shutdowns during a power failure. Many companies select peer networks for their ease of installation, but they fail to realize that the duties of the network administrator, while simplified, are pretty much the same whether the LAN comprises five or five hundred stations.

9 CHAPTER

Microsoft Mail

Windows for Workgroups includes an excellent electronic mail system, Microsoft Mail for Windows, and an office scheduler, Schedule+. The Workgroup Connection installation will install a DOS Mail program so DOS workstations can send and receive mail as well.

HOW MAIL WORKS

The Mail system in Windows for Workgroups consists of a *client piece* and a *mail-server piece*. The mail-server runs on a single enhanced-mode workstation on the network. Windows for Workgroups installs the mail-server files in a subdirectory of Windows, and this directory is set up for sharing. The mail-server directory becomes the "post office" for the workgroup. Every workstation, including the workstation containing the post office, uses the client piece to create, send, and receive messages.

The mail system uses a "store and forward" design. When a user creates a message off-line and then connects to the mail-server, the message is forwarded to the post office. At the same time, any waiting messages for the user are copied to his or her workstation. The uploaded message remains in the post office until the addressee logs into Mail, when it is forwarded to that user's workstation. This design allows portable PC users to create, delete, and read messages off-line. When the portable PC user reconnects to the mail-server, the post office downloads all unsent mail and uploads the user's pending mail.

Differences with MAIL for PC LANs

The Mail application in Windows for Workgroups is similar to Microsoft's MAIL for PC LANs but not identical. Microsoft provides an upgrade path to the full functionality of Mail for PC LANs via MAIL 3.x and Schedule+ Extensions for Windows for Workgroups. The primary differences between these two products are:

- Windows for Workgroups post offices cannot connect to other post offices or gateways.

- Windows for Workgroups does not use an ADMIN account.

- Windows for Workgroups does not use a separate Admin program for maintaining the post office.

- Windows for Workgroups' Mail lacks some additional features of Mail 3.x, such as spell-checking and the on-line tutorial.

In summary, the Mail 3.x product allows your electronic mail system—by way of connections to external post offices and gateways—to extend the mail system beyond the workgroup. Since Schedule+ uses the mail system to coordinate with other users, the Windows for Workgroups version of the program is limited to coordinating schedules within a single workgroup. You can extend the reach of the Windows Mail and Schedule+ programs by using the MAIL and Schedule+ Extensions for Windows for Workgroups. This product extends Windows Mail in three ways:

Microsoft Mail

9

- multiple post offices can be connected,

- support for e-mail gateways to other mail systems is provided,

- remote dial-in support for Mail is provided.

CREATING A POST OFFICE

You may have already discovered that the first time you access Mail, you are prompted to create a post office. It is difficult to move a post office later, so careful selection of the post office server is advised. The post office must be installed on a system running in enhanced mode, since the post office directory must be shared by all Mail users. The Mail application is not CPU-intensive unless several users access Mail simultaneously, so you may be able to combine the post office function with one or more other server tasks.

When the Mail application is started, it looks for a mail initialization file called MSMAIL.INI in the Windows directory. If this file does not exist, you are presented with the option box shown in Figure 9-1.

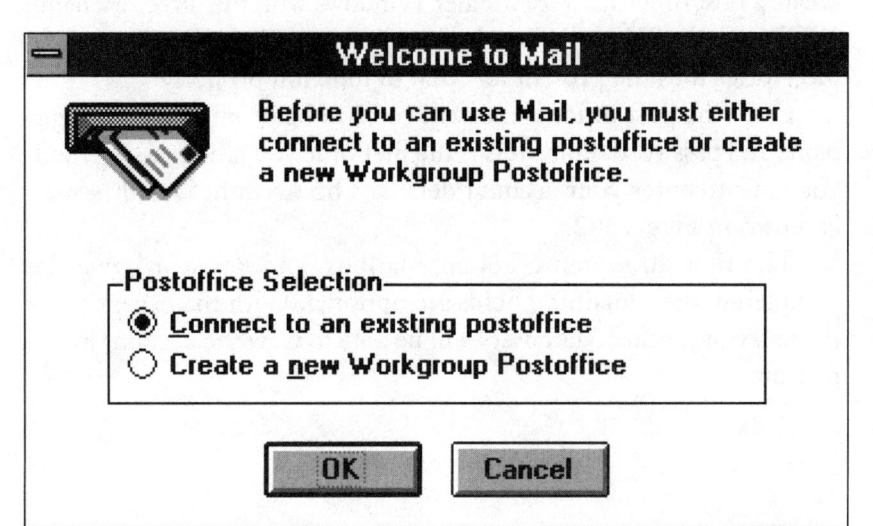

Figure 9-1. Starting Mail the first time. One user on the network will create a workgroup post office on his or her local drive. This PC must be able to share its post office directory with the workgroup.

109

If this is the first time you have run Mail on any workgroup station and you intend to create a post office for your workgroup, your PC must meet the following requirements:

- You are running Mail at the workstation that will act as the post office.

- This system is capable of running Windows in enhanced mode and will be running in enhanced mode whenever users connect to Mail.

- No other workstation has already been designated as the WorkGroup post office.

- The user name used to log on to Windows will be the user who acts as the Mail Administrator.

Select Cancel if the above requirements are not met.

However, if you are satisfied that all the above conditions are correct, select Create a new Workgroup Postoffice. The program will create a post office directory under Windows with the directory name WGPO, and will install several other directories in WGPO. All these directories must be present for Mail to function properly.

Once the post office is created, you will be prompted for a login name and password. Since this is the first time you are accessing Mail, you have to enter your account details. The Account Details screen is shown in Figure 9-2.

The first three items, Name, Mailbox, and Password, *must* be completed; the remaining fields are optional. With the exception of the password, other Mail users will be able to view the account information.

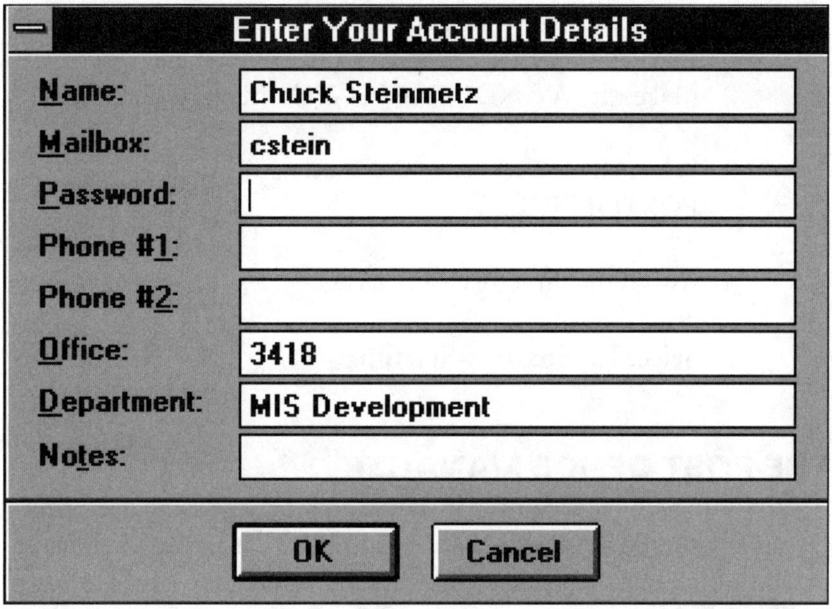

Microsoft Mail

Figure 9-2.
Setting up a Mail account. Unlike most mail systems, Windows for Workgroups Mail allows each user to set up an account, which reduces the workload on the network/mail administrator.

- *Name:* Typically, you'll want to enter your first and last name in the Name field. You can enter up to 30 characters.

- *Mailbox:* The Mailbox name is the name you will actually use to sign on to Mail, and is limited to 10 characters.

- *Password:* The Password field is limited to 8 characters. When you enter the password the first time, you will see what you type. Afterwards, however, the password field will display a series of asterisks.

After you have created the post office and logged onto Mail, you need to make the post office directory accessible to the workgroup.

1. Using the File Manager, select the **Share As...** command.

2. Make the \WINDOWS\WGPO directory sharable.

3. Select an easy-to-recognize sharename, such as POSTOFFICE.

4. Assign the directory **Full** access.

5. Select **Re-Share at Startup**.

THE POST OFFICE MANAGER

Once logged in, the post office manager has the same user interface as all other Mail users, with one exception. Under the Mail menu, an additional option called Postoffice Manager... appears, as shown in Figure 9-3.

Figure 9-3. Accessing the Post office management functions. The first user of Mail is, by default, the Mail administrator.

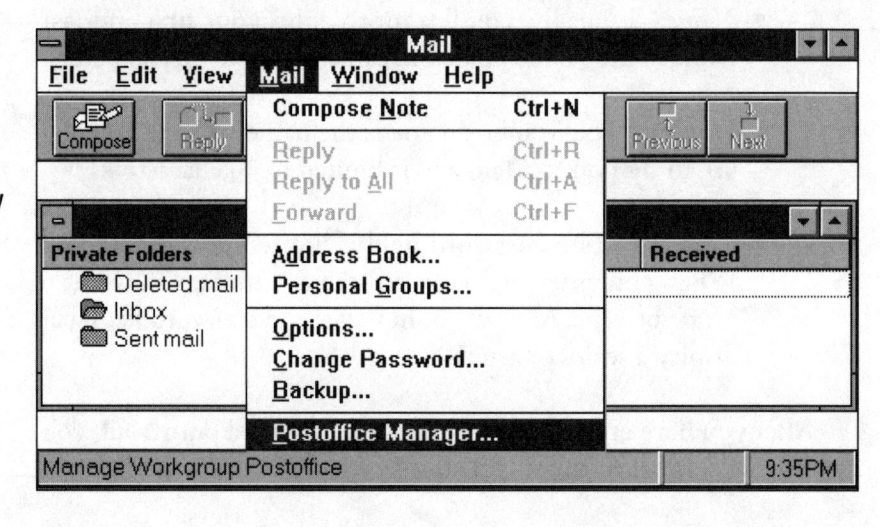

Microsoft Mail

9

Selecting the Postoffice Manager... option brings up the Postoffice Manager screen. Figure 9-4 shows the Postoffice Manager screen. From here you can create Mail users, remove users, and reset Mail passwords.

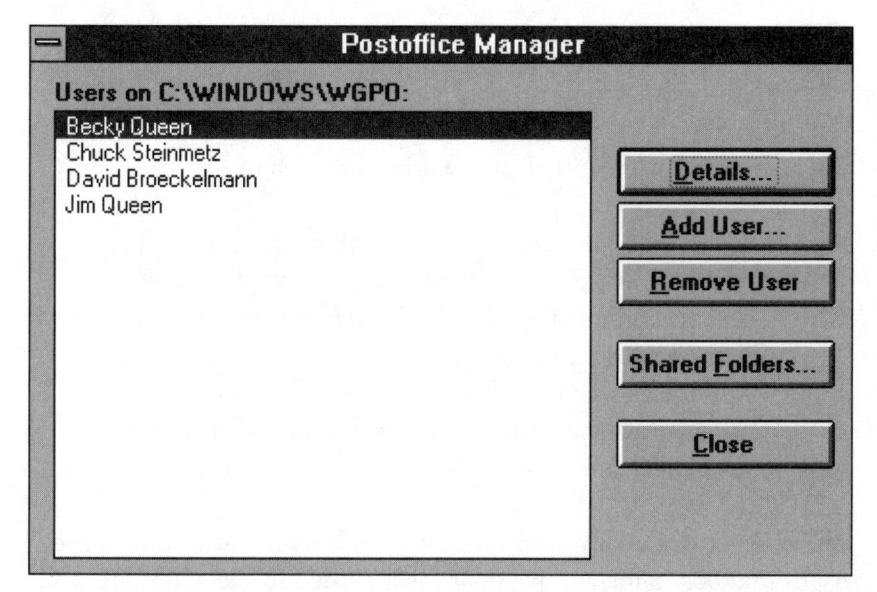

Figure 9-4. Mail administrative functions. Highlight the user name and click the Details... box to modify user information. Other options include adding new users, removing users, and defining shared mail folders.

The Details... button allows you to view the Account Details screen (see Figure 9-2). Although you cannot view the user's Mail password, you can reset the password here, if necessary.

You can also add or remove users with the Postoffice Manager. Although you could add each Mail user at this point, you may prefer to let each user sign on to Mail from their individual workstations. Mail will ask users if they are a new account and create the mailbox at that time, and allow users to complete the Account Details screen.

The Shared folders... button allows the post office manager to compress shared folders to reduce disk-space requirements. Shared folders will be discussed later in this chapter. Just be aware that if you have a significant amount of shared folder usage—that is, lots of messages added and deleted—you should compress them at least once a month.

Before you can start using Mail, you'll need to create some additional accounts. Use the Postoffice Manager to create these accounts, or start Mail on other workstations in the workgroup.

USING MAIL

When a workstation invokes Mail for the first time, it looks for the MSMAIL.INI file and then asks if you are connecting to an existing post office or creating a new workgroup post office.

> CAUTION: Be sure to connect to the existing post office. Never, under any circumstances, should multiple post offices be in the same workgroup. While each workgroup can have only one post office, you can create multiple workgroups with their own post offices. However, if you need to pass mail between these workgroups, you'll need additional software and a dedicated PC to act as a mail gateway.

When users create accounts from their own workstations, each user's mailbox name and password is included in the MSMAIL.INI file. If multiple users will be accessing Mail from the same workstation, however, you need to remove the password to the right of the

```
ServerPassword=
```

entry in the MSMAIL.INI file. Mail will continue to display the name of the last user at login, but the new user can erase the login (Mailbox) name and enter his or her new name and password at the workstation.

Once logged on to Mail, users should see a display similar to Figure 9-5. From here they can use the pull-down menus and "smart icons" to create messages, send messages, receive messages, create folders (either shared or private), export folders (or import folders previously exported), move messages into folders, or delete old messages.

Microsoft Mail

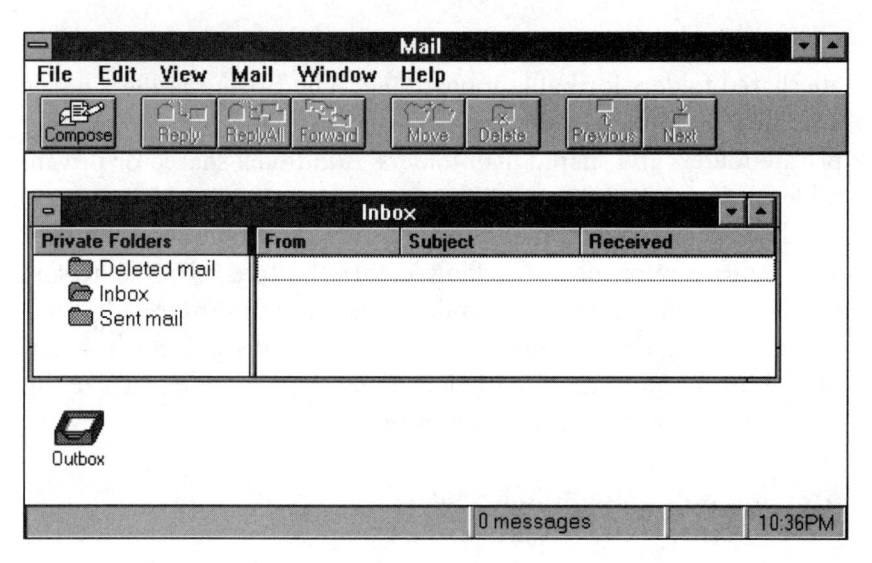

Figure 9-5.
The Mail program window. Both the Inbox and Outbox windows can be reduced to an icon, or expanded to the full window. Note that the button bar below the main menu contains frequently used commands that may or may not be available depending on the active table.

In Figure 9-5, the Outbox has been reduced to an icon using the down-arrow on the Outbox title bar. The Outbox acts as a storage device for sent mail that has not been picked up by the recipient.

Just like a real outbox, you can trash a message sitting in the outbox up until the time it is forwarded, simply by selecting the message and pressing the delete button. Outgoing mail messages that are deleted before delivery are maintained in the Deleted mail folder, just like deleted incoming messages. The Deleted mail folder is purged when the user exits the Mail program.

The Inbox actually consists of three items, the Deleted mail folder, the Inbox, and the Sent mail folder. Double-clicking on one of these folders causes the window title to switch to the selected item. Reducing the window to an icon at this point causes the icon to switch to the appropriate icon. The icon for Deleted mail is a small folder with an *X* slashed across it, the Sent mail icon is a plain folder, and the Inbox icon is a box that looks just like the Outbox.

Only one icon will be displayed when the Inbox, Deleted mail, or Sent mail folders are displayed, but you can double-click on the appropriate icon to open one of these three windows.

Building Local Area Networks with Windows for Workgroups

In addition to these private folders, users on the network can create shared folders for bulletin board use. The Private Folders box is actually a button. Click on this command to toggle between viewing private folders and shared mail folders. Additional shared or private folders can be created at any time.

The From, Subject, and Received boxes are also buttons, but they serve a different purpose. Clicking on these buttons tells Mail to sort the messages in the folder by sender, subject, or date/time. Additionally, by placing the mouse cursor on the vertical separator between these buttons and pressing the left mouse button, you can size the width of each button to suit your taste.

Creating and Sending a Message

To create a message, click on the Compose button just below the menu bar. Like most Windows applications, Mail supports shortcut keys. If a menu command supports a shortcut key, it is displayed to the right of the command in the pull-down menu bar. Besides clicking on Compose to create a message, you can press Ctrl-N. This brings up the Send Note window, as shown in Figure 9-6.

Figure 9-6. Creating a mail message. Multiple addressees can be added to both the To: and Cc: address lines.

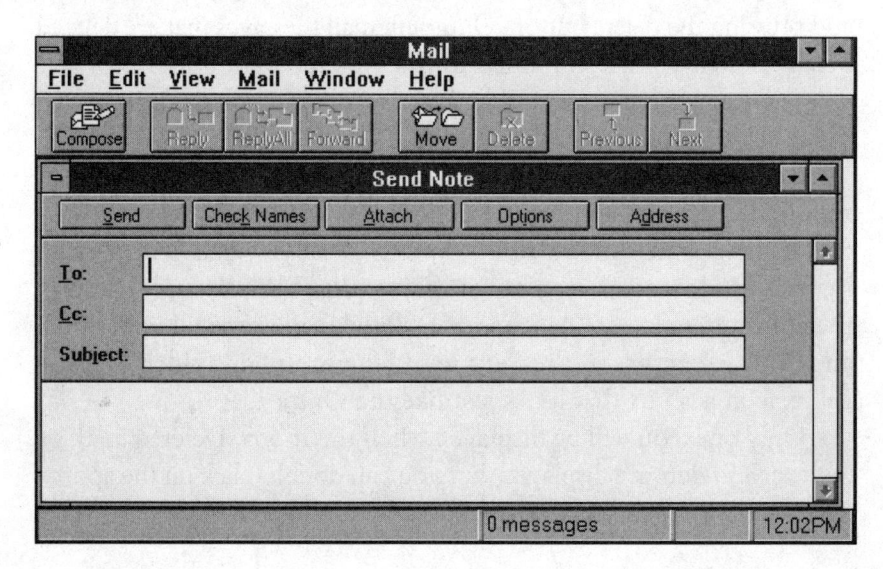

Microsoft Mail

The button bar offers the following commands:

- *Send* allows you to send a message.

- *Check Names* checks for the existence of a user based on a partial spelling.

- *Attach* attaches a file to the message.

- *Options* lets you select more message options.

- *Address* lets you select destination addresses from the address book.

To use the Check Names command, enter the first letter or letters of a mail user's first or last name in either the To: or Cc: box and click the Check Names button. If Mail can find a match, it automatically enters the name when you click the Check Names button. If more than one match is found, Mail displays a list of matching users and allows you to choose the correct recipient. You can add additional destinations by entering partial names after each successful match and selecting Check Names again.

The Attach command allows you to attach a DOS file to the message. Selecting this command brings up a dialog box similar to the one in Figure 9-7. Notice the Network... button. With this button, you can assign network drive letters and attach files from other locations on the network without switching to the File Manager. To attach a file, browse through the drive letters and directories until you locate the correct file, highlight it, and then select Attach. You can continue to attach files in this manner. When you're finished, select Close.

Building Local Area Networks with Windows for Workgroups

**Figure 9-7.
Attaching a file to a message. Using the Network... common dialog button, you can attach files from shared directories on the network without switching to the File Manager.**

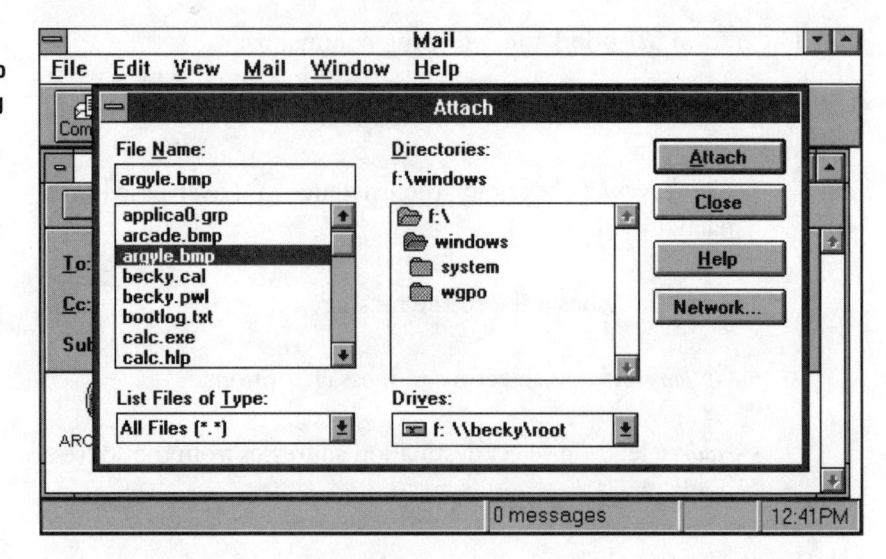

If Windows recognizes the file type (based on the file name extension), it will place an icon of the application in the mail document. When the user receives the document, he or she can launch the application from within Mail and view the attached file, assuming the user has the application needed in the local path. For example, the document created in Figure 9-8 has a Windows Paint bit-mapped image (BMP) and a DOS executable (EXE) file in addition to a text message.

**Figure 9-8.
Attached files in a Mail message. Windows data files that have an associated program type will display the icon for the program used to create the file.**

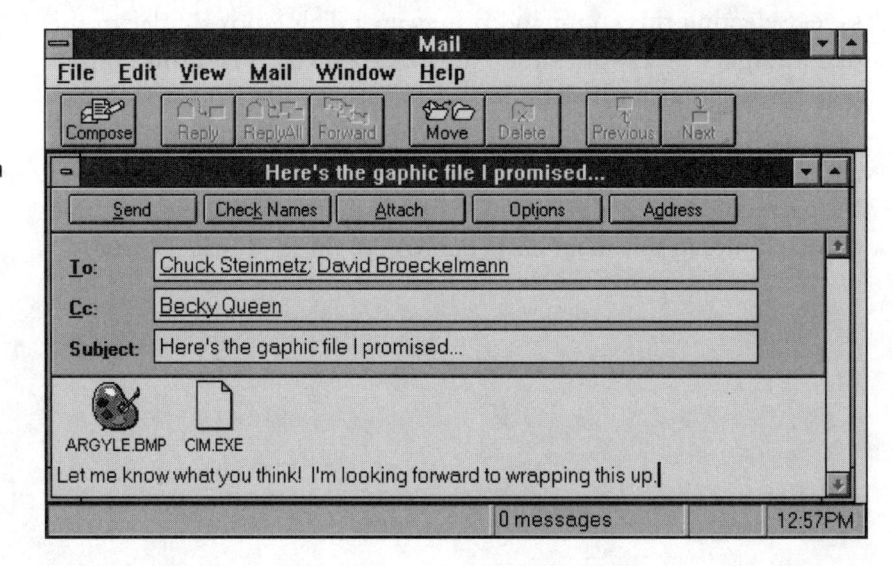

118

Microsoft Mail

When the recipient reads this message, he or she will be able to click on the ARGYLE.BMP icon and launch Paint from within Windows, if Windows can locate the application in the path. Exiting Paint will return them to the Mail message. A DOS application will launch a DOS session, execute the DOS program, and return to Mail upon exit.

The Options button displays the dialog box shown in Figure 9-9. The options are:

- Return receipt tells the receiving Mail program to automatically return a message to you when the recipient opens his or her mail.

- Save sent messages places a copy of your message in your Sent mail folder.

- The Priority button does not affect the speed at which your message is sent—it places an icon next to the message to alert the receiver to the priority you have assigned to it. A low-priority message has a small arrow pointing down next to it, a normal message does not have a priority icon, and a high-priority message has a red exclamation point next to it, as in Figure 9-10.

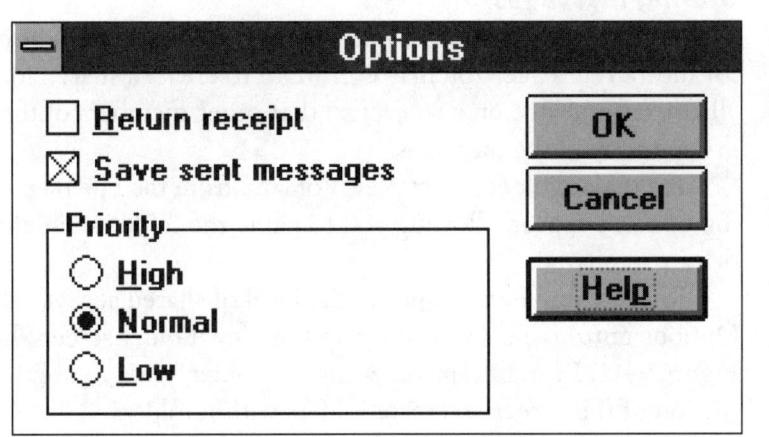

Figure 9-9. Mail options. Check the Return receipt box to have a mail message sent back with a time- and date-stamp when the mail recipient reads your mail.

Figure 9-10.
The mail inbox. Notice the mail slot in the lower-right corner of the window. The letter sticking out of the slot indicates that you have unread mail.

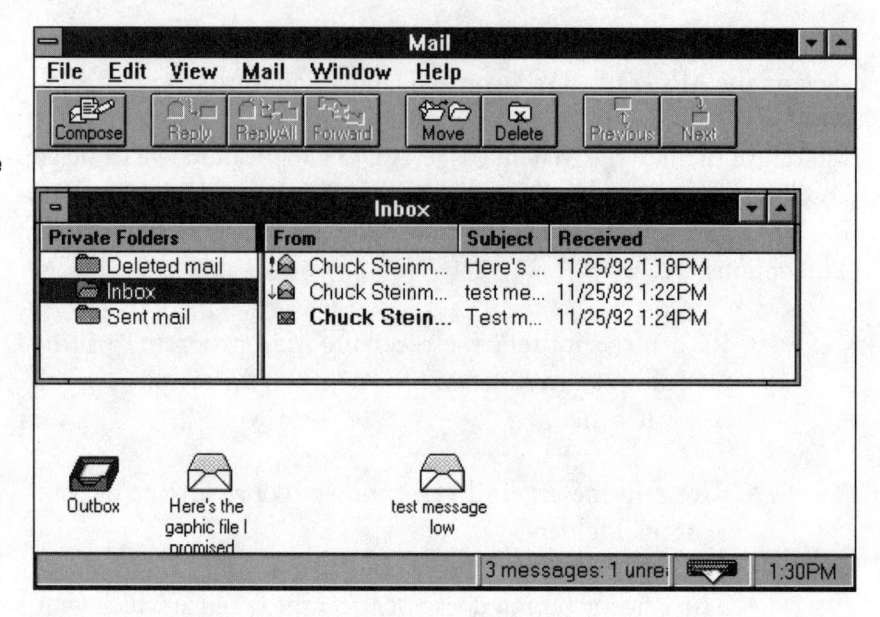

Reading Messages

Reading messages is as simple as double-clinking on the message in your Inbox. Once read, you can use the button bar to delete the message, reply to the sender, reply to the sender and all other users in the To: and Cc: box, or forward the message to another user.

Storing Messages

As you receive messages, you'll probably want to file some of them for future reference. You may even want to create a shared folder for all correspondence on a subject so that other members of the workgroup can read the messages.

To create a folder, select New Folder... from the File menu. A dialog box will appear, allowing you to name the folder and define it as private or shared.

To add comments or specify the level of shared access, select the Options button. This will bring up the New Folder screen shown in Figure 9-11. In addition to creating the folder, you can use the Level section of this screen to create folders within folders.

Microsoft Mail

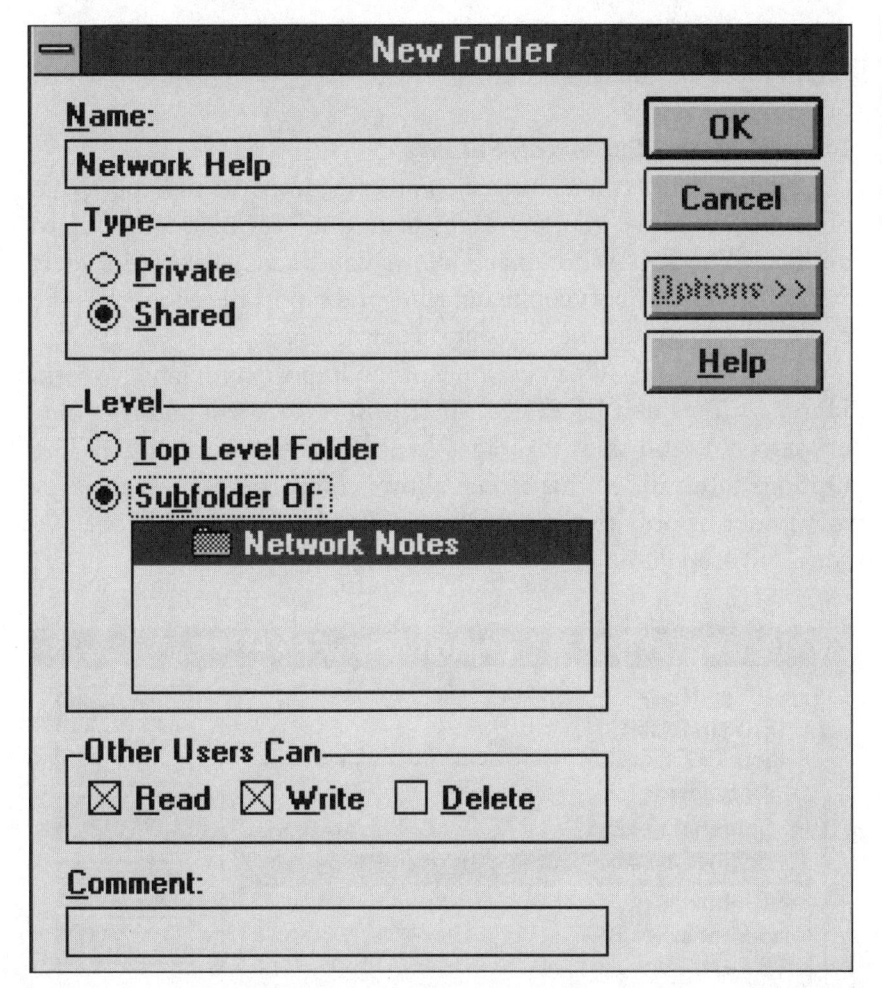

Figure 9-11.
Creating a folder.
Folders can be nested inside of other folders by using the Subfolder button.

Once a folder is created, you can drag and drop messages from folder to folder by selecting the message with the mouse. Move the cursor to the message you wish to file, and press and hold the left mouse button. Moving the mouse will cause a small letter icon to appear. This letter represents the actual message. Drag this icon over to the appropriate folder and release the mouse button. The message will immediately be filed. You can open this folder and use the same method to move the message to another folder, or simply highlight

Building Local Area Networks with Windows for Workgroups

the message and press the Delete key when you no longer wish to retain the message.

Importing and Exporting Folders

Mail supports two additional commands, Import and Export, that allow you to move mail messages from one user or workgroup to another. The Export command allows you to copy selected folders into a file. The Import command reads the export file and moves the exported folders and messages into your mailbox.

Figure 9-12 shows an example of the Export command at work. Here, a file named EXPORT.MMF will be created, and the folders selected (and their messages) will be written to this file. The Options... button on this screen allows you to specify all messages in a folder or only those messages received or modified between a start and stop date.

Figure 9-12. Exporting folders. The Export command places all the selected mail folders into a single file, which can be copied or mailed to another workstation.

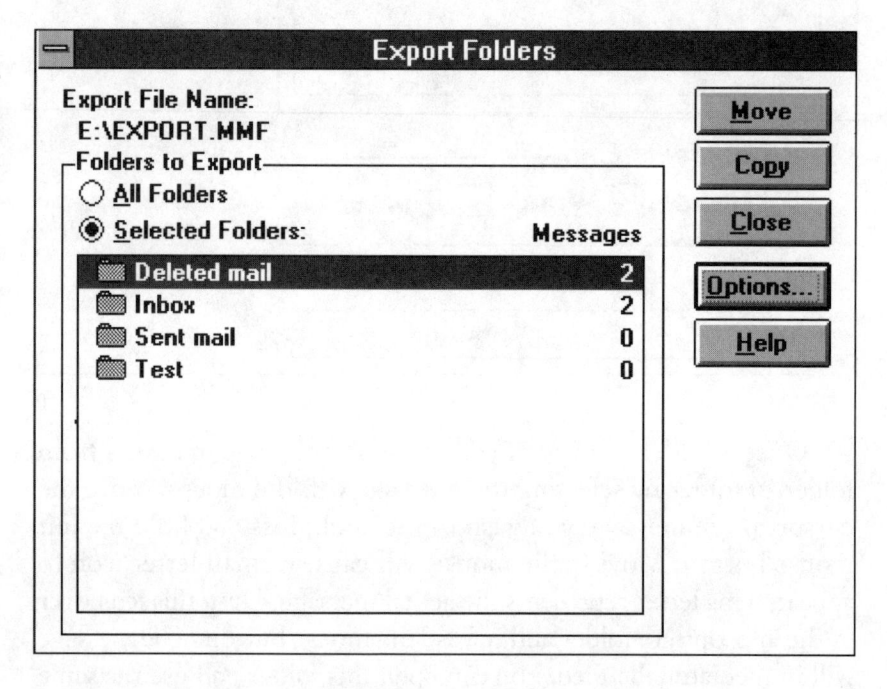

```
┌─────────────────── Export Folders ───────────────────┐
 Export File Name:                           ┌─────────┐
 E:\EXPORT.MMF                               │  Move   │
 ┌─Folders to Export──────────────────────┐  └─────────┘
 │ ○ All Folders                          │  ┌─────────┐
 │ ● Selected Folders:         Messages   │  │  Copy   │
 │ ┌────────────────────────────────────┐ │  └─────────┘
 │ │ 📁 Deleted mail                 2  │ │  ┌─────────┐
 │ │ 📁 Inbox                        2  │ │  │  Close  │
 │ │ 📁 Sent mail                    0  │ │  └─────────┘
 │ │ 📁 Test                         0  │ │  ┌─────────┐
 │ │                                    │ │  │ Options..│
 │ └────────────────────────────────────┘ │  └─────────┘
 └────────────────────────────────────────┘  ┌─────────┐
                                             │  Help   │
                                             └─────────┘
```

9

Microsoft Mail

Once exported, this file can be copied to disk and transferred to another workstation, or it can even be sent to another user as a Mail message with the File Attach command. The Import command will create the necessary folders and copy the messages into the new mailbox.

> **NOTE:** The Export command offers an excellent means of filing old messages off-line. Consider creating a JAN.MMF file, etc., for archiving old messages monthly.

Customizing Mail

The main menu Mail submenu includes an Options... command that allows you to customize Mail for sending messages, checking for new mail, or emptying the Deleted Mail folder. The Options dialog box is shown in Figure 9-13.

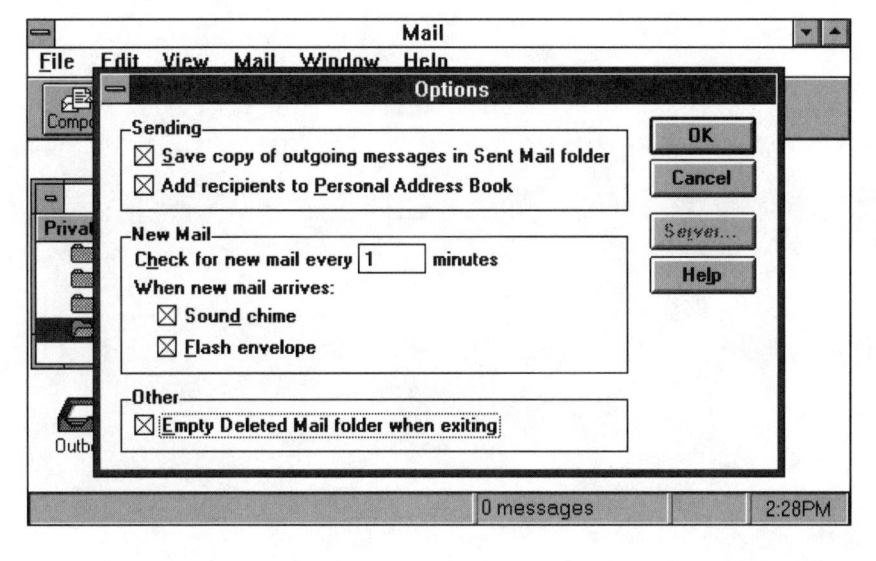

Figure 9-13. Mail options. The chime option will generate a beep whenever mail is received, so you can be notified of new mail even if you have another window open in full-screen mode.

The easiest way to use Mail is to log in to the Mail system the first thing in the morning, and then use the Minimize command to reduce the Mail application to an icon. Based on the options selected for New Mail, the application will check your post office as frequently as you specify. New mail will be copied to your system, and the workstation speaker will beep and the mail icon will display a small envelope in the mail slot if both the Sound chime and Flash envelope options are checked.

CHAPTER 10

Schedule+

Schedule+ is a personal planner for tracking appointments and tasks and keeping notes on your meetings. If you desire, Schedule+ will also notify you of upcoming appointments or events. On the network, Schedule+ can coordinate your schedule with the schedules of other members of your workgroup. Resources such as conference rooms can have their own account, so you can easily determine if a resource is available at a particular time. Networked user and resource schedules can be overlaid to find available time-slots.

Although Schedule+ can function as a standalone application, for maximum benefit you need to use it along with the Microsoft Mail software. The Mail engine provides the means of transmitting meeting requests and replies. Portable PC users can maintain two copies of their schedule, however, and configure Schedule+ so they can work off-line and update the network copy of their schedule when they reconnect to the LAN. With Schedule+ running on the network, you can designate an assistant to schedule appointments for you. Each user on the network can set up access rights for viewing or modifying his or her schedule.

Schedule+ also allows you to print out your calendar for reference and for recording appointments when you can't access your PC.

SETTING UP SCHEDULE+

If you installed the Microsoft Mail engine as discussed in Chapter 9 and you have a mailbox, you can use Schedule+. Which opening screen you see in Schedule+ depends on the current status of your Microsoft Mail signon. Unless you are already running Mail, Schedule+ always prompts you to sign in to the Mail engine. Schedule+ will *not* prompt you to sign in to Mail under the following conditions:

- You already logged into Mail but have switched it to a background window or icon.

- You exited Mail or Schedule+ previously and did not sign out.

The Exit command will retain your connection and ID with the Mail engine, but the Exit and Sign-Out options will sever the connection to Mail. If you use the Sign-Out command in either Mail or Schedule+, you will not be notified when you receive new mail or schedule requests.

If Schedule+ cannot access the Mail engine, it generates an error message and asks if you want to work off-line. You can elect to work off-line on your schedule using the local drive. When you reconnect to the network, Schedule+ will merge your off-line schedule with your network schedule.

AN OVERVIEW OF SCHEDULE+

Schedule+ tasks are broken into two types: maintaining your schedule and communicating with members of your workgroup. Each task has its own window. The opening window for Schedule+ defaults to scheduling appointments, as shown in Figure 10-1. The messages window is used to review schedule requests or replies from other members of the workgroup.

Schedule+

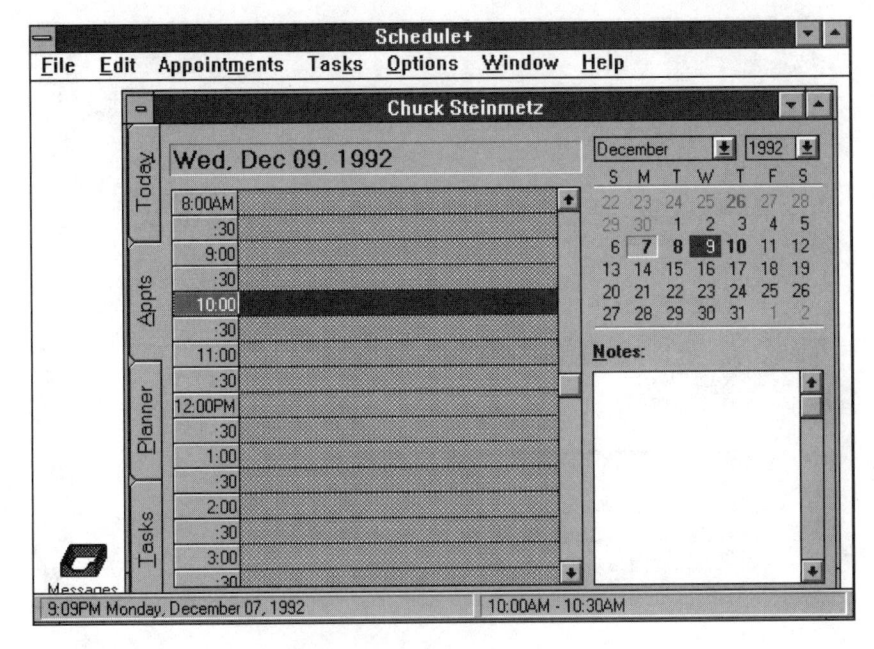

Figure 10-1. Schedule+ scheduling window. The date you are viewing is displayed in the calendar box on the right side of the window. All dates with appointments appear in bold-face.

Notice the tabs—Tasks, Planner, Appts (Appointments), and Today—along the left side of the appointment book. By using the mouse to click on a tab or pressing an Alt-key combination, you can jump to a portion of the appointment book. For example, by pressing Alt-P or clicking on the Planner you can access the Planner. Choosing the Today tab brings up the scheduling window. Let's examine the other tabs.

Scheduling Appointments

Click on Appts to display the appointment book, which shows your daily schedule, notes, and the types of appointments scheduled for the highlighted day, as in Figure 10-2.

Appointments can be either normal or tentative. *Tentative appointments* appear in gray and do not appear as busy times on your schedule. In Figure 10-2, the Microsoft sales presentation is tentative and all other meetings, in white, are *normal meetings*.

Figure 10-2. Chuck's calendar for December 10. The time-slot from 1:30 to 2:30 shows three conflicting meetings.

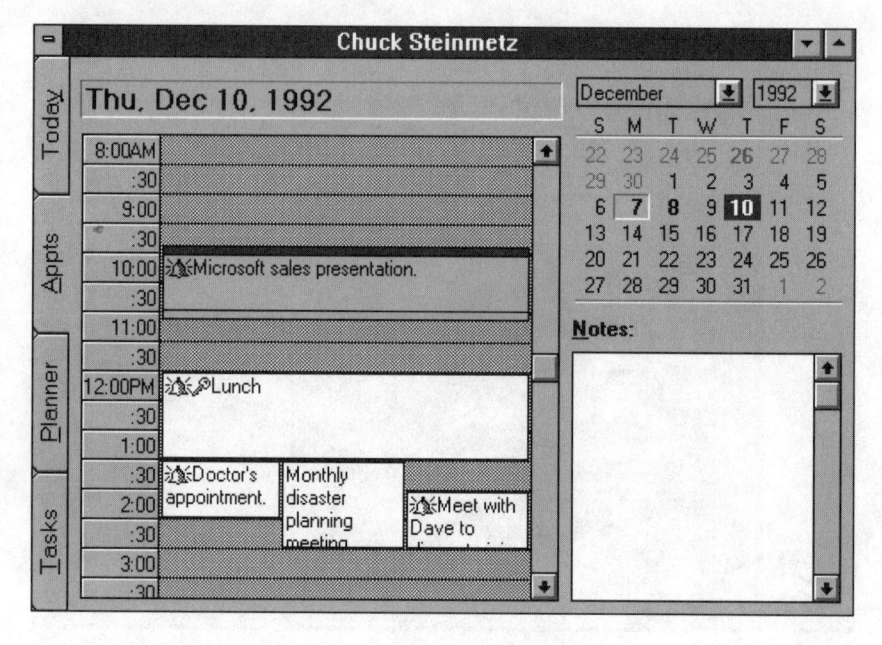

Notice the key and bell icons.

- The key in the box for Chuck's lunch meeting indicates that this is a private meeting. Other users who access Chuck's schedule will not be able to see this meeting.

- The bell icon indicates that Chuck has requested an alarm prior to a meeting.

Although you can add to the appointment book at any time by selecting New Appointment from the Appointments pull-down menu, the easiest way to block a time period is from the Appts tab.

1. Click on **Appts** or press **Alt-A**.

2. Place the mouse cursor on a time-slot.

3. Press and hold the left mouse button to highlight a time-block.

4. Release the mouse button.

Schedule+

Once the time-block is highlighted, the next appointment you add will appear in this time-block. Figure 10-3 shows the Appointment screen with a time-block from 8:30 to 12:00 already selected.

```
┌─────────────────── Appointment ───────────────────┐
│ ┌─When──────────────────────────────────┐   ┌──OK──┐ │
│ │ Start: [8:30AM▼] [Wed 12/9/92▼] [Choose Time...] │ │      │ │
│ │ End:   [12:00PM▼] [Wed 12/9/92▼] ☐ Tentative │   ├Cancel┤ │
│ └───────────────────────────────────────┘   │      │ │
│ Description:                                 ├Invite┤ │
│ ┌────────────────────────────────────┐↑     └──────┘ │
│ │                                    │              │
│ │                                    │↓             │
│ └────────────────────────────────────┘              │
│ ☒ Set Reminder for [15] [minute(s)▼] Beforehand     │
│ ☐ Private                                           │
└─────────────────────────────────────────────────────┘
```

Figure 10-3. Entering the time for an appointment. You can modify the Start and End date and time by using the up or down button bars, or with the Choose Time button. Choose Time will display a box from five days before to five days after the date selected. Using the mouse, you can then select a new time block or date.

Selecting the Appointment from the main menu and adding an appointment brings up the Appointment screen. Here you can set an alarm for 1 to 99 minutes, hours, days, weeks, or even months before the meeting with the Set Reminder for Beforehand button.

> **NOTE:** The option in Schedule+ to Exit without signing out allows the Alarm to sound even when Schedule+ is not loaded. Signing out of Schedule+ unloads the Alarm feature.

From the Appointment screen, you can define the meeting as Tentative (in which case it will appear in gray in the appointment book) or Private (in which case a key icon will appear in the meeting box). The Tentative box is located under the Choose Time box. The Private box is at the bottom of the screen.

The Invite button will read the Mail engine directory and allow you to select other workgroup members to attend the meeting. Other users who are selected automatically receive a mail message inviting them to this meeting. When inviting others, be sure to use the description box—the invitation will include this description.

The Planner

The Schedule+ Planner allows you to scan your appointments for several days and overlay other schedules to determine when users or resources such as conference rooms are available. To use the Planner, click on the Planner tab or Press Alt-P in the appointment book.

To overlay schedules, select the Attendees: Change... button and add the users or resources defined in Mail. Assuming you have at least read-access to the selected calendars, you'll be able to compare schedules, as shown in Figure 10-4. Each potential attendee's schedule will appear in a different color, and overlapping appointments among users will appear in a pattern of diagonal stripes. Empty time-slots indicate available meeting times.

Figure 10-4. Comparing calendars. The Planner tab is the only way in Schedule+ to directly compare your schedule with others'.

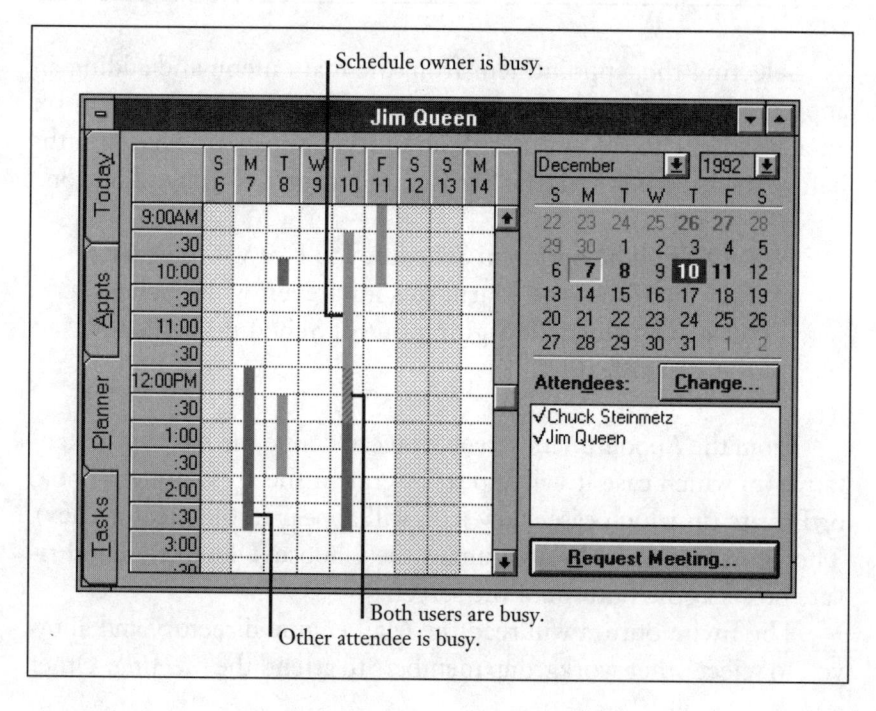

Schedule+

Notice the check mark next to each name in the Attendees box. The check indicates that that user's calendar is being displayed. When evaluating meeting times, you can click on each name and toggle the display for that user or resource off and on. Once you have chosen the attendees and picked a time frame for the meeting, you can click the Request Meeting... button to send all the selected users a mail message inviting them to the meeting.

Maintaining a Task List

The Tasks tab in the appointment book brings up the Task List Manager, as shown in Figure 10-5. From here, you can create task descriptions and track them with Schedule+. Tasks can be copied into appointment book time-slots so you can plan to work on them at specific times. If you are sharing your schedule, this will prevent others from attempting to schedule while you are completing a task.

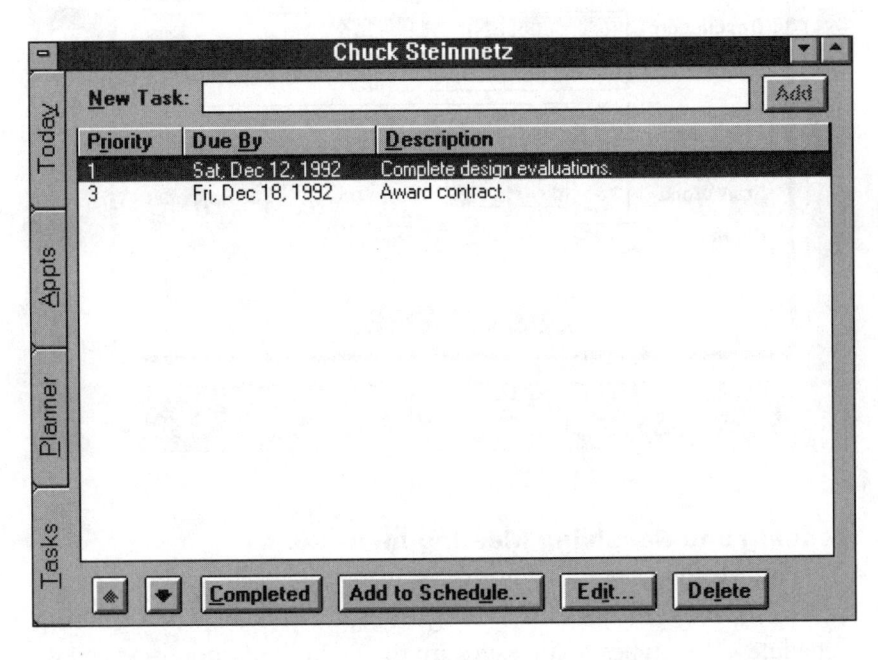

Figure 10-5. Task List Manager. The large arrows in the lower-left corner of the screen are for modifying the priority level of the highlighted task.

Building Local Area Networks with Windows for Workgroups

Tasks can be assigned a priority number from 1 to 9 or a letter from A to Z with the large arrows in the lower-left corner of the screen. You can assign due dates to each task, and tasks can be grouped into projects. Finally, you can sort and print tasks by priority, due date, description, or project. Figure 10-5 shows a sample task list. Tasks marked as completed are deleted from the task list.

The Edit function allows you to modify a task and assign it to a project, as in Figure 10-6. Select Add to Schedule... to bring up the Planner and assign a time-block. Multiple time-blocks can be assigned by selecting Add to Schedule... again. This dialog box also allows you to set due dates, project names, priority, and alarms.

Figure 10-6. Editing a task entry. Assigning related tasks to the same project will keep them grouped together on the task list screen.

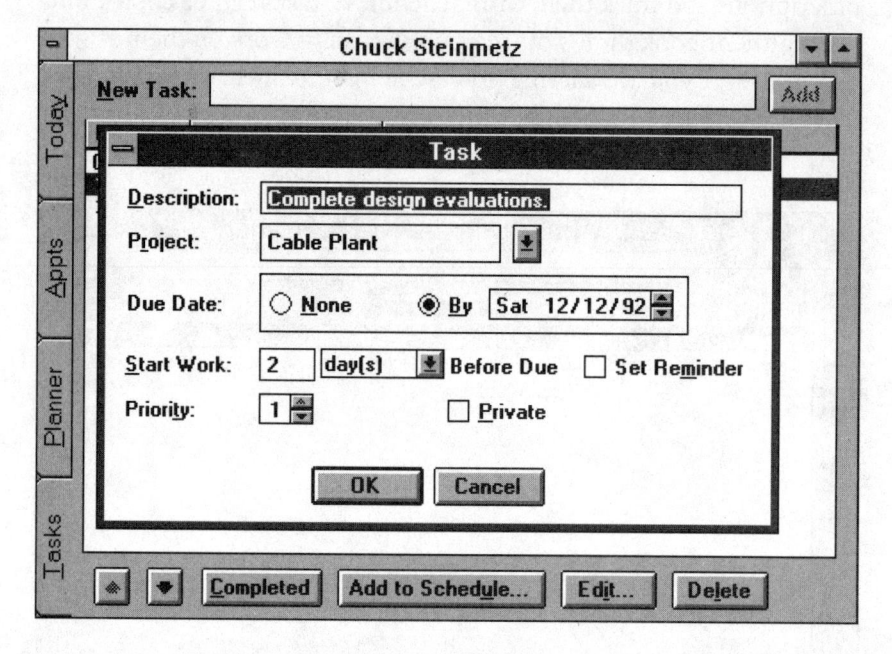

Sending and Receiving Meeting Invitations

The Messages window is always available to users who are connected to the Windows for Workgroups mail server when running Schedule+. Two types of messages are shown in this window—requests for a meeting and responses to meeting requests. Since Schedule+ uses

Schedule+

the mail server to send these messages, you can also read, respond to, and delete Schedule+ messages from within Mail. Figure 10-7 shows a sample mail message created by Schedule+.

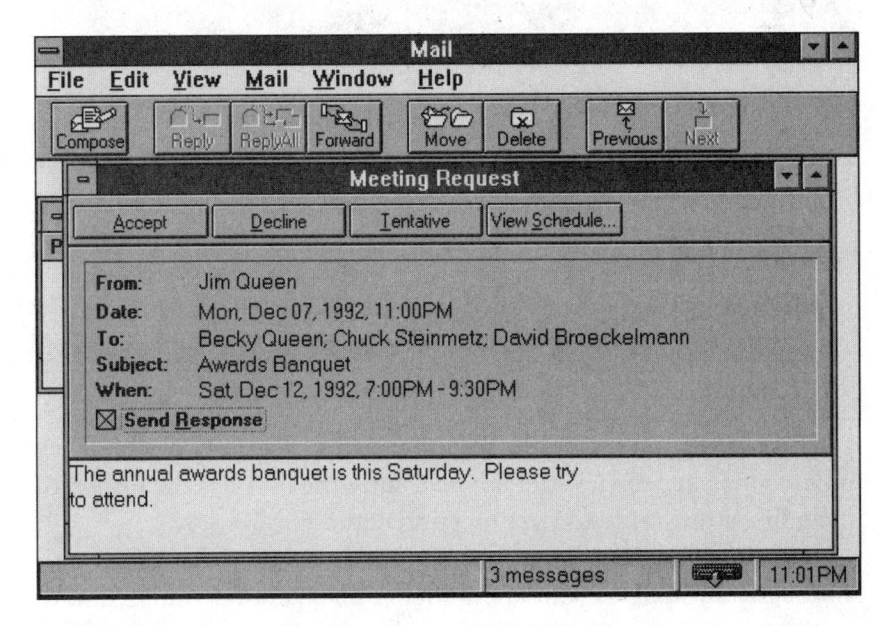

Figure 10-7. Mail message from Schedule+. Within Mail, users can accept, decline, tentatively accept, or check their schedules without switching to the Schedule+ program.

Responses to a request for a meeting appear both in your Windows Mail mailbox and in the messages box in Schedule+. Clicking on the Messages box icon will open the Messages box. In the Messages box, a question mark, X, or check mark icon appears next to the reply to indicate the sender's response, as in Figure 10-8.

> ? Indicates that the sender has placed the meeting in his or her schedule as tentative.
>
> X Means the sender will not attend the meeting.
>
> ✓ Indicates the sender will attend the meeting.

Unread messages appear in boldface.

Building Local Area Networks with Windows for Workgroups

Figure 10-8. Viewing Schedule+ messages. Unread messages appear in boldface. In this example, David might be able to attend (?), Chuck will not attend (X), and Becky will attend the banquet (✓).

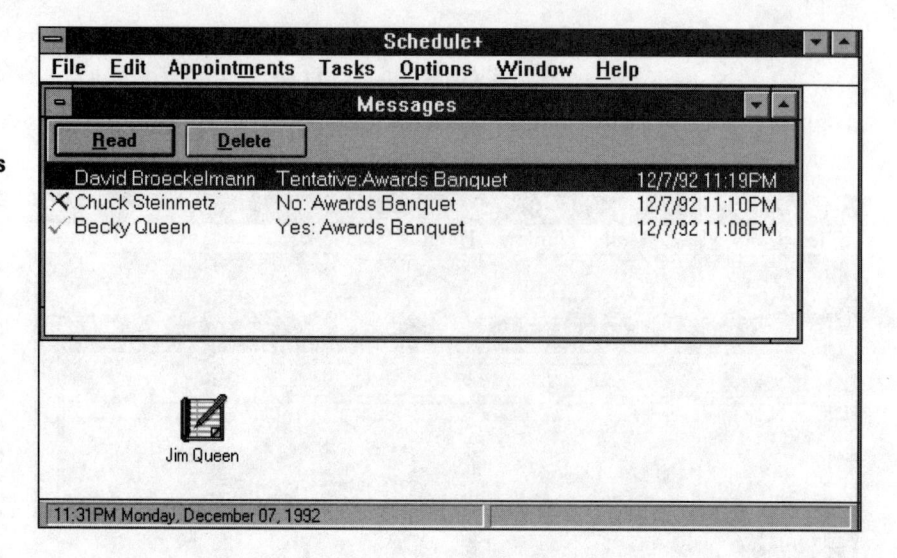

In addition to viewing the response, you will want to double-click on each message to view the full text, since the user has the option of including a text reply to your meeting request.

When you accept a request, Schedule+ notifies the sender and automatically updates your appointment book, even if you used Mail to respond (it is not necessary to use the message function in Schedule+). A tentative acceptance will be entered as a tentative appointment. Declining a meeting request will make no changes to the appointment book.

SCHEDULE+ AND THE NETWORK

Using Schedule+ off-line gives you the ability to setup and maintain a personal schedule and task list. Running Schedule+ on the network provides additional functions, including

- access to other workgroup members' schedules, based on individual access lists;

- tracking workgroup resources, such as a meeting rooms and equipment;

Schedule+

- allowing others to update your schedule;

- merging off-line and network schedules;

- sending and receiving meeting requests and responses.

Each of these functions is described below.

Accessing Workgroup Schedules

As mentioned earlier in this chapter, Schedule+ allows you to access other workgroup members' schedules. The level of access depends on the access privileges you define in your copy of Schedule+.

By default, Schedule+ lets other users view your free/busy times. However, the Set Access Privileges... command on the Options menu allows you to revoke this access or grant additional access on a user-by-user basis. Selecting this menu option displays the dialog box shown in Figure 10-9.

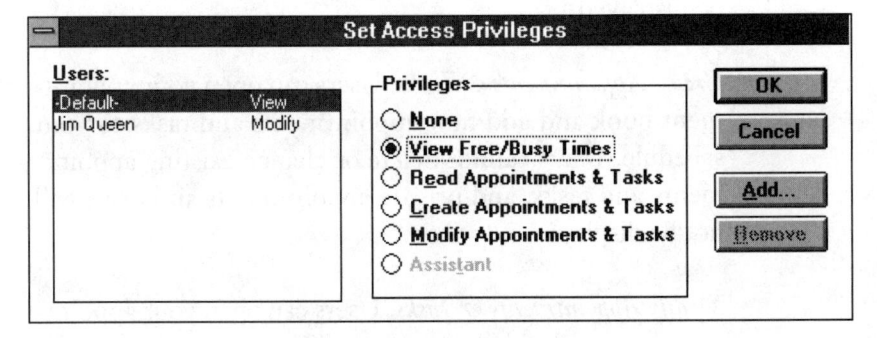

Figure 10-9. Schedule+ Access List. In this example, Jim has been added to the access list, and he has the ability to modify this user's schedule. All other users can only view this user's free/busy times.

While the ability to view free/busy times may be the most common level of access, several other levels can be assigned. In the Set Access Privileges dialog box, you can click on any of the boldface privileges to change your *default* level of access for all users. Click on the Add... button to assign *specific* privilege levels for individual workgroup members. For example, you could set the default level for all users to

135

read-only, add user Becky and give her no access at all, and define user Bill as your assistant.

Following is a list of access levels:

- *None.* The specified user (or default users) cannot access any portion of your scheduler.

- *View Free/Busy Times.* Users can use their Planners to view your free/busy times. Meetings defined as private will not display on the Planner. The Open Other's Appt. Book... command will not work with this access level; users can add you to the list of attendee's in their Planner and your available time-slots will be displayed.

- *Read Appointments & Tasks.* Users can open your appointment book and use the tab keys to switch to your Planner, Appointments, and Tasks. Users cannot modify any of these areas, however, and private appointments or tasks will not be displayed.

- *Create Appointments & Tasks.* Users can open your appointment book and add new appointments and tasks to your schedule. Users cannot delete or change existing appointments and tasks, and private appointments and tasks will not be displayed.

- *Modify Appointments & Tasks.* Users can open your appointment book and add, delete, or modify appointments or tasks. The contents of private appointments and tasks will not be displayed.

- *Assistant.* The assistant has the same access privileges as any user with modify access, but there are several key differences. Only one person can be designated as your assistant,

Schedule+

and this person will receive copies of any meeting requests sent to you. Under Options, you can even tell Schedule+ to send the meeting requests directly to the assistant. The assistant can accept or decline meeting requests on your behalf, and appointments that your assistant makes on your behalf are identified as being handled by the assistant. The assistant cannot, however, view or modify your private appointments or tasks.

A note on private meetings: users with view, read, create, modify, or assistant privileges can see the time frames assigned to private meetings, but they can't view the text fields for these meetings or modify the time-blocks assigned to them.

Tracking Workgroup Resources

Schedule+ allows you to track workgroup resources, such as conference rooms and audio-visual equipment, by setting up a Schedule+ for the resource. This entails creating a Microsoft Mail account for the resource, and then starting Schedule+ and using this mailbox ID and password to initialize the Schedule+ files. Once this is completed, select General Options... from the Schedule+ Options menu, and select This Account is for a Resource. This will assign a default access-level of Create for all workgroup members. The General Options screen is shown in Figure 10-10.

After defining this account as a resource, you should select an assistant for this resource, especially if you want to limit the number of users who can create appointments for this account. Limiting the users who can create appointments will require restricted users to send a request each time they want to use the resource in a meeting. This request will automatically be forwarded to the assistant, who can accept or decline on behalf of the account. By selecting the Send Meeting Messages Only to my Assistant option, it will not be necessary to log in to Schedule+ with this account and respond to or purge meeting requests periodically.

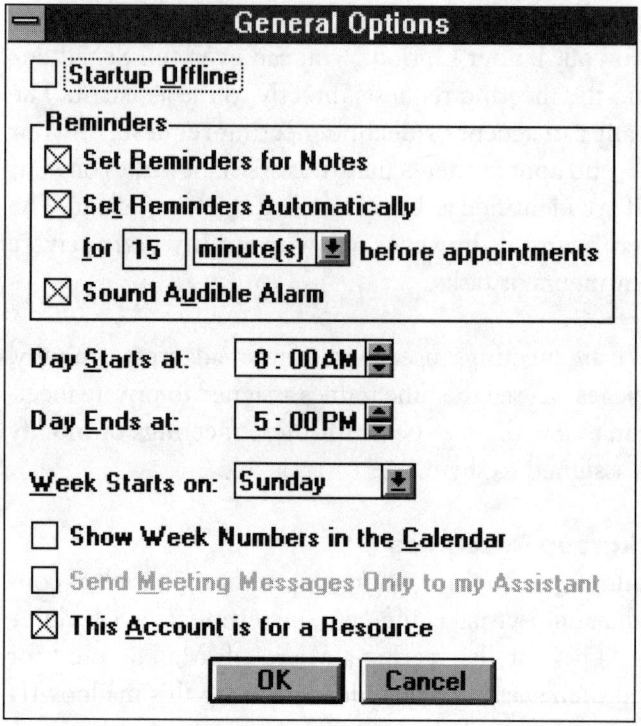

Building Local Area Networks with Windows for Workgroups

Figure 10-10. Defining a resource account. You should set up an assistant for this account—meeting requests for this resource will be copied to the assistant. Check the Send Meeting Messages Only to my Assistant box once an assistant has been assigned.

Allowing Others to Update Your Schedule

As mentioned earlier in this chapter, Schedule+ has extensive access privileges you can assign to other members of your workgroup.

Schedule+ maintains two copies of your schedule—the network copy that other users can access, and a local copy for use off-line. A user with a portable computer can continue to use Schedule+ while away from the office, and upon return, Schedule+ will automatically merge the changes made to the off-line schedule with the network copy.

Merging Off-Line and Network Schedules

Since you can assign other workgroup members the rights to add to the network copy of your schedule, it's possible that the merge

Schedule+

process will generate schedule conflicts. However, Schedule+ simply places both on- and off-line meetings side-by-side in the same time-blocks, and it updates both the on- and off-line copies of your schedule accordingly. Moreover, the merge is completely transparent to the user.

The first time you use an account under Schedule+, a dialog box will appear asking you to specify the name and location of the local copy of the schedule, as shown in Figure 10-11. You must locate the existing local calendar file or create a new one. You cannot cancel this dialog box and continue to use Schedule+.

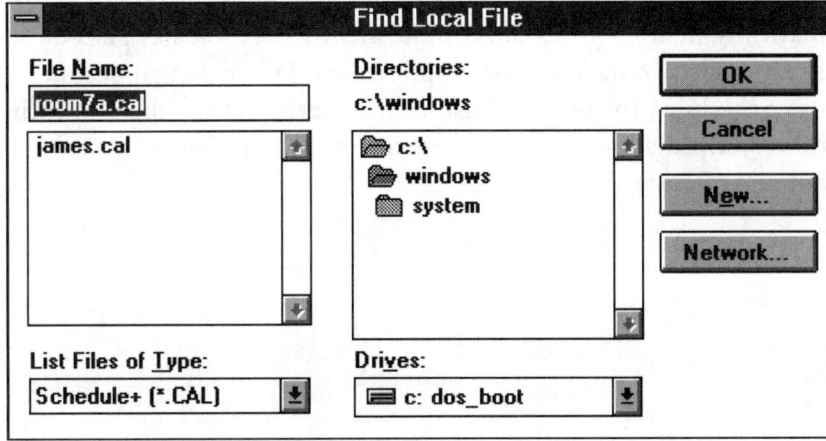

Figure 10-11. Creating a local calendar file. All Schedule+ accounts, even resource accounts, must have a local calendar file. If the calendar file has been moved, scroll through the directories and locate the file, or select New... to copy the network copy of the calendar to the local drive.

Once Schedule+ locates your local calendar file, it will determine if the network file is available. The network copy is maintained under the WGPO\CAL directory on the system acting as your mail server. If the network file can be located, Schedule+ will merge any additions or changes in your local calendar file with the network file. However, if the network file cannot be located, Schedule+ will display a dialog box alerting you to the fact. You'll be given the option to continue working off-line.

SCHEDULE+: A SOLID PERFORMER

Schedule+ offers tight integration with Microsoft Mail so you can send meeting requests and acknowledgments from within the Scheduler. By defining accounts for both resources and users, and by using the assistant function, you can not only schedule meetings with your workgroup members, but you can confirm the availability of meeting rooms and equipment.

Like its Microsoft Mail counterpart, Schedule+ is a feature-rich application that demonstrates Microsoft's understanding of the capabilities of the Windows environment. Schedule+ is exceptionally easy to use, while providing outstanding calendar functionality. The ability to maintain two copies of the calendar and merge them automatically demonstrates the commitment Microsoft has placed on functionality in its Windows applications. Whether you decide to use Schedule+ for personal use or for sharing your schedule with others, it provides an excellent means of maintaining both a calendar and task list.

11 CHAPTER

Windows INI Files

Virtually all the changes you make to the Windows environment are stored in initialization (INI) files in the Windows directory. Windows for Workgroups uses several initialization files by default. As you add additional Windows programs, other INI files will be added to the Windows directory as well.

This chapter describes INI files and tells you how to work with them. It offers advice and instruction on the WIN.INI, SYSTEM.INI, and PROGMAN.INI files.

WORKING WITH INI FILES

Table 11-1 lists the default INI files in Windows for Workgroups. Windows INI files are plain-text (ASCII) files. If you decide to edit these files, use a word processor or text editor that can save them in plain-text format. Failure to save an INI file in ASCII format will render the file unusable. In addition, modifications to INI files can result in undesirable results, so you should make a backup of INI files before making changes.

Building Local Area Networks with Windows for Workgroups

Table 11-1. Windows for Workgroups Default INI Files

INI File	Purpose
CONTROL.INI	Entries defining the color scheme and wallpaper pattern for Windows, as well as printer settings and installable drivers.
MSMAIL.INI	Entries defining the appearance and behavior of Mail.
PROGMAN.INI	Entries defining the content of the workstation's program groups.
PROTOCOL.INI	Entries defining the network protocol and drivers.
SCHDPLUS.INI	Entries defining the appearance and behavior of Schedule+.
SHARED.INI	Entries for sharing Mail custom commands and messages with other workgroup members.
SYSTEM.INI	Entries defining system hardware settings.
WIN.INI	Modifiable entries for the Windows for Workgroups environment. Applications sometimes add their settings directly to WIN.INI instead of maintaining their own file.
WINFILE.INI	Entries defining the appearance and behavior of items in the File Manager.

INI files have a specific format, as follows:

```
[section name]
keyname=value
;comment
```

- Text within the square brackets ([]) denotes the name of a section within the INI file; the brackets are required. The leftmost bracket must be in the first column of the line.

Windows INI Files

- Below the section name are one or more line entries, or *keynames*, and their associated settings.

- Any line that starts with a semicolon (;) is either a comment field or a line entry that has been disabled. Windows will ignore any line beginning with a semicolon.

The sections in an INI file do not have to be in any specific sequence—Windows will search the entire file for the appropriate sections, as necessary.

Windows INI files can be modified several different ways:

- By using the Windows Control Panel, Program Manager, File Manager, Mail, or Schedule+ to change settings

- By running Windows Setup to change hardware settings, network drivers, or printer definitions

- By using commands such as Printer Setup from the File Menu and specifying new options

- By using a text editor to modify the files directly

- By adding application programs which rewrite or append entries to the files during installation

Windows includes a system editor utility to help you edit the AUTOEXEC.BAT, CONFIG.SYS, WIN.INI, and SYSTEM.INI files easily from a local workstation. To invoke the editor,

1. Choose **Run** from the File menu in the Program Manager.

2. Type **sysedit** in the command line box.

Building Local Area Networks with Windows for Workgroups

The editor will load all four files, and you can click on the window containing the file you want to edit, as in Figure 11-1.

**Figure 11-1.
The system editor.** The system editor uses the same commands and editing techniques used by Windows' Notepad.

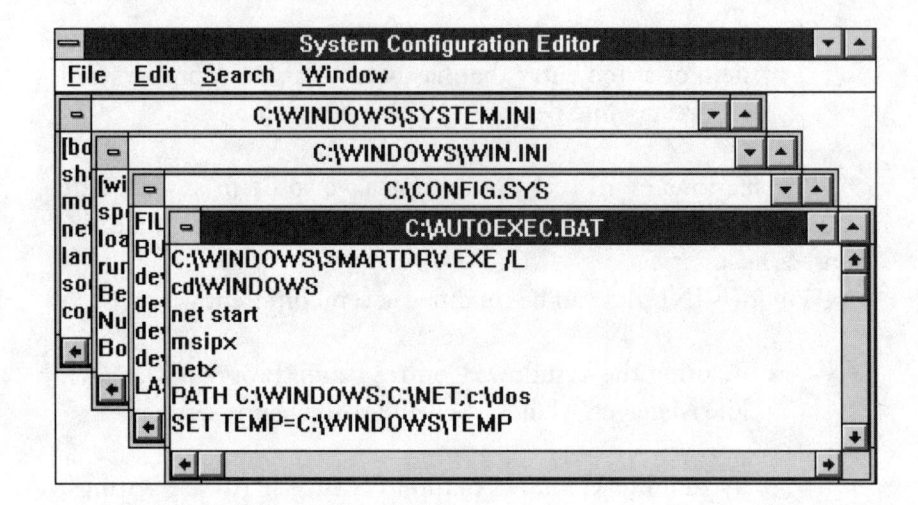

```
System Configuration Editor
File  Edit  Search  Window
    C:\WINDOWS\SYSTEM.INI
    C:\WINDOWS\WIN.INI
    C:\CONFIG.SYS
    C:\AUTOEXEC.BAT
C:\WINDOWS\SMARTDRV.EXE /L
cd\WINDOWS
net start
msipx
netx
PATH C:\WINDOWS;C:\NET;c:\dos
SET TEMP=C:\WINDOWS\TEMP
```

Changes made to WIN.INI and SYSTEM.INI will not take effect until you restart Windows. Changes to CONFIG.SYS and AUTOEXEC.BAT will not take effect until you reboot the workstation.

> **NOTE:** While it is possible to run the AUTOEXEC.BAT, some entries may conflict with existing drivers. You should always reboot after modifying the AUTOEXEC.BAT file.

A comprehensive explanation of all the options available in Windows for Workgroups INI files would require a book in itself. The rest of this chapter discusses some of the more important settings, with emphasis on network features.

WIN.INI

As a general rule, WIN.INI is used to perform customization of the software environment under Windows. Table 11-2 lists the sections available in WIN.INI and a brief description of their purpose.

Windows INI Files

Table 11-2. WIN.INI Section Headings

Section	Purpose
[colors]	Defines the colors used in Windows displays.
[desktop]	Controls the appearance of the desktop.
[devices]	Lists active output devices (for compatibility with earlier Windows applications).
[embedding]	Lists server objects used in OLE.
[extensions]	Associates file extensions with applications.
[fonts]	Describes the screen fonts used by Windows.
[FontSubstitutes]	Lists pairs of fonts that Windows recognizes as interchangeable.
[Hearts]	Used to define the appearance and behavior of the Hearts application.
[intl]	Describes how to display settings for countries outside the United States.
[Mail]	Lists global variables used by Mail.
[mci extensions]	Associates file types to Media Control Interface drivers.
[MRU_Files]	Maintains the 12 most recently used (MRU) file share connections for this workstation. Used by the Connect Network Drive dialog box.
[MRU_Printers]	Maintains the 12 most recently used (MRU) printer share connections for this workstation. Used by the Connect Network Printer dialog box.
[network]	Describes network settings and previous network connections.
[ports]	Lists available output ports.
[programs]	Lists additional paths for Windows to search to locate applications associated with a data file.

Table 11-2, continued

Section	Purpose
[PrinterPorts]	Lists active and inactive output devices.
[sounds]	Lists the sound files associated with specific events.
[spooler]	This section is used by the Print Manager.
[TrueType]	Describes options for displaying TrueType fonts.
[Windows]	Affects several elements of the Windows for Workgroups environment.
[WindowsHelp]	Describes default size, color, and placement of help files and dialog boxes.

In addition to the sections shown in Table 11-2, applications can add their own sections to WIN.INI during installation. For assistance with a specific section not shown here, consult the documentation for the application. The [section] portion of WIN.INI will provide the application name.

SYSTEM.INI

What WIN.INI is to the Windows software environment, SYSTEM.INI is to the hardware and network. SYSTEM.INI tells Windows what the system hardware configuration is and the device drivers to use to support the hardware configuration. Table 11-3 outlines the section headings in SYSTEM.INI and provides a brief description of their purpose.

Windows INI Files

Table 11-3. SYSTEM.INI Section Headings

Section	Purpose
[386Enh]	Contains information used by Windows when running in enhanced mode.
[boot]	Lists drivers and Windows modules.
[boot.description]	Lists devices you can change via Windows setup.
[ClipShares]	Identifies the names of ClipBook pages shared by this workstation.
[DDEShares]	Identifies the DDE shares defined in the DDE database that can participate in a DDE conversation.
[drivers]	Contains a list of aliases (or names) assigned to device drivers.
[keyboard]	Contains information for the keyboard.
[mci]	Lists Media Control Interface drivers.
[network]	Contains information about the workstation network configuration.
[NonWindowsApp]	Contains information used by DOS applications.
[PasswordLists]	Specifies the location of the password list files.
[standard]	Contains information used by Windows when running in standard mode.

Under each of the section headings in WIN.INI and SYSTEM.INI are a variety of line entries that allow you to customize your Windows environment. The Windows manual, however, does not include explanations for each entry, and you won't find them in this book, either.

The reason for this is simple: Microsoft includes a full description of each option in the WININI.WRI and SYSINI.WRI files that you copied to your network as part of the Windows installation. You can access these files by double-clicking on them in the File Manager or by opening them from the Write program in the Accessories group.

You may notice that not all sections or options are listed in your copy of the SYSTEM.INI and WIN.INI files. Many are only used during customization or have default values if they do not exist.

PROGMAN.INI

While it is certainly possible to edit the remaining Windows for Workgroups default INI files, in most cases you will want to use the Control Panel or the application to make these changes, since they will select the correct values automatically. One INI file called PROGMAN.INI, however, includes features that can be useful in a Windows for Workgroups environment, particularly if you have a "dedicated" Windows server. The PROGMAN.INI file is used by the Program Manager to store information about the groups defined on the desktop and their associated icons. In addition, undocumented options in PROGMAN.INI can be used to limit the Program Manager's functions. PROGMAN.INI normally looks something like this:

```
[Settings]
Window=20 26 597 427 1
display.drv=vga.drv
Order= 2 3 4 5 1

[Groups]
Group1=C:\WINDOWS\MAIN0.GRP
Group2=C:\WINDOWS\ACCESS00.GRP
Group3=C:\WINDOWS\GAMES0.GRP
Group4=C:\WINDOWS\STARTUP0.GRP
Group5=C:\WINDOWS\APPLICA0.GRP
```

Windows INI Files

In the [Settings] section, the Window= line indicates the location of the Program Manager window the last time Windows was exited with Save Changes set to ON. The five numbers on the line indicate:

- The horizontal distance of the window from the upper-left corner of the screen.

- The vertical distance of the window from the upper-left corner of the screen.

- The height of the Program Manager window.

- The width of the Program Manager window.

- Whether or not the Program Manager should load as a window or an icon. A value of 0 means to load it as an icon, and a value of 1 means to load it as a window.

Distance values are measured in pixels. A *pixel* is a single dot on the screen.

The [Groups] section of this file defines the location of each group's definition file. In some instances, you may be able to use this section to point several workstations to the same group. Since each group is essentially a menu, this will allow you to have a network menu system under Windows. For example, if several members of your workgroup will access an applications group on a shared directory, assign a drive letter to this directory and edit each user's PROGMAN.INI to point to this drive letter. It is possible to access group files from different locations at the same time. Your modified PROGMAN.INI might look something like this:

```
[Settings]
Window=20 26 597 427 1

[Groups]
Group1=D:\MAIN0.GRP
Group2=C:\WINDOWS\ACCESS00.GRP
Group3=C:\WINDOWS\GAMES0.GRP
Group4=C:\WINDOWS\STARTUP0.GRP
Group5=E:\APPLICA0.GRP
```

In this example, the user has two drive letters assigned to a shared directory on another workstation (or workstations). The Main program group will load from the shared directory mapped to drive D:, and the applications group will load from a directory mapped to drive E:. These groups contain information describing the path and where each application in the group can be found, so you will have to match these paths with the drive mappings for the remote users. Since you can define these shared directories as read-only, you can in effect create Windows menu groups that cannot be modified (or damaged) by the user. Changes or additions to these groups will automatically be distributed network-wide.

When the user exits Windows with Save Changes ON, any groups that are read-only will generate an error message "Program group file *XXXXXX*.GRP is write protected," where *XXXXXX* is the name of the shared group. Inform your users in advance that this is not an error—their personal groups and Program Manager settings will be saved.

In addition to the ability to share groups using PROGMAN.INI, I mentioned several undocumented settings you can use to control your Windows environment. PROGMAN.INI does not have a section called [restrictions] when Windows is installed, but you can manually add this section and set several options under this heading. When this section is absent, Windows assumes the following default values:

Windows INI Files

```
[restrictions]
NoRun=0
NoClose=0
NoFileMenu=0
NoSaveSettings=0
EditLevel=0
```

Let's look at each of these restrictions and their possible values. Most of these arguments use a YES/NO setting, where 1 is YES and 0 is NO. The EditLevel has multiple setting values.

- *NoRun.* Setting the NoRun value to 1 disables the Run command on the File menu. This prevents a user from using the Run command to execute a program from the command line. The user can still execute a program by clicking on it from the File Manager.

- *NoClose.* Setting the NoClose value to 1 disables the Exit Windows menu item on the File menu, and the Close option on the Control menu. It also disables the Alt-F4 keyboard shortcut, which normally exits Windows. The user would have to reboot the workstation to exit Windows.

- *NoFileMenu.* Setting the NoFileMenu value to 1 completely removes the File menu from the Program Manager. A value of NoClose=0 will still allow the user to exit Windows with the Alt-F4 key combination.

- *NoSaveSettings.* Setting the NoSaveSettings value to 1 disables the ability to write changes to icon locations to PROGMAN.INI. The user can move icons around, but their original positions are restored when Windows is exited and restarted.

- *EditLevel*. Setting the EditLevel determines the user's ability to modify group windows, icons, and icon properties: the default value of 0 allows the user full editing of these items; 1 prevents the user from deleting, creating, or changing group window names; 2 prevents the creating or deleting of program items; 3 prevents the user from changing the command line of program items; 4 prevents the modification of *any* program item properties.

As you can see, the restrictions section of PROGMAN.INI can be very useful in a network environment, particularly on a server PC. By setting the NoClose option ON, for example, you can prevent users from exiting to DOS on a server. The EditLevel line can be used to prevent users from modifying program item properties.

SUMMARY

It should be noted that you may never have to modify the INI settings in your Windows environment because Windows and Windows applications generally handle most settings changes transparently. Still, understanding the location and purpose of Windows INI files will help you understand where to look if you have problems down the road. You'll want to print out the contents of the SYSINI.WRI and WININI.WRI files for future reference, particularly if you have problems with running Windows in enhanced mode.

In Chapter 13, about troubleshooting Windows, I refer to the enhanced mode section of SYSTEM.INI, since this is where most enhanced mode troubles can be resolved.

12 CHAPTER
DOS Applications in a Windows Environment

An old computer joke asks how God was able to create the world in only seven days. The answer—because He didn't have an installed base—refers to the difficulty in bringing out a new software release while continuing to support previous versions. For Windows to gain acceptance in the marketplace, it needed to provide significant advantages over DOS and still maintain compatibility with the thousands of DOS-based applications already in use. Windows 2.x and 3.0 provided some DOS compatibility and Microsoft refined the DOS interface in 3.1. However, successfully using DOS applications under Windows remains one of the most difficult tasks you may have to perform.

The difficulty in using DOS applications is primarily a function of how DOS and Windows applications view the system hardware. Many DOS applications were written on the assumption that they would have complete control of the system, and they don't behave properly in a multitasking environment such as Windows. In contrast, Windows-based applications work directly with the Windows operating system and access memory and hardware through the Windows interface. It is extremely unlikely that you will ever experience compatibility problems when running multiple Windows-based programs, but you're almost certain to experience some Windows problems when running DOS applications.

While a variety of factors, including software costs and training, can keep you from converting from DOS to Windows applications, you should consider converting as many of your current applications as possible. Most Windows applications use a fairly similar graphical interface and tend to group common commands under the same headings, so the training costs of using Windows applications should be lower than your initial investment in DOS applications, and eventually the most die-hard DOS fanatic can become a Windows convert.

WINDOWS AND THE PIF FILE

Since a DOS application doesn't talk directly to Windows, Windows needs several pieces of information to allocate the necessary resources for the DOS program to run. This information is stored in a *program information file*, or *PIF*. PIF files include information about the amount of memory needed by the DOS application, the video modes used, and the location of the program. Because it's possible to run many DOS programs directly from the Run command in the File menu, a common misconception is that not all DOS applications require a PIF. In actuality, Windows still needs to allocate resources for the program, and it uses a default PIF provided with Windows if a PIF is not specified. If you only have one or two DOS applications and their system requirements are similar, you may be able to run these applications without creating a custom PIF file. In this instance, Windows will use the default settings, and you can edit the default PIF, if necessary. Some applications, however, require a custom PIF file (and many DOS programs now provide recommended PIF settings or an actual PIF file for Windows).

DOS APPLICATIONS IN WINDOWS' STANDARD AND ENHANCED MODES

Although Windows applications can run concurrently under either standard or enhanced mode, DOS applications are treated differently, depending on the mode Windows is using. In standard mode, DOS

12

DOS Applications in a Windows Environment

applications must run in full-screen mode, and when a DOS program is active, all other tasks—such as background Windows programs—are suspended. To switch to another task from a DOS program, press Ctrl-Esc. This both brings up the Task List dialog box and minimizes the DOS application to an icon. From there you can select another application or return to the Windows desktop. To return to the DOS application, double-click on its icon.

In enhanced mode, Windows is able to run both a DOS and Windows applications concurrently, and will even allow you to run a DOS application in its own window. There is a performance penalty associated with this, however, and many DOS applications don't work well with this setting. Most DOS applications can work quite well in a window, but the increased complexity involved in running active DOS applications alongside active Windows programs increases the likelihood of problems. You can eliminate some of these problems by adjusting the DOS program PIF file to tell Windows to suspend all background tasks when the DOS application is active, and leave the DOS application full-screen.

WORKING WITH PIF FILES

The Windows for Workgroups installation procedure automatically searches your disk during the installation for PIF files. PIF files found during this search can be added to your desktop automatically, if the associated program is found. For example, if Lotus 1-2-3 is installed on your system, Windows automatically adds Lotus 1-2-3 to the desktop by using a PIF supplied with Windows. Windows includes PIF files for many popular programs, but the settings may not always provide the optimum configuration for your environment.

The PIF files provided with Windows can be easily modified—or created—by using a Windows application called the PIF Editor (located in the Main program group). Double-clicking on the PIF editor icon will launch the application. Windows PIF files can have different settings, depending on the Windows operating mode, and the PIF Editor is sensitive to the current operating mode when it is started. Figure 12-1 shows the PIF Editor when running under enhanced mode. The various fields on this screen are discussed later in this chapter in the "Enhanced Mode PIF Settings—Standard Options" section.

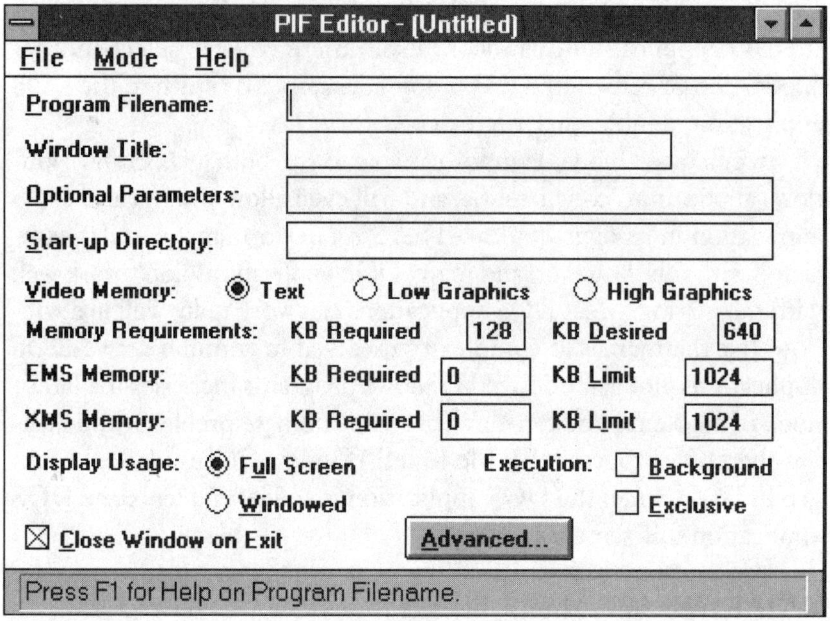

Figure 12-1. Enhanced mode PIF Editor. The primary difference between the standard and enhanced mode PIF Editors is that the enhanced mode PIF Editor includes the Advanced... button, which brings up the Advanced Options screen.

Although you'll typically want to set up a PIF for the same mode you are running, there may be instances when you'll want to set up a PIF for another mode. Select the Mode menu option to toggle the PIF Editor between standard and enhanced mode. A PIF created in either standard or enhanced mode will work regardless of the actual mode running, but Windows will make certain settings assumptions, if necessary. Since these assumptions may not be correct, it is up to you to create the PIF for the mode you intend to use. The PIF for standard modes is largely a subset of the enhanced mode settings, so creating a PIF for enhanced mode operations provides you with the greatest compatibility between modes. Keep in mind if you're running in standard mode that you should develop a PIF specifically for the modes you plan to use.

12

DOS Applications in a Windows Environment

Creating or Modifying a PIF

When you start the PIF Editor, Windows creates a new, untitled PIF file with a set of default settings. To modify an existing PIF,

1. Select the **Open** command from the File menu in the PIF Editor. This brings up the Windows dialog box with a list of the PIF files in the Windows directory.

2. Select the PIF you wish to view or modify.

3. Click the **OK** button.

There are two PIF files in the Windows directory you should know about—the DOSPRMPT.PIF and the _DEFAULT.PIF. Even if you didn't install any DOS applications as part of your Windows installation, the DOSPRMPT.PIF should have been installed in the Main program group as the MS-DOS Prompt icon. Clicking on this icon should invoke the standard MS-DOS prompt in a full-screen. If, for example, you want to have your DOS prompt in a window or force the DOS prompt to run as an exclusive task, you can edit the DOSPRMPT.PIF appropriately.

Editing the _DEFAULT.PIF file will provide the same functionality both for any DOS program invoked using the Run command on the File menu, or for a DOS program that does not have an associated PIF file in either the Windows directory or its own directory.

After making your changes, select Save to save changes to an existing PIF file or Save As... to save the changes to a new file. Be sure to save the PIF either in the Program directory or the Windows directory, and do not add an extension to the PIF file name. PIF files must have the extension .PIF, and the editor will add this extension automatically.

Prior to saving, the PIF Editor will check the Program Filename you have entered in the PIF. Program Filenames must end with a valid extension for a DOS executable file (.BAT, .COM, or .EXE).

The PIF Editor will not check for the actual existence of the program, however.

To use the PIF, modify the program item properties for the associated application and replace the command line parameter with the name of your PIF. Figure 12-2 shows the program item properties for the MS-DOS Prompt icon.

Figure 12-2. Entering a PIF as the command line. Replacing the PIF with the name of an executable file (such as COMMAND.COM) would tell Windows to use the _DEFAULT.PIF. Adding the PIF to the command line allows you to create custom PIF files for each DOS application.

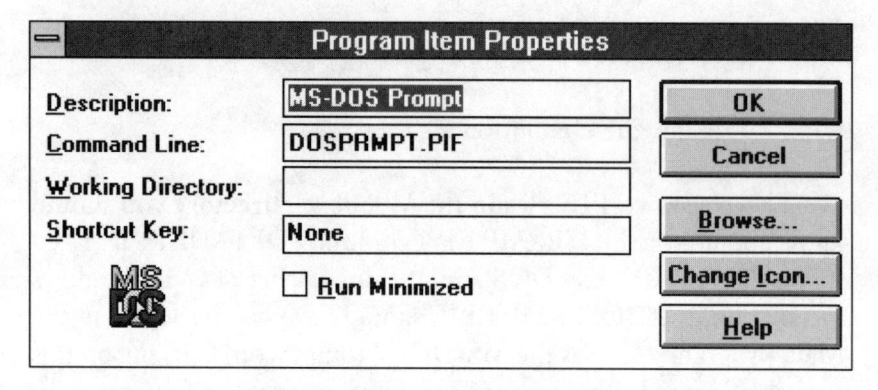

Even though the PIF defines the settings Windows should use when starting the application, it is still possible to perform some tuning after a DOS application is running. To do so,

1. Press **Ctrl-Esc** once the application is started to switch back to Windows.

2. Reduce the DOS application to an icon (if you were running the DOS application in a window).

3. Click the mouse once on the DOS program's icon.

A menu will appear. Two options on this menu are specific to DOS applications—the Settings option and the Fonts option. Selecting the Settings option will give you a dialog box similar to the one in Figure 12-3.

DOS Applications in a Windows Environment

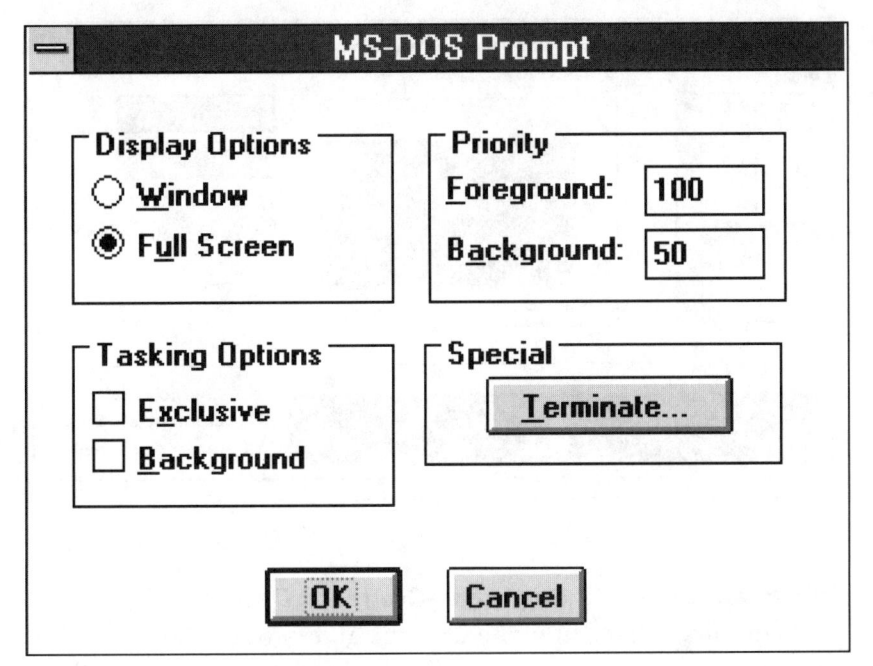

Figure 12-3.
The Settings box for a DOS application. Regardless of the PIF settings, a DOS application running on a system operating in enhanced mode can be "tuned" while the application is running.

From this box, you can switch the DOS application from windowing to full-screen, set its operation as exclusive or background, and set the CPU priority when running the application as either a foreground or background task. The Terminate button allows you to force the application to close. However, this will not properly close the application, so it should only be used if you know the application does not have any open files.

The Fonts option will display a dialog box similar to the one in Figure 12-4. Choose a font size in the Font box. The font you choose will only be used when the application is run in a window mode, not in a full-screen mode. Additionally, many DOS applications bypass the system BIOS and write directly to the screen hardware. While Windows can still force these applications to run in a window, the font selection will be ignored. Select Save Settings on Exit to make the font change permanent.

Building Local Area Networks with Windows for Workgroups

Figure 12-4.
The Font Selection box. Selecting a font from the left column will generate a sample font in the Selected Font box.

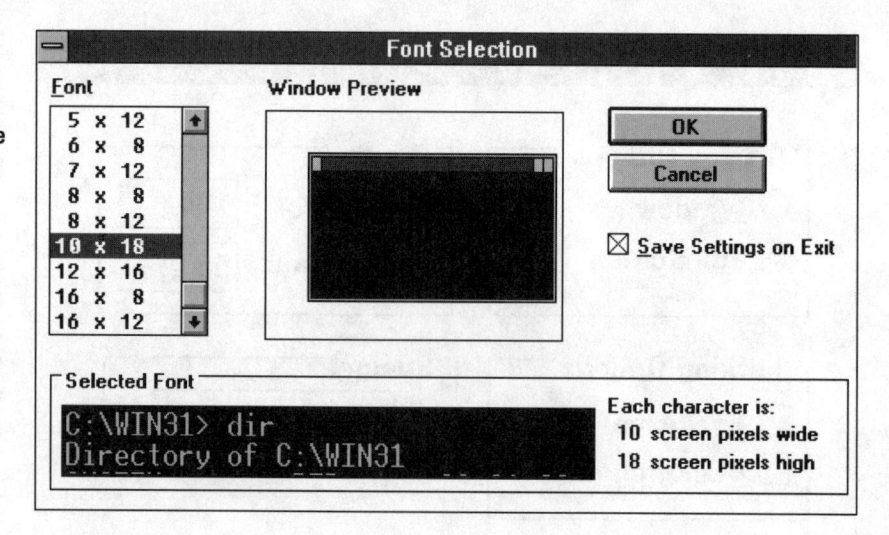

Enhanced Mode PIF Settings—Standard Options

Windows enhanced mode uses the ability of the 80386/80486 microprocessor to create a "virtual" machine for every DOS application you run. The processor performs this feat by assigning each program a block of physical memory, and then mapping each block to the same set of logical memory addresses. While no two programs can be mapped to the same address space concurrently, the processor switches blocks so quickly that the apparent result is the ability to run two or more tasks simultaneously. Advanced memory management functions in the 80386/80486 can also allow the operating system to use XMS memory to emulate either conventional or extended memory, and release this memory when the application no longer requires it.

Applications running under Windows need to be able to tell the operating system just how much memory they require, as do programs written for Windows. As I mentioned earlier, DOS applications don't provide this information, and Windows uses a PIF to decide what resources to give to the DOS application. A DOS application given insufficient resources may overwrite memory locations that belong to Windows, resulting in a system crash.

12

DOS Applications in a Windows Environment

This problem is only prevalent in enhanced mode operation, so let's examine the enhanced mode PIF file to determine the appropriate settings for DOS applications in this environment. Figure 12-1 showed the opening screen for the PIF Editor. From this screen, you can begin defining a DOS application's PIF requirements.

- *Program Filename* requires the full path and executable file name for your DOS program. This file name must end in a valid DOS executable file name extension (.BAT, .COM, or .EXE).

- *Window Title* stores the name that should appear in the application's title bar. If this field is blank, Windows will use the file name from the Program Filename field (minus the extension).

- *Optional Parameters* allows you to add command line options or switches to the program file name. This field will accept up to 63 characters for command line options. If you'd like Windows to prompt you for the command line options, place a question mark in this field.

- *Start-up Directory* specifies what directory you want to be in when the program loads. This will normally be either the Program directory or the directory used for data files for this program.

- *Video Memory buttons* tell Windows how much memory to initially reserve for the application's display. Low Graphics refers to applications that use CGA-equivalent graphic displays. High Graphics refers to applications that use EGA or VGA video modes. Windows monitors the application's use of video and will allocate additional memory, if necessary (assuming the memory is available). Windows will also free up video memory if it detects that the application is no longer using it. By selecting the Retain Video Memory button in the Advanced section of the PIF Editor and setting video memory requirements there (see the next section of this chapter), you can select the minimum amount of video memory reserved for the application, regardless of the mode the application is currently using.

- *Memory Requirements* has two settings, one for the amount of memory required by the application and another for the desired amount of memory. The Required memory field simply tells Windows not to attempt to run the program unless this amount of memory is available. The Desired memory setting is the amount of memory you want Windows to allocate to the application, if available. These fields refer to conventional memory only, so the maximum value for desired memory is 640 (kilobytes). Ordinarily, you'll want to leave this field at the maximum value. You only need to reduce it if you are low on memory and want to run additional applications.

- *EMS Memory* has two sections, one for the amount of memory required by the application and another for the maximum amount of EMS memory to allocate to the program. EMS (expanded memory specification) is used by applications that require expanded memory. Just like video memory, Windows can allocate additional EMS memory to an application if the application needs it (assuming the memory is available). Windows will continue to allocate EMS memory up to the limit specified in the EMS KB Limit field.

- *XMS Memory* works just like the EMS section, but is for applications that require extended memory. Again, the KB Required field tells Windows not to load the program unless this minimum amount of memory is present.

    Although many DOS applications can use either EMS or XMS memory, most do not require this memory in order to operate. You can generally set the KB Required fields to 0.

DOS Applications in a Windows Environment

Use a higher number only if the program absolutely requires it, or you need to guarantee the presence of this memory in order to load your data files.

- *Display Usage* determines if Windows will run the DOS application in a window or in a full screen. Not all programs can run in a window, and the screen refresh is slower. You can improve screen refresh by increasing the priority of DOS screen updates in a window. Do this by adding the line WindowUpdateTime=*XX* in the [386Enh] section of your WIN.INI. The value for *XX* can range from 20 to 1000. The default value (if this line doesn't exist) is 50, and increasing this number to around 200 should provide good performance without significantly impacting Windows itself. When an application is placed in a window, you can toggle between the window and the full-screen by pressing Alt-Enter.

- *Execution boxes* determine how the application interacts with Windows and with other applications running on your system. Check the Background box if you want your application to run in the background while you are using another program. If this box is blank (the default), the application will be suspended when you switch to another program. The Exclusive box is the opposite of the Background box, in that it suspends all other DOS applications whenever this application is in the foreground, regardless of the other application's Background option setting.

- *Close Window on Exit* instructs Windows to close the application's "session" when you exit the program. If this box is checked—regardless of whether the program is running in full-screen or a window—the session will close when the program is terminated.

- *Advanced...* The Advanced options are explained below.

Enhanced Mode PIF Settings—Advanced Options

The PIF Editor provides Windows with sufficient information to allow a DOS application to run. The Advanced option in the PIF Editor, however, allows you to perform some additional tuning of your DOS session. Select the Advanced button on the PIF Editor main screen and you'll see an additional set of parameters, as shown in Figure 12-5.

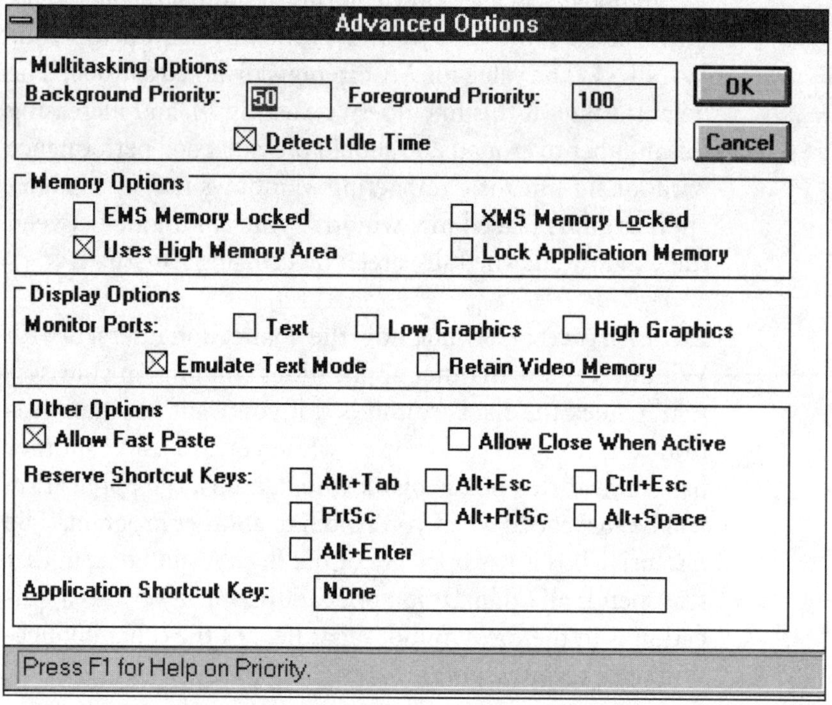

Figure 12-5. Advanced settings for enhanced mode PIFs. You cannot select Advanced settings unless the PIF Editor is set for 386 enhanced mode. These settings are not applicable when running DOS applications under Windows standard mode.

The Multitasking Options box allows you to set priorities for foreground and background operations for your DOS applications. These values can range from 1 to 10,000, but are also dependent on the values set for other PIF files that are run concurrently. To determine the comparative priority of a DOS application, divide its priority by the total of all the active DOS application's priority values. For example,

12 DOS Applications in a Windows Environment

if the foreground application has a Foreground Priority of 100, and two background tasks each have a Background Priority of 50, then the total priority is 200 (100+50+50). Divide the foreground task's priority of 100 by the total, and the result is the amount of CPU allocated by the foreground task. Divide each background task's priority by the total, and you'll have the amount of CPU allocated to each background task. In our example, the foreground DOS application gets half the CPU time, and each background application gets one-fourth the CPU.

Check the Detect Idle Time box if you want to allocate fewer CPU cycles to this program when the program is idle (typically when it is waiting for keyboard input).

The Multitasking Options settings defined here only affect the amount of CPU cycles shared by multiple DOS applications running concurrently. If you only have one DOS application running in Windows at any one time, these settings are not used. The amount of CPU time shared between Windows programs and DOS was set in the Scheduling portion of the Control Panel's 386 Enhanced dialog box.

Following is an explanation of the Memory Options boxes.

- *EMS Memory Locked* prevents Windows from swapping this program's expanded memory to disk. Disk swapping of a program's expanded memory reduces the performance of the application but gives you additional memory for running applications.

- *XMS Memory Locked* prevents Windows from swapping this program's extended memory to disk.

- *Uses High Memory Area* tells Windows that this application can use the *high memory area*, or *HMA*. The HMA is the first 64K of extended memory. Although this setting is checked by default, you must turn this function off if MS-DOS 5.0's ability to load in the HMA is activated or you use a memory manager to load other programs in the HMA. Only one application can use the HMA.

- *Lock Application Memory* prevents Windows from swapping the application to disk. Swapping the application to disk will suspend the program, but will give you additional memory for other programs.

The Display Options portion of the Advanced Options screen tells Windows how to handle the video display in your system.

- *Monitor Ports* instructs Windows to attempt to monitor instructions to the video display in each of the video modes—Text, Low Graphics, and High Graphics. If you experience problems with an application display in full-screen mode, try running the application after turning on the appropriate box for the video mode used by the program. Since this can affect the overall performance of Windows, don't use these selections unless you are experiencing problems. These settings are not used when a DOS application is running in a window.

- *Emulate Text Mode box* allows Windows to handle screen displays when in text mode. This provides for much better screen updates. Leave this option checked unless you experience problems with the display or cursor location.

- *Retain Video Memory box* instructs Windows to retain the video memory for a DOS application, once the application requests this memory. Normally, when an application switches to a lower video mode, Windows will release this memory for use by other applications. If you are low on memory, it is conceivable that the application could lose some of its display when it attempts to switch back to the higher video mode.

DOS Applications in a Windows Environment

Following is an explanation of boxes in the Other Options section of the Advanced Options screen.

- *Allow Fast Paste*. Most DOS applications can accept data pasted from the Clipboard as fast as Windows can send it. If you experience difficulties pasting from Windows to your DOS application, turn this setting off.

- *Allow Close When Active*. When you exit Windows, any active Windows application will warn you if you have unsaved information. DOS applications, however, do not provide this information to Windows. If you attempt to exit Windows with an active DOS application, Windows will instruct you to close the application, and try again. Checking this box tells Windows not to worry about this application and to proceed with the Exit command. Any unsaved data in the DOS application will be lost, and it is even possible to corrupt open data files by exiting improperly. Don't check this box unless you are sure you can exit this program without saving and closing the program.

- *Reserve Shortcut Keys*. The shortcut keys listed in this section are used by Windows for a variety of tasks. Some DOS applications use the same keystroke combinations, however, and this section allows you to disable the Windows shortcut keystroke in favor of the DOS application shortcut keystroke. Disabling a Windows keystroke only takes affect while in the application associated with this PIF.

- *Application Shortcut Keys*. This option allows you to define a shortcut key for your application. With this shortcut key, you can jump to your DOS application from within any other program. You must start the application in order to jump to it later. The shortcut key you assign must include either the Alt or Ctrl key and cannot include the Esc, Enter, Tab, Space,

Building Local Area Networks with Windows for Workgroups

PrtSc, or Backspace keys. Once you start an application to which you have assigned a defined shortcut key, you can press the shortcut key to jump to your program even if it normally has another meaning to the application you are using.

Standard Mode PIF Settings

Figure 12-6 shows the PIF Editor for creating a PIF in standard mode operation. Since most of the settings here were covered under the discussion of enhanced mode PIF operations, we'll concentrate on the settings that are unique to standard mode PIFs.

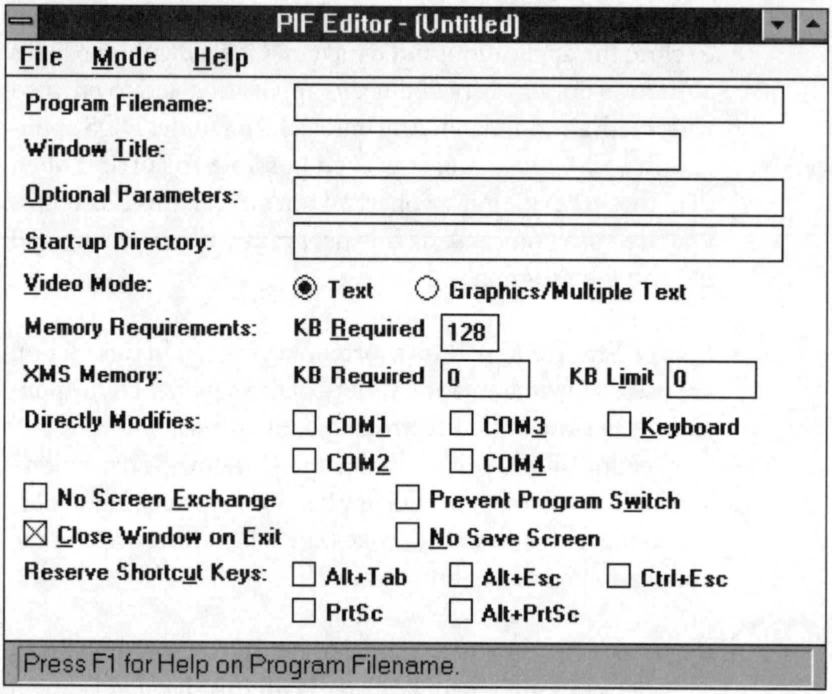

Figure 12-6. Standard mode PIF. A PIF created in either standard or enhanced mode will still function if Windows is running in a different mode—but it will use Windows defaults for the differences.

DOS Applications in a Windows Environment

Following is an explanation of several key settings in the PIF Editor dialog box.

- *Video Mode* determines whether the application will use graphics. Windows in standard mode does not dynamically map video memory to the application as required.

- *Memory Requirements* does not have a maximum value field, since only one DOS application can run at a time. Windows will verify that the minimum amount of memory is available, and then provide all the conventional memory in the system to the DOS application.

- *Directly Modifies* tells Windows that the application talks directly to the device, and prevents the user from switching to another program without quitting the application.

- *No Screen Exchange box* prevents you from pressing PrtSc or Alt-PrtSc to copy the application's screen to the Clipboard (DOS applications typically use these key combinations to send screen output to the printer).

- *Prevent Program Switch box* prevents Windows from switching to another application without exiting the current program.

- *No Save Screen box* instructs Windows not to save the current screen image when switching to another application. If the application stores its own screen image and can refresh the screen, you can select this option to free up memory for other programs.

SELECTING APPLICATIONS FOR THE NETWORK

Windows 3.1 and Windows for Workgroups have made significant improvements in the handling of DOS applications. Still, when you consider upgrading your existing software and evaluate new applications, your selection criteria should include the availability of a Windows version of the program. You selected Windows for several reasons, including its graphical interface and the ability to multitask your system while using applications that can access more than 640K of memory. DOS applications lack these features. Fewer and fewer development dollars are being spent to upgrade DOS programs. PIF files may allow you to "get by" for now with your DOS applications, but if DOS applications are your primary programs you would be better served by running a DOS-based network. I included this chapter to help you use existing DOS software until you are ready to upgrade. However, the real benefits of the Windows environment are realized through Windows applications, not the operating system.

13 CHAPTER

Troubleshooting Windows for Workgroups

In this chapter, we'll examine some of the common problems that you may experience with Windows for Workgroups. After describing the problem, I'll suggest possible causes as well as solutions and ways to work around problems. At the end of this chapter is a list of resources you can use to get additional help.

COMMON PROBLEMS WITH USING WORKGROUPS FOR WINDOWS

This section examines the kinds of problems that come up most often with Workgroups for Windows, including problems with installation, printing, and network communication.

The Setup Program Fails to Work

Problem: During installation, Setup hangs the system or reports a memory-resident program conflict during loading.

The Setup program is incompatible with many *terminate and stay resident* (TSR) programs. The SETUP.TXT file on Setup disk 1 discusses specific TSR programs that can cause Setup to fail. Remove

Building Local Area Networks with Windows for Workgroups

any unnecessary TSR's from the CONFIG.SYS and AUTOEXEC.BAT files and reboot the system before running Setup again. If this fails to correct the problem, try using

```
setup/i
```

instead of

```
setup
```

The /i switch tells Setup to select a standard hardware configuration instead of attempting to detect your existing hardware configuration. When Setup loads with these settings, the auto-detection portion of Setup may not be able to correctly identify portions of your configuration. After changing the standard hardware configuration to suit your system, proceed with Setup.

The Setup Program for the Network Fails
Problem: When running SETUP/N for a network copy, Setup fails.

Setup/N allows you to install a portion of the Windows files to a local directory, while accessing Windows from a shared network directory. To verify that all the necessary files are in the shared directory, Setup will not allow you to use the /N parameter when installing from floppies. Setup can also fail if you set up an ArcNet or Ethernet adapter using a RAM address of D000. Reset the adapter to D800 and rerun Setup. ArcNet adapters may also have problems with auto-detection, so use Setup /I /N to bypass detection.

The Video Display Goes Blank or Is Incorrect
Problem: After displaying the Windows logo, the video display goes blank or the display is incorrect.

Troubleshooting Windows for Workgroups

Try running Windows in standard mode, using the

```
win/s
```

command. If Windows works properly in this mode, you may be using a Windows 3.0 display driver. Many video drivers used with Windows 3.0 won't work with Windows for Workgroups. If your video adapter and monitor supports 800x600 16 color resolution, you should be able to substitute the Windows for Workgroups SuperVGA driver for the 3.0 video driver.

This problem can also occur if Windows fails to detect all of the video memory on your display card. Typically, this memory will be in the C000-CFFF range. You can instruct Windows not to use this entire memory range by adding

```
emmexclude=C000-CFFF
```

to the [386enh] section of the SYSTEM.INI file.

Windows Does not Work in Enhanced Mode

Problem: Windows works in standard mode, but not enhanced mode.

This problem usually results from a conflict with a hardware device that uses upper memory. To determine if this is the problem, run Windows using the

```
win /d:x
```

command. This instructs Windows not to use any upper memory. You can make this change permanent by changing or adding

```
emmexclude=A000-FFFF
```

to the [386enh] section of the SYSTEM.INI file.

If you can identify the specific memory address range or ranges that conflict with Windows, you can exclude each range by adding multiple emmexclude= statements to the SYSTEM.INI file.

Windows Does not Start in Enhanced Mode

Problem: The workstation has at least 3Mb of memory, but Windows will not start in enhanced mode.

The 3Mb memory specification is the absolute minimum in order for Windows to load in enhanced mode. Memory-resident programs that load prior to starting Windows (including Windows for Workgroups network drivers) will reduce the available memory for Windows. Try using the command

```
WIN/3
```

to force Windows to run in enhanced mode. If this works, your system has just enough memory to run in enhanced mode, but performance will suffer. You may also be able to free up additional memory by removing unnecessary TSR's from the AUTOEXEC.BAT file.

A Disk Error Is Reported when Accessing the Local Hard Drive

Problem: The workstation reports a disk error when attempting to access the local hard drive.

In enhanced mode, Windows requires that SMARTDrive (Windows disk-caching software) be used with any hard drive controller that doesn't emulate a standard ST506 controller. If you have replaced or disabled SMARTDrive, try running Windows with SMARTDrive reinstalled. If you continue to experience problems, place the command

```
VirtualHDirq=off
```

in the [386enh] section of the SYSTEM.INI file.

13
Troubleshooting Windows for Workgroups

The Workstation Can't Access the Network

Problem: The workstation reports an error when attempting to access the network.

On a network that has been in operation, this error can usually be traced to one of three things—cable, cable, or cable. The network cable is the weakest link in your network environment. If you experience a network outage, start looking for workstations that have been moved. The network cable may have been incorrectly disconnected, or the cable may been have stretched and broken internally. I once experienced a network outage on a token-ring network when a secretary set her purse on a cable and caused the cable to come partway out of the data connector.

In a new installation, network errors at a specific workstation can be caused by interrupt, I/O port address, or shared-memory address conflicts with other devices in the system. You need to choose network adapter settings that do not conflict with other hardware in your system. EMM386, the memory manager provided with Windows, may require an X= option on the command line to exclude your network driver shared memory. You may also need to exclude this area in the [386enh] portion of the SYSTEM.INI by using the

```
EMMEXCLUDE=
```

entry. Finally, if your system is able to use shadow RAM or shadow ROM, try turning off these options.

One Workstation Can't Attach to Another

Problem: The workstation generates an error attempting to attach to a specific workstation.

When Windows for Workgroups loads, it attempts to connect to all directories and printers defined for the user. If one of the remote "servers" is unavailable, the workstation will generate an error and ask if it should continue to attempt to connect to other network devices.

Building Local Area Networks with Windows for Workgroups

Selecting No will prevent Windows for Workgroups from connecting to any remaining resources, even if they are available. Make sure all workstations that will be acting as servers are running Windows in enhanced mode, and restart Windows on the affected workstation.

The Workstation Can't Print a Document

Problem: The workstation generates an error when attempting to print a document.

If the printer is locally attached, it may simply be off-line or out of paper. Verify that the printer is on-line and check the printer cable. The Windows Print Manager spools print jobs to disk before printing, and places these jobs in the directory specified by the TEMP= variable in the AUTOEXEC.BAT file. Make sure that this variable points to an existing directory and that the directory's drive has disk space available. If this directory is on a network drive, verify that the user has write-access to the directory.

An Error Message Appears when Printing to the Network Printer

Problem: The workstation generates an error message in the middle of printing a document to a network printer.

This is usually caused by a time-out in the Print Manager. Increase the Transmission Retry setting in the Printers section of the Control Panel. This setting determines the amount of time the printer can remain busy before the Print Manager reports an error.

The Mouse Doesn't Work in Windows Applications

Problem: The mouse doesn't work in Windows.

The MS-DOS version of the Microsoft Mouse driver must be 7.04 or later. The Logitech DOS driver must be version 6.0 or later.

Troubleshooting Windows for Workgroups

For other mice, try removing the MS-DOS level driver. You may also have a device interrupt conflict. Verify the interrupt level of the serial port or bus card used by the mouse. PS/2 mouse-compatible systems typically use interrupt 12.

The Mouse Doesn't Work in DOS Applications

Problem: The mouse doesn't work when running DOS applications under Windows.

DOS applications that support mouse functions can continue to use a mouse with Windows for Workgroups. The mouse driver must be loaded before running Windows and the application must be in full-screen mode. If you don't need mouse support for your DOS applications, don't load the DOS mouse driver.

The DOS Application Crashes or Reports Insufficient Memory

Problem: A DOS application reports insufficient memory or crashes when running under Windows.

The amount of conventional memory available to each DOS application under Windows will always be somewhat less than the memory available outside of Windows, although on a highly tuned system this loss can be as little as 10K. The best way to resolve these problems is to reconfigure the system to get as much available memory before Windows loads. On an 80286 system, there is little you can do except switch to MS-DOS 5.0 and use its memory manager to load a portion of DOS in upper memory. On an 80386/80486 system, some third-party memory managers can provide you with additional memory. For example, QEMM386, from Quarterdeck, offers a STEALTH mode that will remap ROM addresses to the page frame. Combining MS-DOS 5.0's features with QEMM386 can result in DOS windows as large as 600K.

While most DOS-based business applications should work with this configuration, some programs just won't work under Windows. Many high-resolution games, for example, talk directly to the video adapters, sound cards, and mice or joystick ports. This combination is almost certainly fatal to Windows.

The DOS Communications Program Is Performing Poorly

Problem: DOS communications programs lose data or perform poorly under Windows.

Running DOS communications programs in Windows at baud rates higher than 2400bps can be tricky. In addition, never attempt to switch away from a DOS communications program when running in standard mode, since this suspends the DOS application. When running DOS communications programs in a windowed DOS session, using the mouse to highlight text (with the Edit Mark command) will also suspend the DOS session until the highlight function is complete.

DOS applications cannot reliably support baud rates higher than 9600bps when run under Windows, and this speed requires an 80386 running at 20mhz or higher. You can improve your odds of successfully running DOS communications programs at 9600bps by increasing the communications buffer in the [386enh] section of the SYSTEM.INI file. Add the

```
COMxBuffer=256
```

line in this file (x represents the serial port number, 1 or 2). This increases the buffer from the default of 128, and this value can be further increased in 128-byte increments. You can also increase the amount of time Windows allows a DOS application to process characters by adding a second line to the [386enh] section. Place the command

```
COMBoostTime=
```

in this section followed by a time value (in milliseconds). A value of 4 will double the Windows default of 2 milliseconds.

13

Troubleshooting Windows for Workgroups

Finally, create a PIF file for the DOS communications program. Set the execution to Exclusive and, under the Advanced Options, select Lock Application Memory. This will suspend other DOS applications but provide for more reliable communications, while preventing Windows from inadvertently moving memory and disrupting the communications program.

Specific DOS and Network Applications Are Experiencing Problems

Problem: Specific DOS and network applications experience problems under Windows for Workgroups.

Windows for Workgroups includes information files for using certain applications. Check the README.WRI and NETWORKS.WRI files for current notes on specific applications.

The Mail Program Cannot Access the Mail Directory

Problem: When starting Mail for the first time, the program indicates that it cannot access the Mail directory.

This is an apparent bug in the Windows for Workgroups Mail software—the only bug I found during testing. Mail creates and reads the MSMAIL.INI file to determine the location of the Mail files. The version of Windows for Workgroups I used while preparing this book put the *universal naming convention* (UNC) name in the MSMAIL.INI, and Mail apparently has trouble with this setting. My solution was to replace the UNC name with a drive letter and tell the File Manager to assign the POSTOFFICE to this drive for each user. For example, if the POSTOFFICE is on \\BECKY\POSTOFFICE, edit the

```
ServerPath=
```

entry in MSMAIL.INI to read E:\, and use the File Manager to assign drive E: to \\BECKY\POSTOFFICE.

Netware Users Cannot See the Workgroup

Problem: On a NetWare network, some users cannot see the workgroup.

NetWare supports what Novell calls "internal routing," the ability to install two or more network adapters in a server and route traffic from one network cable to another through the server. NetWare will only route IPX/SPX traffic, not Windows for Workgroups NETBEUI packets. Unless you are willing to install special hardware and software, all Workgroup members must be on the same cable segment.

Users Can't Connect to a CD-ROM Drive on a Workstation

Problem: The CD-ROM drive on a workstation has been defined as a shared device, but other users get "error reading device" when attempting to connect to this drive.

Setup will install a new version of MSCDEX (2.21) if it detects MSCDEX running on a system. If MSCDEX was not already loaded, however, you can manually expand this file from the diskette. Locate the file MSCDEX.EX_ on the Windows diskettes, place it in the A: drive, and from the Windows directory, type

```
EXPAND A:\MSCDEX.EX_ C:\WINDOWS\MSCDEX.EXE
```

The command line that loads MSCDEX should be modified to point to the new driver, and the parameter /S should be added to enable sharing. The CD-ROM drive still must be shared through the File Manager.

13

Troubleshooting Windows for Workgroups

Difficulties with TrueType Fonts

Problem: Windows or the printer driver experiences problems with TrueType fonts.

TrueType fonts allow Windows to display the same fonts on-screen that will print to the printer. Any printer capable of printing graphics can, with the correct driver, print TrueType fonts. There are several "gotchas" though, since TrueType fonts require the video adapter driver and printer adapter driver to work hand-in-hand.

If you are using a font that has been converted from another font program, the converter may have corrupted the font. Converted fonts often generate a General Protection fault. To isolate the font, create a full one-page document in a standard font and save it. Highlight the entire text and change it to one of your converted fonts. Continue the process until you find the corrupted font.

Some third-party video drivers are not compatible with TrueType. Try switching to a video driver shipped with Windows or contact the manufacturer for assistance.

Do not use Windows 3.0 print drivers with Windows 3.1. Windows 3.0 drivers do not support TrueType.

System Integrity Violations

Problem: Windows reports that "This application has violated System Integrity."

If the application is a Windows program, the problem is probably due to a corrupt program or data file. Try reinstalling the application. DOS applications may not correctly handle EMS or XMS memory. Create a PIF for this program and set the maximum values for EMS and XMS memory to 0. If this doesn't help, examine your CONFIG.SYS and AUTOEXEC.BAT files for TSRs or device drivers that conflict with the application.

General Protection Faults
Problem: The workstation crashes with a "General Protection Fault."

General Protection faults occur when an application attempts to write to memory occupied by another program. While its difficult for the typical user to determine the root cause of this error, Windows for Workgroups includes an application called Dr. WATSON that can be used to help determine the source. Start Dr. WATSON by selecting the File/Run command and entering

```
drwatson
```

in the Command box. When the error occurs, Dr. WATSON will create a text file called DRWATSON.LOG in the Windows directory. The first lines in this file should point to the either the program or the Windows driver at fault. Windows 2.x programs will not run under Windows 3.0 or later. Contact the program manufacturer or device driver manufacturer for additional assistance.

If General Protection faults occur in a specific application, the program or its data files may be corrupt. Exit Windows and run CHKDSK on the hard drive. Cross-linked files are a typical symptom of corrupted data files.

General Protection faults can also occur as a result of hardware conflicts. Try adding these three lines to the [386enh] section of the SYSTEM.INI file:

```
EMMEXCLUDE=A000-FFFF
VirtualHDIRQ=OFF
SYSTEMROMBreakPoint=False
```

GETTING ADDITIONAL HELP

Microsoft provides a wide variety of additional support tools for Windows for Workgroups.

Troubleshooting Windows for Workgroups

- Microsoft FasTips is an automated system that provides answers to common questions via phone recordings or faxes. Technical notes are available via fax. The support number is (206) 635-7245. The service is free to all callers and is available 24 hours a day.

- Microsoft Bulletin Board is also available 24 hours a day. The bulletin board provides technical notes and printer drivers at no charge. The BBS number is (206) 936-6735. Modem settings are 1200, 2400, or 9600 baud, no parity, 8 data bits, 1 stop bit.

- Telephone support is available Monday through Friday, 6 a.m. to 6 p.m. Pacific Standard Time, excluding holidays. The number is (206) 637-7098.

- TDD/TT (Text Telephone) support for all Microsoft products is available for the deaf and hard of hearing. This service requires a special TDD/TT modem, and is available Monday through Friday, 6 a.m. to 6 p.m. Pacific Standard Time, excluding holidays. The number is (206) 635-4948.

MICROSOFT RESOURCE KITS

Microsoft provides in-depth technical resource manuals for both Windows and Windows for Workgroups. The *Windows Resource Kit* provides technical information on all aspects of the Windows operating environment and includes a set of utilities, drivers, and accessories for supporting a Windows environment. The *Windows for Workgroups Resource Kit* is a companion technical reference to the *Windows Resource Kit* and covers additional topics and differences between Windows 3.1 and Windows for Workgroups. These kits are available directly from Microsoft or from your Microsoft reseller.

APPENDIX A
Windows Shortcut Keys

Windows for Workgroups provides alternate key combinations you can use to perform certain tasks without relying on the mouse. Table A-1 lists the key combinations you can use in most windows.

Table A-1. Shortcut Keys Used within a Window

Key Combination	Function
F1	Activate on-line Help
Shift-F1	Activate context-sensitive Help (in some, but not all, Windows applications)
Alt-F4	Close the active Windows application
Ctrl-F4	Close the active document or Group
Ctrl-F6	Jump to the next document in an application or Group icon in the File Manager
F10	Select the first menu item on the menu bar
PrtScn	Copy the current screen image to the Clipboard
Alt-PrtScn	Copy the contents of the current active window to the Clipboard
Alt-Esc	Select the next application window or icon
Ctrl-Esc	Open the Task List window

Table A-1, continued

Key Combination	Function
Alt-hyphen (-)	Open an application's Command menu
Alt-spacebar	Open an applicaton's Control menu
Alt-Tab	Jump between applications
Alt-X	Open the menu item X, where X is the underlined letter in a menu option

Table A-2 lists shortcut keys commonly used in dialog boxes.

Table A-2. Shortcut Keys Used within Dialog Boxes

Key Combination	Function
Alt-F4	Cancel the dialog box
Alt-X	Select the item, where X is the underlined letter in the item
Alt-down arrow key	Open the selected drop-down list
Alt-up arrow key	Close a drop-down list
End	Move to the last position in a data-entry box
Home	Move to the first position in a data-entry box
Enter	Execute the command corresponding to the dialog box settings
Esc	Cancel the dialog box
Tab	Move to the next field in the dialog box
Shift-Tab	Move to the previous field in the dialog box
spacebar	Select or deselect (toggle) a button style command

APPENDIX B

Windows for Workgroups Files

The "master" Windows installation server described in this book copies all files from the Windows for Workgroups diskettes to the server, regardless of each file's function.

This appendix describes the files installed in the Windows for Workgroups WINDOWS and SYSTEM directories. Using this information, you can delete unnecessary files and reduce the amount of disk space required for the "master" Windows for Workgroups installation server.

The Windows for Workgroups files can be divided into six primary areas, as follows:

- WIN.COM file.

- Dynamic-link libraries with code and data for Windows.

- Font and driver files for the keyboard, display, mouse, printers, network, system, multi-media, and fonts.

- Files supporting MS-DOS functions under Windows.

- Files enabling network support in terms of sharing files and printers under Windows.

- Files used by Windows applications, utilities, and accessories.

WIN.COM

Windows for Workgroups is loaded by the WIN.COM file. This file determines the appropriate operating mode, and then executes either DOSX.EXE for standard mode operation or WIN386.EXE for enhanced mode operation.

THE CORE FILES

The Windows core components are as follows:

- The kernel files (KRNL286.EXE or KRNL386.EXE) allocate computer resources for managing memory and scheduling program tasks.

- USER.EXE creates and maintains the screen windows and icons, and directs input from the mouse and keyboard to the appropriate application.

- GDI.EXE controls the graphical interface.

SYSTEM DRIVER AND FONT DRIVER FILES

Windows for Workgroups ships with only two system drivers:

- SYSTEM.DRV, a driver for most hardware systems.

- HPSYSTEM.DRV, a driver for HP Vectra systems running in standard mode.

B

Windows for Workgroups Files

The following keyboard drivers are shipped with Windows for Workgroups:

- KEYBOARD.DRV, the standard keyboard driver.

- KBDHP.DRV, the keyboard driver for all Hewlett-Packard machines.

These keyboard drivers use keyboard tables to refer to a language library. Following is a list of the keyboard tables:

Table	Language Library
KBDBE.DLL	Belgian keyboard
KBDCA.DLL	French-Canadian keyboard
KBDDA.DLL	Danish keyboard
KBDDV.DLL	U.S.-Dvorak keyboard
KBDFC.DLL	Canadian multilingual keyboard
KBDFI.DLL	Finnish keyboard
KBDFR.DLL	French keyboard
KBDGR.DLL	German keyboard
KBDIC.DLL	Iclandic keyboard
KBDIT.DLL	Italian keyboard
KBDLA.DLL	Latin American keyboard
KBDNE.DLL	Dutch keyboard
KBDNO.DLL	Norwegian keyboard
KBDPO.DLL	Portuguese keyboard
KBDSF.DLL	Swiss-French keyboard
KBDSG.DLL	Swiss-German keyboard
KBDSP.DLL	Spanish keyboard
KBDSW.DLL	Swedish keyboard
KBDUK.DLL	British keyboard
KBDUS.DLL	U.S. keyboard
KBDUSX.DLL	U.S.-international keyboard

Building Local Area Networks with Windows for Workgroups

Mouse Driver Files

The mouse driver files in Windows for Workgroups support pointing devices for Windows and Windows-based programs.

Driver	Mouse or Pointing Device
HPMOUSE.DRV	Hewlett-Packard mouse (HP-HIL)
LMOUSE.DRV	Logitech Serial mouse
MOUSE.DRV	Logitech, PS/2, or Microsoft mouse
MSC3BC2.DRV	Mouse Systems COM2/3 button mouse
MSCMOUSE.DRV	Mouse Systems Serial/Bus mouse
NOMOUSE.DRV	No mouse attached to system

Display Driver Files

The display drivers support the system display and cursor. This driver is not used by DOS applications running full-screen.

Driver	Supported Display Adapter
8514.DRV	IBM 8514/a
EGA.DRV	EGA
EGAHIBW.DRV	EGA with 128K RAM
EGAMONO.DRV	Monochrome EGA
HERCULES.DRV	Hercules monochrome display
MMTLLO.DRV	ET4000 (small fonts)
MMTLHI.DRV	ET4000 (large fonts)
OLIBW.DRV	Olivetti/AT&T monochrome or PVC
PLASMA.DRV	Compaq Portable Plasma
SUPERVGA.DRV	Super VGA (800x600, 16 color)
TIGA.DRV	TIGA
VGA.DRV	VGA
VGAMONO.DRV	Monochrome VGA
V7VGA.DRV	Video 7 VGA with 512K RAM
XGA.DRV	XGA

B

Windows for Workgroups Files

Other Driver Files

Driver	Function
COMM.DRV	Supports serial/parallel ports
POWER.DRV	Advanced Power Management driver (for laptops and notebook PCs)

Printer Driver Files

Printer drivers provide support for printer and plotter devices. Some printer drivers in Windows for Workgroups include soft-font installation files and help files.

Driver	Supported Printer
CANON10E.DRV	Canon Bubble-Jet BJ-10e
CANON130.DRV	Canon Bubble-Jet BJ-130e
CANON330.DRV	Canon Bubble-Jet BJ-300/330
CIT24US.DRV	Citizen 24-pin
CIT9US.DRV	Citizen 9-pin
CITOH.DRV	C-Itoh 8510 or AT&T 470/475
DICONIX.DRV	Kodak Diconix
DM309.DRV	Olivetti DM309
DMCOLOR.DLL	Universal color printing library
EPSON24.DRV	Epson 24-pin
EPSON9.DRV	Epson 9-pin
ESCP2.DRV	Epson ESC2P dot matrix
EXECJET.DRV	IBM ExecJet
GENDRV.DLL	Generic library
HPDSKJET.DRV	Hewlett-Packard DeskJet
HPPCL.DRV	HP LaserJet II series
HPPCL5MS.DRV	HP LaserJet III series
HPPLOT.DRV	HP Plotter

Driver	Supported Printer
IBM4019.DRV	IBM Laser Printer 4019
IBM5204.DRV	IBM Quickwriter 5204
IBMCOLOR.DRV	IBM Color
LBPII.DRV	Canon LBP-8 II
LBPIII.DRV	Canon LBPIII
NEC24PIN.DRV	NEC 24-pin
OKI24.DRV	Okidata 24-pin
OKI9.DRV	Okidata 9-pin
OKI9IBM.DRV	Okidata 9-pin IBM Graphics Printer
PAINTJET.DRV	HP PaintJet
PANSON24.DRV	Panasonic 24-pin
PANSON9.DRV	Panasonic 9-pin
PROPRINT.DRV	IBM Pro series
PROPRN24.DRV	IBM Pro 24-pin series
PS1.DRV	IBM PS/1
PSCRIPT.DRV	PostScript
PSCRIPT.HLP	PostScript Help file
QWIII.DRV	IBM QuietWriter III
THINKJET.DRV	HP ThinkJet
TI850.DRV	Texas Instruments TI850/855
TOSHIBA.DRV	Toshiba p351/1351
TTY.DRV	Generic/Text only
TTY.HLP	Help file for TTY
UNIDRV.DLL	Microsoft universal library
UNIDRV.HLP	Help file for UNIDRV.DLL

Soft-Font Installer	Related Printer
CAN_ADF.EXE	Canon LBP-8 or LBIII
FINSTALL.DLL	HPPCL5/MS
FINSTALL.HLP	Help file for FINSTALL.DLL
SF4019.EXE	IBM Laser Printer 4019

B

Windows for Workgroups Files

PostScript Description	Related Printer
40291730.WPD	IBM Laser Printer 4029 (17 fonts)
40293930.WPD	IBM Laser Printer 4029 (39 fonts)
DEC1150.WPD	Digital DEClaser 1150
DEC2150.WPD	Digital DEClaser 2150
DEC2250.WPD	Digital DEClaser 2250
DEC3250.WPD	Digital DEClaser 3250
DECCOLOR.WPD	Digital ColorMate PS
DECLPS20.WPD	Digital LPS Print Server
EPL75523.WPD	Epson EPL-7500
HERMES_1.WPD	Hermes H606PS (13 fonts)
HERMES_2.WPD	Hermes H606PS (35 fonts)
HPELI523.WPD	HP LaserJet IIISi
HPIID522.WPD	HP LaserJet IID PostScript
HPIII522.WPD	HP LaserJet III PostScript
HPIIP522.WPD	HP LaserJet IIP PostScript
HP_3D522.WPD	HP LaserJet IIID PostScript
HP_3P522.WPD	HP LaserJet IIIP PostScript
IBM17521.WPD	IBM 4019 (17 fonts)
IBM39521.WPD	IBM 4019 (39 fonts)
L100_425.WPD	Linotronic 100 v42.5
L200230&.WPD	Linotronic 200/230
L300_471.WPD	Linotronic 300 v47.1
L300_493.WPD	Linotronic 300 v49.3
L330_52&.WPD	Linotronic 330
L500_493.WPD	Linotronic 500 v49.3
L530_52&.WPD	Linotronic 530
L630_52&.WPD	Linotronic 630
MT_TI101.WPD	Microtek TrueLaser
N2090522.WPD	NEC Silentwriter2 90
N2290520.WPD	NEC Silentwriter2 290
N2990523.WPD	NEC Silentwriter2 990
N890X505.WPD	NEC Silentwriter LC890XL
N890_470.WPD	NEC Silentwriter LC890
NCM40519.WPD	NEC Colormate PS/40
NCM80519.WPD	NEC Colormate PS/80

Building Local Area Networks with Windows for Workgroups

PostScript Description	Related Printer
O5241503.WPD	OceColor G5241 PS
O5242503.WPD	OceColor G5242 PS
OL840518.WPD	Oki OL840/PS
OLIVETI1.WPD	Olivetti PG306PS (13 fonts)
OLIVETI2.WPD	Olivetti PG306Ps (35 fonts)
P4455514.WPD	Panasonic KX-P4455
PHIIPX.WPD	Phaser II PX
Q2200510.WPD	QMS-PS 2200
Q820_517.WPD	QMS-PS 820
SEIKO_04.WPD	Sieko ColorPoint PS Model 04
SEIKO_14.WPD	Sieko ColorPoint PS Model 14
TIM17521.WPD	Texas Instruments MicroLaser PS17
TIM35521.WPD	Texas Instruments MicroLaser PS35
TKPHZR21.WPD	Phaser II PX 1
TKPHRZ31.WPD	Phaser III PX 1
TRIUMPH1.WPD	Triumph Adler SDR 7706 PS (13 fonts)
TRIUMPH2.WPD	Triumph Adler SDR 7706 PS
U9415470.WPD	Unisys AP9415

Network Driver Files

The network interface to Windows for Workgroups is provided by the network driver files. These drivers can be divided into three groups, those that support Windows for Workgroups, Microsoft LAN Manager-based networks, and NetWare. Following are the file names and associations:

B

Windows for Workgroups Files

Driver	Function	Network Supported
WFWNET.DRV	Network driver	Windows
WFWNET.HLP	Network driver help file	Windows
NETAPI.DLL	Network API library	Windows
PMSPL.DLL	Printer API library	Windows
MSNET.DRV	Generic network driver	LAN Manager-based
LMSCRIPT.EXE	LAN Manager Scripts	LAN Manager-based
LMSCRIPT.PIF	LAN Manager Scripts	LAN Manager-based
NETWARE.DRV	Network driver	NetWare
NETWARE.HLP	Network driver help file	NetWare
NWPOPUP.EXE	Supports pop-up messages	NetWare
NETX.COM	Workstation shell	NetWare
ROUTE.COM	Token Ring Source route	NetWare
MSIPX.COM	NDIS-compliant IPX	NetWare
MSIPX.SYS	NDIS pointer for MSIPX	NetWare

Multimedia Driver Files

The following drivers support the audio functions of Windows for Workgroups:

Driver	Purpose
MCICDA.DRV	MCI CD-audio driver
MCISEQ.DRV	MCI driver for MIDI driver
MCIWAVE.DRV	MCI driver for waveform audio
MIDIMAP.DRV	Driver for MIDI Mapper
MMSOUND.DRV	Multimedia sound driver
MPU401.DRV	MIDI driver for MPU401 compatibles
MSADLIB.DRV	MIDI driver for Adlib compatibles
SNDBLST.DRV	SoundBlaster 1.5 DSP driver
SNDBLST2.DRV	SoundBlaster 2.0 DSP driver
TIMER.DRV	Multimedia timer driver

Font Files

Windows for Workgroups has several different font types, which are used for a variety of purposes. The system font files are used by Windows itself, and include system, fixed, and OEM fonts. Raster, vector, and TrueType fonts are used by applications. In addition, Windows for Workgroups contains font files for MS-DOS applications running in a window.

System Font File	Supported Display Resolution
8514SYS.FON	8514/A (1024x768) resolution system font
EGASYS.FON	EGA (640x350) resolution system font
EGASYS.FON	AT&T (640x400) resolution system font
VGASYS.FON	VGA (640x480) resolution system font

Fixed Font File	Supported Display Resolution
8514FIX.FON	8514/A (1024x768) resolution fixed font
EGAFIX.FON	EGA (640x350) resolution fixed font
EGAFIX.FON	AT&T (640x400) resolution fixed font
VGAFIX.FON	VGA (640x480) resolution fixed font

OEM Font File	Supported Display Resolution
8514OEM.FON	8514/A (1024x768) resolution OEM font
EGAOEM.FON	EGA (640x350) resolution OEM font
EGAOEM.FON	AT&T (640x400) resolution OEM font
VGAOEM.FON	VGA (640x480) resolution OEM font

B

Windows for Workgroups Files

Raster font file resolutions are identified by a letter appended to the file name. The letter identifies the resolution of the associated font. The letter assignments for Windows raster fonts are as follows:

Letter	Output	Resolution	Height/Width in Pixels
A*	CGA	2:1	96/48
B	EGA	1.33:1	96/72
C*	Printer	1:1.2	60/72
D*	Printer	1.66:1	120/72
E	VGA	1:1	96/96
F	8514	1:1	120/120

From this table, substitute the appropriate letter for the lowercase *x* in the raster font file list in the following table. Font resolutions marked with an asterisk (*) are not included in Windows for Workgroups.

Following are the raster font files:

Font	File Name	Character	Font Description
Courier	COUR*x*.FON	ANSI	Fixed-width serif
MS Sans Serif	SSERIF*x*.FON	ANSI	Proportional
MS Serif	SERIF*x*.FON	ANSI	Proportional serif
Small	SMALL*x*.FON	ANSI	Proportional small
Symbol	SYMBOL*x*.FON	Symbol	Math symbols

Vector Font Files

Windows for Workgroups includes three vector font files: ROMAN.FON, SCRIPT.FON, and MODERN.FON. These fonts are scalable and can be created in any size desired, although some applications or print devices may limit the font sizes supported.

TrueType Font Files

The TrueType fonts shipped with Windows for Workgroups support Arial, Courier, Symbol, and Times New Roman fonts, as well as a symbol and graphic character font. Each font requires two files, a .TTF and a .FOT file.

TrueType File Names	Font Name
ARIAL.FOT/ARIAL.TTF	Arial
ARIALBD.FOT/ARIALBD.TTF	Arial Bold
ARIALBI.FOT/ARIALBI.TTF	Arial Bold Italic
ARIALI.FOT/ARIALI.TTF	Arial Italic
COUR.FOT/COUR.TTF	Courier
COURBD.FOT/COURBD.TTF	Courier Bold
COURBI.FOT/COURBI.TTF	Courier Bold Italic
COURI.FOT/COURI.TTF	Courier Italic
TIMES.FOT/TIMES.TTF	Times New Roman
TIMESBD.FOT/TIMESBD.TTF	Times New Roman Bold
TIMESBI.FOT/TIMESBI.TTF	Times New Roman Bold Italic
TIMESI.FOT/TIMESI.TTF	Times New Roman Italic
SYMBOL.FOT/SYMBOL.TTF	Math symbols
WINGDING.FOT/WINGDING.TTF	Graphic characters/dingbats

Font Files for MS-DOS

The following files are used when displaying MS-DOS applications in a window while running Windows in enhanced mode. Font files marked with an asterisk (*) are installed by default.

B

Windows for Workgroups Files

Font file	Associated Font Table	Configuration
APP850.FON		U.S., enhanced mode
DOSAPP.FON*		U.S., enhanced mode
CGA40850.FON	XLAT850.BIN	Multilingual
CGA40WOA.FON*		U.S.
CGA80850.FON	XLAT850.BIN	Multilingual
CGA80WOA.FON*		U.S.
EGA40850.FON	XLAT850.BIN	Multilingual
EGA40WOA.FON*		U.S.
EGA80850.FON	XLAT850.BIN	Multilingual
EGA80WOA.FON*		U.S.
HERC850.FON	XLAT850.BIN	Multilingual
HERCWOA.FON*		U.S.
VGA850.FON	XLAT850.BIN	Multilingual
VGA860.FON	XLAT860.BIN	Portuguese
VGA861.FON	XLAT861.BIN	Icelandic
VGA863.FON	XLAT863.BIN	French Canadian
VGA865.FON	XLAT865.BIN	Norwegian/Danish

International Support Files

Windows for Workgroups provides the following libraries to support the indicated languages:

File Name	Language Supported
LANGDUT.DLL	Dutch language driver
LANGENG.DLL	International English driver
LANGFRN.DLL	French language driver
LANGGER.DLL	German language driver
LANGSCA.DLL	Scandinavian languages driver
LANGSPA.DLL	Spanish language driver

MS-DOS SUPPORT FILES FOR WINDOWS FOR WORKGROUPS

The MS-DOS support files in Windows for Workgroups include MS-DOS drivers and grabber files that allow data exchange between DOS and Windows applications.

MS-DOS Driver Files

Following is a list of MS-DOS Driver files and their functions:

Driver	Function
EGA.SYS	EGA MS-DOS driver
EMM386.EXE	Microsoft MS-DOS 386 EMS Manager
HIMEM.SYS	Microsoft MS-DOS XMS Manager
RAMDRIVE.SYS	Microsoft RAMDrive utility
SMARTDRV.EXE	Microsoft SMARTDrive Disk-Cache 4.0
LMOUSE.COM	DOS driver for Logitech mouse
MOUSE.COM	DOS driver for Microsoft mouse
MOUSE.SYS	DOS driver for Microsoft mouse
MOUSEHP.COM	DOS driver for Hewlett-Packard mouse
MOUSEHP.SYS	DOS driver for Hewlett-Packard mouse
MSCDEX.EXE	Microsoft CD-ROM Extensions 2.21 driver
NET.EXE	WfW MS-DOS network redirector
NET.MSG	WfW network redirector message file
NETH.MSG	WfW network redirector help message file
PROTMAN.EXE	WfW protocol manager TSR
WORKGRP.SYS	Real-mode pointer for WfW network redirector

B

Windows for Workgroups Files

NDIS Network Adapter Card Drivers

The following drivers support Windows for Workgroups compatible network adapters:

Driver	Network Adapter Supported
AM2100.DOS	Advanced Micro Devices AM2100/PCnet
DEPCA.DOS	DEC EtherWorks
E20NDIS.DOS	Cabletron E2010-X
E21NDIS.DOS	Cabletron E2112
ELNK16.DOS	3Com EtherLink 16
ELNK3.DOS	3Com EtherLink III
ELNKII.DOS	3Com EtherLink II
ELNKMC.DOS	3Com EtherLink/MC
ELNKPL.DOS	3Com EtherLink Plus
EVX16.DOS	Everex SpeedLink/PC16 (EV2027)
EXP16.DOS	Intel EtherExpress 16
HPLANB.DOS	HP LAN
I82593.DOS	Intel Motherboard Module
IBMTOK.DOS	IBM Token Ring
MAC586.SYS	DCA 10Mb
NDIS39XR.DOS	Proteon Token Ring
NE1000.DOS	Novell/Anthem NE1000 or compatible
NE2000.DOS	Novell/Anthem NE2000 or compatible
NI6510.DOS	Racal-Interlan NI6510
OLITOK.DOS	Intel or Olicom 16/4 Token Ring
PE2NDIS.DOS	Xircom Pocket Ethernet II
PRO4.DOS	Proteon ISA Token Ring
SMC3000.DOS	SMC 3000 series
SMCMAC.DOS	SMC/Western Digital EtherCard PLUS
SMC_ARC.DOS	SMC ArcNet
STRN.DOS	NCR Token Ring
TCCARC.DOS	Thomas Conrad TC6x4x (enhanced mode)
TLNK.DOS	3Com TokenLink

WinOldAp and the Grabber Files

These files provide Windows for Workgroups with the ability to exchange data with DOS applications. The WinOldAp files come in two versions, WINOLDAP.MOD for standard mode operation and WINOA386.MOD for enhanced mode. The grabber file used by your system is dependent on your display adapter, as follows:

Standard Mode Grabber Files	Video Display Supported
CGA.2GR	CGA
EGACOLOR.2GR	EGA
EGAMONO.2GR	EGA monochrome
HERCULES.2GR	Hercules monochrome
OLIGRAB.2GR	Olivetti/AT&T monochrome
VGACOLOR.2GR	VGA
VGAMONO.2GR	VGA monochrome

Enhanced Mode Grabber Files	Video Display Supported
EGA.3GR	EGA
HERC.3GR	Hercules monochrome
PLASMA.3GR	Compaq Portable Plasma
V7VGA.3GR	Video 7 VGA
VGA.3GR	VGA
VGA30.3GR	VGA (version 3.0)
VGADIB.3GR	DIB (8514/a monochrome)

Files for Standard Mode Operation

Windows uses two additional files to handle task swapping in standard mode. WSWAP.EXE handles the swapping of Windows applications in standard mode, and DSWAP.EXE handles the swapping of DOS applications in standard mode.

B

Windows for Workgroups Files

Files for Enhanced Mode Operation

When Windows loads in enhanced mode, it reads SYSTEM.INI and loads the files identified in the [386enh] portion of this file. Examine the contents of the [386enh] section of the SYSTEM.INI prior to deleting any of the following files.

File Name	Virtual Device Supported
LANMAN10.386	LAN Manager version 1.0 support
LVMD.386	Logitech mouse
HPEBIOS.386	EBIOS for Hewlett-Packard machines
MONOUMB2.386	UMB driver for monochrome video space
MSCVMD.386	Mouse Systems mouse
V7VDD.386	Video Seven display adapter
VADLIBD.386	Adlib sound card
VCD.386	Communications driver
VDD8514.386	IBM 8514/a display
VDDCGA.DRV	CGA display
VDDEGA.386	EGA display
VDDHERC.386	Hercules monochrome display
VDDTIGA.386	TIGA video adapter
VDDTLI4.386	Tseng ET4000 Super VGA adapter
VDDVGA30.386	VGA version 3.0 video
VDDXGA.386	IBM XGA display
VIPX.386	Novell NetWare IPX support
VDMAD.386	DMA device driver
VNETWARE.386	Novell NetWare support
VPD.386	Printer device support
VPICD.386	Interrupt controller support
VPOWERD.386	Advanced Power Management for laptops
VSBD.386	SoundBlaster sound card
VTDAPL.386	Multimedia timer
VBROWSE.386	WfW network browse device
VNB.386	WfW virtual NETBEUI

Building Local Area Networks with Windows for Workgroups

File Name	Virtual Device Supported
VNETBIOS.386	WfW virtual NETBIOS
VNETSUP.386	WfW virtual network support
VREDIR.386	WfW virtual network redirector
VSERVER.386	WfW virtual network server
VSHARE.386	WfW virtual file sharing
VWC.386	WfW virtual workgroup client
WIN386.PS2	Support driver for IBM PS/2

FILES FOR WINDOWS FOR WORKGROUPS APPLICATIONS

Windows for Workgroups includes several applications, utilities, and games. The following table lists these applications and their associated files. All files used by an application are grouped together.

File Name	Associated Application
CALC.EXE CALC.HLP	Calculator
CARDFILE.EXE CARDFILE.HLP	Cardfile
CHARMAP.EXE CHARMAP.HLP	Character Map
CLIPBRD.EXE CLIBBRD.HLP CLIBSRV.EXE	Clipboard Viewer
CLOCK.EXE	Clock
CONTROL.EXE CONTROL.HLP CONTROL.INI	Control Panel

B

Windows for Workgroups Files

File Name	Associated Application
CPWIN386.CPL DRIVERS.CPL LSEXPAND.DLL MAIN.CPL MIDIMAP.CFG SND.CPL WFWSETUP.DLL	Control Panel
DRWATSON.EXE	Dr. Watson diagnostic utility
EXPAND.EXE LZEXPAND.DLL	Windows installation utility
MPLAYER.EXE MPLAYER.HLP MMSYSTEM.DLL MMTASK.TSK	Media Player
MSD.EXE MSD.INI	Microsoft diagnostic utility
MSHEARTS.EXE MSHEARTS.HLP CARDS.DLL	Hearts game
MSMAIL.EXE MSMAIL.HLP SENDFILE.DLL AB.DLL DEMILAYR.DLL FRAMEWRK.DLL IMPEXP.DLL MAILMGR.DLL MAILSPL.EXE MAPI.DLL MSSFS.DLL STORE.DLL VFORMS.DLL WGPOMGR.DLL	Microsoft Mail

Building Local Area Networks with Windows for Workgroups

File Name	Associated Application
NETDDE.EXE NDDEAPI.DLL NDDENB.DLL	Network Dynamic Data Interchange
NETWATCH.EXE NETWATCH.HLP	Net Watcher
NOTEPAD.EXE NOTEPAD.HLP	Notepad
PACKAGER.EXE PACKAGER.HLP	Object Packager
PBRUSH.EXE PBRUSH.DLL PBRUSH.HLP	Paintbrush
PIFEDIT.EXE PIFEDIT.HLP	PIF Editor
POWER.HLP SL.DLL SL.HLP	Advance Power Management support
PRINTMAN.EXE PRINTMAN.HLP	Print Manager
PROGMAN.EXE PROGMAN.INI PROGMAN.HLP	Program Manager
RECORDER.EXE RECORDER.HLP RECORDER.DLL	Recorder (desktop macros)
REGEDIT.EXE REGEDIT.HLP REGEDITV.HLP	Applications Registration Editor

B

Windows for Workgroups Files

File Name	Associated Application
DDEML.DLL OLECLI.DLL OLESRV.DLL	Applications Registration Editor
SCHDPLUS.EXE SCHDPLUS.HLP SCHDPLUS.INI MSREMIND.EXE SCHEDMSG.DLL TRNSCHED.DLL	Schedule+
SHELL.DLL	Shell library
SOL.EXE SOL.HLP	Solitaire game
SMARTDRV.EXE	SMARTDrive disk-cache software
SOUNDREC.EXE SOUNDREC.HLP	Sound Recorder
SYSEDIT.EXE	Windows System Editor
TASKMAN.EXE	Windows Task Manager
TERMINAL.EXE TERMINAL.HLP	Terminal communications program
TOOLHLP.DLL	Windows Tool Helper library
WINCHAT.EXE WINCHAT.HLP	Chat
WINFILE.EXE WINFILE.HLP	File Manager

Building Local Area Networks with Windows for Workgroups

WINHELP.EXE	Windows on-line help engine
WINHELP.HLP	
GLOSSARY.HLP	
WINMETER.EXE	System performance meter
WINMINE.EXE	MineSweeper game
WINMINE.HLP	
WINTUTOR.EXE	Windows Tutorial
WINTUTOR.DAT	
WRITE.EXE	Windows Write
WRITE.HLP	

SETUP FILES

Setup has several files for its own use. These include several files with the extension .LGO and .RLE. Depending on the display adapter, the appropriate LGO and RLE files are combined with WIN.CNF to create WIN.COM. Setup also uses the following files:

APPS.INF	SETUP.REG
CONTROL.INF	SETUP.SHH
CONTROL.SRC	SETUP.TXT
EXPAND.EXE	SYSTEM.SRC
NETWORK.INF	VER.DLL
PRTUPD.INF	WIN.CNF
SETUP.EXE	WIN.SRC
SETUP.HLP	WINVER.EXE
SETUP.INF	XMSMMGR.EXE
SETUP.INI	

B

Windows for Workgroups Files

OTHER FILES

Windows for Workgroups also comes with custom support files and various miscellaneous files. Custom files are as follows:

Custom Support Files

File Name	Purpose
386MAX.VDX	Qualitas 386MAX standard mode driver
BLUEMAX.VDX	Qualitas BlueMAX virtual driver
COMMCTRL.DLL	WfW internal custom-control interface
COMMDLG.DLL	WfW Common Dialogs library
WIN87EM.DLL	80x87 math coprocessor emulator library
WINDOWS.LOD	Qualitas 386MAX/BlueMAX loadable module

Miscellaneous Files

Windows includes several remaining files that serve a variety of functions. The MORICONS.DLL is a collection of icons that you can assign to DOS or Windows applications. Several files ending in the extension .BMP (for bit-mapped graphics) are available for Windows wallpaper. The files ending in the extension .SCR are Windows screen-saver files, while the files ending in .WAV are wave-form sound files that can be used to assign sounds to system events, if the workstation is equipped with a soundboard. The CANYON.MID file is a MIDI sound file for Canyon. Finally, there are several WRITE documents with the extension .WRI that provide read-me documentation for certain aspects of Windows for Workgroups.

DELETING FILES

While the Windows for Workgroups installation does not normally copy unnecessary files to the workstation during setup, subsequent updates, such as a new video adapter or mouse driver, will not delete the old driver but will simply copy the new driver into the system. Additionally, the 20Mb disk requirement for the "master" Windows server directory can be significantly reduced by deleting printer and display drivers for hardware you do not support. You may also choose to delete specific accessories, such as wallpaper, games, screen savers, and sound files.

Finally, there may be some trash files in your WINDOWS or TEMP directories, usually as a result of exiting Windows for Workgroups improperly. These files can easily be identified by either a prefix of ~WOA or ~GRB. These are swap files and grabber files used by Windows. You can also delete any files in the TEMP directory—Windows for Workgroups should delete these files when exited. Exiting Windows improperly may also leave a WIN386.SWP file, a temporary swap file, on the disk, and it should also be deleted.

> **CAUTION:** These files are used by Windows when in operation. You should only delete them if you exit Windows and they still exist. Do not attempt to delete them from within Windows.

APPENDIX C

Network Cabling Specifications

This appendix describes the network cabling specifications for Token-Ring, ArcNet, and Ethernet cabling.

TOKEN-RING CABLE SPECIFICATIONS

The IEEE 802.5 specification provides for a logical ring using a token-passing protocol. While the specification is limited to 4 Mb/sec on shielded twisted-pair cabling, new developments in token-ring design now support unshielded twisted-pair cabling, and speeds of either 4 or 16 Mb/sec.

The logical layout of a token-ring network is a ring, but the network is physically wired in a star topology with the network cables from each workstation running to a central location. The hubs in a token-ring environment are typically referred to as multistation access units (MSAUs), after the original IBM Model 8228 MSAU.

Figure C-1 shows a typical layout for a token-ring network. The ring-in/ring-out ports are used to create the logical ring. The network will still function if the last MSAU ring-out is not connected to the first MSAU ring-in, but the ring will operate in *loop-back mode*. A cable fault occurring between any other ring-in and ring-out ports will effectively separate the network into two separate rings. When the first and last MSAUs are connected, a cable fault between any two MSAUs will force the ring into loop-back, but no workstations will be affected.

Building Local Area Networks with Windows for Workgroups

**Figure C-1.
Token-Ring cable topology**

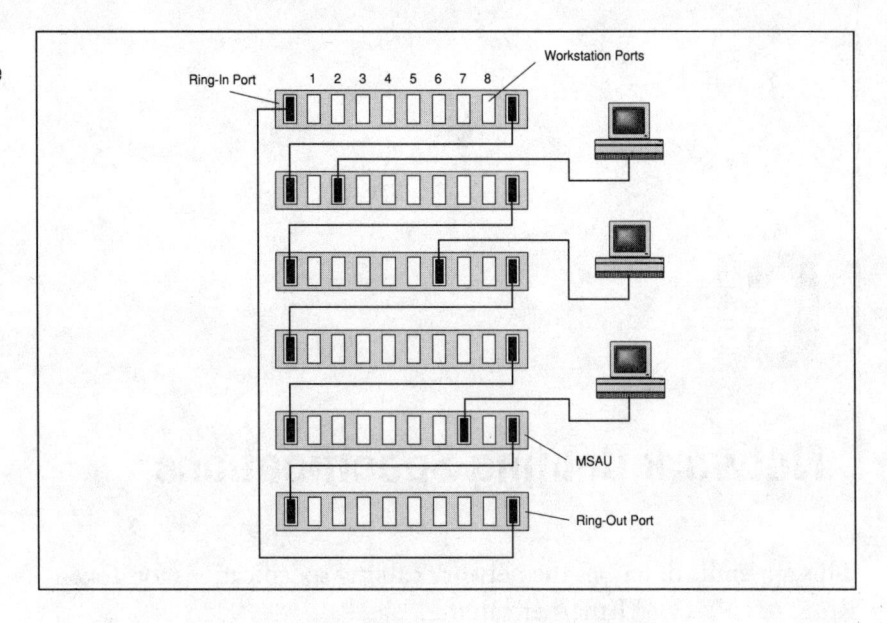

The diagram in Figure C-1 shows the workstation connected directly into the MSAU, but in larger environments the preferred method of cabling is to use several patch cables and a separate patch panel. This method is espoused in IBM's Premise Wiring network design, which specifies the use of IBM data connectors and wall plates. The cable from the wall plate travels to a patch panel co-located with the MSAU rack, and eight-foot patch cables are used to connect both the workstation to the wall plate and the patch panel connector to a port on an MSAU. This method of cabling allows a workstation to be patched to a different MSAU if necessary, while allowing some semblance of order to be maintained in the wiring closet (no easy task in a large token-ring environment).

Basic Specifications

The basic specifications for both 16 Mb/sec and 4 Mb/sec token-ring networks are as follows:

- Maximum number of stations
    Unshielded twisted-pair wiring: 72
    Shielded twisted-pair wiring: 260

Network Cabling Specifications

- Maximum distance between a workstation and MSAU
  Unshielded twisted-pair wiring: 45 meters
  Shielded twisted-pair wiring: 100 meters

- Minimum patch cable length from ring-out to ring-in ports: 2.5 meters

- Maximum patch cable length from ring-out to ring-in ports: 45 meters

- Maximum MSAUs in a single ring: 33

In addition, all network adapters must be configured for the same ring speed, because an adapter set at an incorrect speed will prevent the ring from functioning.

Token-Ring network adapters provide a 9-pin connector for the DB-9 to IBM data connector patch cable. Network adapters that support unshielded twisted-pair cabling use RJ45 (8-wire) telephone style connectors. The pinout for this cable is as follows.

Workstation	Wire Color	MSAU	Usage
Pin 1	not used	Pin 1	
Pin 2	not used	Pin 2	
Pin 3	White/Orange	Pin 3	Primary Transmit
Pin 4	Blue/White	Pin 4	Primary Receive
Pin 5	White/Blue	Pin 5	Backup Transmit
Pin 6	Orange/White	Pin 6	Backup Receive
Pin 7	not used	Pin 7	
Pin 8	not used	Pin 8	

Token-Ring network design provides a fault-tolerant backup path in the event of a cable fault, but some cable, MSAU, and network-adapter faults can prevent the ring from functioning. If a workstation fails to receive its own token within a set period of time, the workstation will begin transmitting "beacon" frames, the presence of which indicates that the ring is unusable, and workstations that attempt to insert into the ring will fail. The workstation transmitting the beacon is not always at fault, however, because it may be that the workstation is detecting a problem caused by the next highest workstation in the ring. The next highest workstation in the ring is referred to as the *next active upstream neighbor*, or *NAUN*. The workstation generating the beacon, as well as its NAUN, and all cables and MSAU ports between the two nodes, are known as the *fault-domain*. Network diagnostic tools for token-ring should be able to determine the network address of any station transmitting beacon frames, as well as the address of the station's NAUN. Trouble-shooting procedures for a beaconing ring should center on testing all components in the fault-domain.

ARCNET CABLE SPECIFICATIONS

ArcNet is one of the oldest existing network topologies. It was developed in 1977 by the Datapoint Corporation. Its popularity stems from the wide variety of system buses it supports, the relative low cost of the network adapters, and its ability to run on virtually any type of cable.

The standard method of wiring workstations in an ArcNet environment is the star topology, or a modified version known as the *star-cluster*. In a star-cluster configuration, hubs are clustered into two or more groups, and each cluster is connected to other clusters in a star pattern. ArcNet's wiring scheme can provide a network cable plant with an overall diameter as large as 20,000 feet. Its relatively low transmission speed (2.5 Mb/sec) makes it far less susceptible to interference from outside sources. Coupled with its token-passing scheme for controlling cable access, ArcNet is ideal for factory environments, where speed is less critical than fair arbitration of the bus.

Despite the number of years that ArcNet has been around, the IEEE has never formally recognized the specification. As such, different vendors offer different implementations of ArcNet. As this book goes to press, however, the IEEE is considering the development of

Network Cabling Specifications   C

a standard for ArcNet. The specifications listed here have been accepted by all ArcNet manufacturers.

Basic Specifications

The basic specifications for ArcNet are as follows:

- Cable type: RG59 or RG62 coaxial

- Termination: RG59: 75 ohm
  RG62: 93 ohm

- Unused ports on active or passive hubs *must* be terminated.

- Maximum length of a segment: Depends on cable type

- Average lengths supported
  Workstation to workstation: 120 meters
  Active hub to active hub: 606 meters
  Passive hub to workstation: 30 meters
  Active hub to passive hub: 30 meters

- Minimum length from workstation and hub or between hubs: .3 meters

- Topology: star or star-cluster

- Maximum computers per segment: Depends on cable type. The absolute maximum computers per segment is 255, based on addressing scheme. ArcNet network adapters have a set of DIP switches to control the workstation network address. These switches can be set for any number from 1 to 255.

    CAUTION: No two devices in a single network should have the same address.

- Passive hub to passive hub connections are not supported.

In addition to these specifications, several vendors have developed extensions to the ArcNet environment. These include:

- *Twisted-pair:* ArcNet boards that support twisted-pair cables allow up to ten adapters to be connected in daisy-chain fashion. The twisted-pair cable can be up to 400 feet in length and only requires one pair of wires. ArcNet on UTP supports either RJ11 (4-wire) or RJ45 (8-wire) telephone-style connectors, and a standard installation uses the two center connectors wired directly across (pin 2 to pin 2, pin 3 to pin 3) without crossing the pinouts.

- *Linear Bus:* Many ArcNet adapters now provide jumpers for configuration in either a star or bus configuration. Linear bus connections use a BNC "T" connector at each card and 93 ohm terminators at each end of the cable. Alternatively, one end of the cable can be connected to an active hub, allowing interconnection with a star topology, or to another linear bus. Only eight cards are allowed on a single linear bus and the bus can be up to 1000 feet in length.

- *Fiber Optic:* Single fiber optic controllers and links can extend the distance between active hubs to 4000 feet, and dual attached fiber can extend the distance between hubs to 11,500 feet.

- *ArcNet Plus:* ArcNet Plus is a 20 Mb/sec version of ArcNet, co-developed by Datapoint Corporation, Standard MicroSystems, and NCR. Although technically a different protocol, ArcNet Plus adapters are designed to coexist on the network cable with ArcNet, and will communicate at the lower speed when talking to "standard" ArcNet devices.

Network Cabling Specifications

Figure C-2 shows an example of an ArcNet network that uses the various extensions to the ArcNet design.

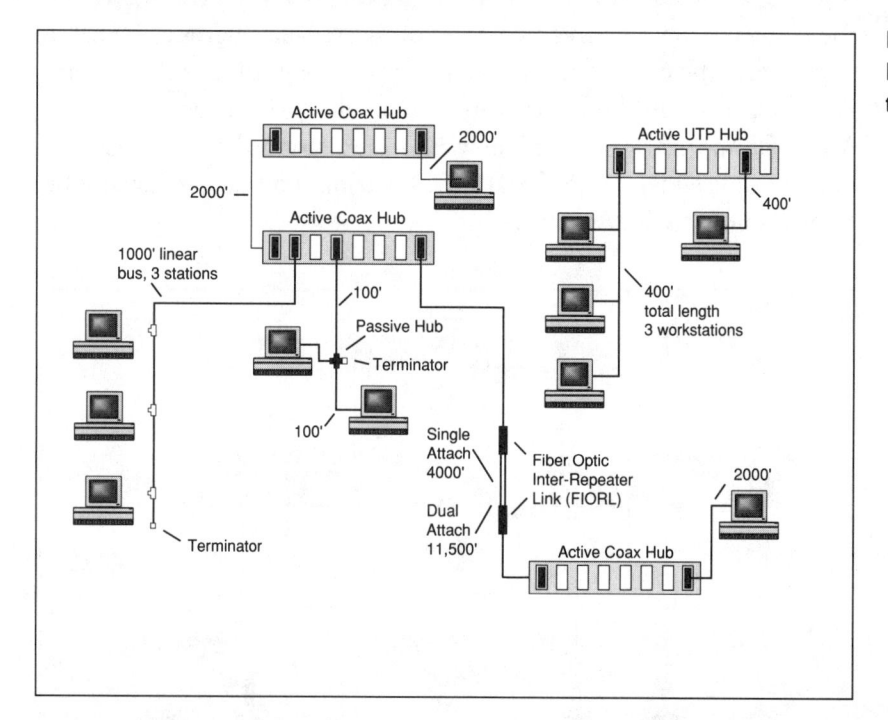

Figure C-2. Extended ArcNet topology

ETHERNET CABLE SPECIFICATIONS

Ethernet cabling specifications vary depending on the type of cable and the wiring topology used. The most common cabling specifications are referred to as 10BaseT, or Ethernet over twisted-pair, 10Base5, or thick Ethernet, and 10Base2, commonly referred to as thin Ethernet. Each cable specification differs in the overall length and number of network devices it supports, but all three methods provide a transmission speed of 10Mbs/sec. From a performance viewpoint, none of these specifications offers any advantage over another.

217

Building Local Area Networks with Windows for Workgroups

10BaseT

The 10BaseT specification connects workstations in a star-wired scheme, as shown in Figure C-3. The cable from the transceiver to the concentrator requires two pairs of twisted-pair wires. The cable connecting the concentrators can be twisted-pair, thin or thick coaxial cable, or even fiber-optic cable, depending on the concentrator. Most commercial-grade phone wiring installations have at least two pairs of unused wires, so the 10BaseT wiring method can usually be implemented with existing wiring.

**Figure C-3.
Ethernet over
10BaseT**

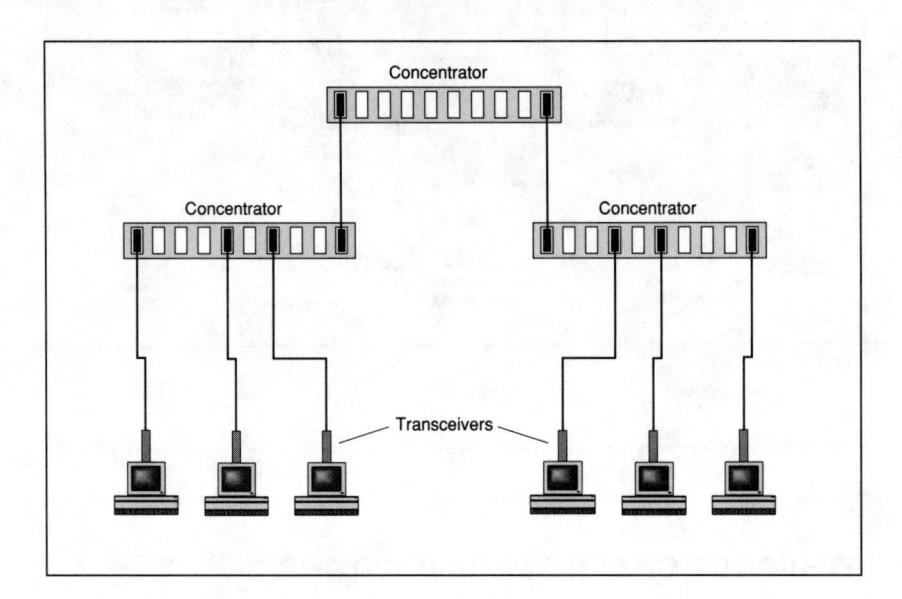

The diagram in Figure C-3 shows an external transceiver connecting each workstation to the concentrator. Many brands of Ethernet adapters now provide an RJ45 (6-wire telephone-style connector) on the card. This connector, as well as the BNC connector used in thin Ethernet installations, uses a transceiver built into the network adapter. If your network card does not have an RJ45 connector, you can purchase external transceivers that connect to the 15-pin thick Ethernet connector on your network card. External transceivers for 10BaseT cost around $60 and are available at most cable supply companies.

Network Cabling Specifications

Basic Specifications

10BaseT cable specifications are as follows:

- Cable type: Unshielded twisted-pair

- Maximum length of a segment: 100 meters

- Minimum length from workstation and concentrator: 2.5 meters

- Topology: star

The specifications listed are those specified in the IEEE specification for 802.3. While technically somewhat different from the specification for Ethernet, the two terms are commonly used interchangeably.

Most 10BaseT concentrators connect the transmit and receive pairs of wires within the concentrator. This is known as an *internal crossover*. It makes the pinout of the RJ45 connectors much simpler. In this environment, the two pairs of wire should be installed as follows:

Workstation	Wire Color	Concentrator	Usage
Pin 1	White/Green	Pin 1	Transmit –
Pin 2	Green/White	Pin 2	Transmit +
Pin 3	White/Orange	Pin 3	Receive –
Pin 4	not used		
Pin 5	not used		
Pin 6	Orange/White	Pin 6	Receive +
Pin 7	not used		
Pin 8	not used		

Building Local Area Networks with Windows for Workgroups

To connect concentrators to each other, or for concentrators that do not provide internal crossover, use a crossover cable as follows.

Concentrator	Wire Color	Concentrator
Pin 1	White/Green	Pin 3
Pin 2	Green/White	Pin 6
Pin 3	White/Orange	Pin 1
Pin 4	not used	
Pin 5	not used	
Pin 6	Orange/White	Pin 2
Pin 7	not used	
Pin 8	not used	

10Base5

The 10Base5 specification is normally wired in a trunk fashion, with drop cables from the trunk connecting to an external transceiver at the workstation. The wiring scheme is shown in Figure C-4.

Figure C-4. 10Base5 cabling

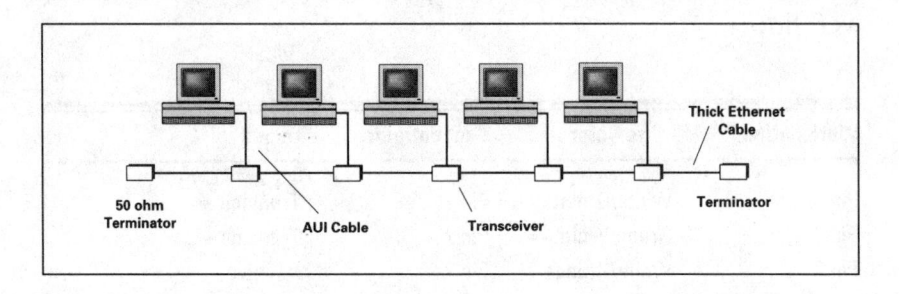

Basic Specifications

The wiring specifications for 10Base5 are as follows:

- Backbone cable type: ThickNet

- Drop cable type: $\frac{3}{8}$-inch shielded twisted-pair

Network Cabling Specifications

- Maximum length of a segment: 500 meters

- Minimum length between computers (excluding AUI cables): 2.5 meters

- Maximum length of AUI cables: 50 meters

- Topology: Bus

- Cable impedance: 50 ohms +/– 2 ohms

- Termination: 50 ohm at each end

- Maximum connected segments: 5 (using repeaters)

- Maximum computers per segment: 100

Thick Ethernet cable is normally banded at 2.5 meter intervals in order to indicate the proper location for the transceiver tap. The AUI cable uses a "vampire-tap" connector, a connector that requires a special tool for drilling into the center conductor of the thick cable. The AUI cable connects directly to the 15-pin connector on the workstation Ethernet adapter, so it is not necessary to build your own cable.

> **NOTE:** Most Ethernet adapters are configured to use the on-board transceiver and the RJ45 or BNC port connector. If you connect a transceiver to the 15-pin port, you will probably need to change jumpers on the network adapter to activate the 15-pin connector.

10Base2

The 10Base2 cable specification is commonly referred to as thinnet, or even cheapernet (due to the low cost of the coaxial cable). 10Base2 networks are a linear bus topology. The network cable travels directly from one station to the next (drop cables are not sup-

Building Local Area Networks with Windows for Workgroups

ported). 10Base2 cabling is inexpensive because no additional hardware is required. The network adapter's on-board transceiver is used and the wiring scheme does not require concentrators. A 10Base2 scheme is shown in Figure C-5.

**Figure C-5.
10Base2 wiring
topology**

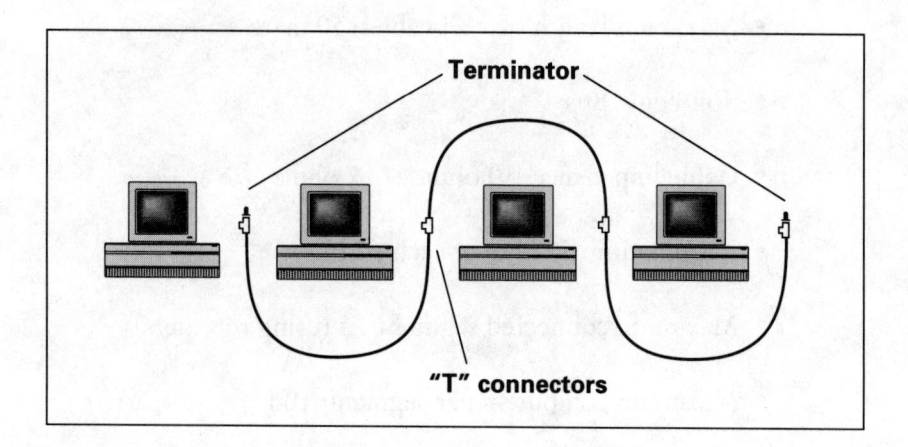

Basic Specifications

The wiring specifications for 10Base2 are as follows:

- Cable type: RG58A/U 50 ohm

- Maximum length of a segment: 185 meters

- Minimum length between computers: .5 meter

- Topology: Linear Bus

- Cable impedance: 50 ohms +/– 2 ohms

- Termination: 50 ohm at each end

- Maximum connected segments: 5 (using repeaters)

- Maximum computers per segment: 30

Network Cabling Specifications

The IEEE specification for 10Base2 specifies RG58A/U cable, but many installers prefer RG58/U. This cable has a solid center conductor, whereas RG58A/U has a stranded center conductor. As long as the distance limitations are met, you should have no problems substituting RG58/U for RG58A/U. Some manufacturers have developed extended length standards for 10Base2 that allow an individual segment to extend to 305 meters (1000 feet). These same vendors may or may not allow additional workstations on the segment (up to 100). If you elect to use the extended specifications provided by a manufacturer, you should do so only if all the network adapters on the segment can support this standard.

Glossary

10BaseT. The IEEE 802.3 standard for Ethernet on unshielded twisted-pair wiring.

10Base2. The IEEE 802.3 standard for Ethernet on thin coaxial wiring.

10Base5. The IEEE 802.3 standard for Ethernet on thick coaxial wiring.

active hub. A multi-port device used in ArcNet networks to connect workstations and other hubs. Active hubs are so named because they amplify the signal on each port.

ArcNet. A token-passing network protocol developed by the DataPoint Corporation. Once extremely popular, its use has declined in recent years.

AUI (attached unit interface) cable. A two-pair cable that attaches an Ethernet adapter to an external Ethernet transceiver.

backbone. Typically, a network design that connects multiple file servers. The backbone provides for communication between servers. Thick Ethernet cable used to connect multiple workstations or subnets is also referred to as a backbone.

base memory address. The starting address in memory used by a network adapter. The base memory address is normally located between C000 and DFFF and can vary in size.

bridge. A device used to connect separate networks. The bridge forwards traffic from one network segment to another, regardless of the frame type.

bus topology. A network cable design where each workstation is directly connected to a single cable, either by drop cables or by direct connection (local bus).

cascade. A Windows Program Manager option that layers all open windows so that each window's title bar is shown. Many applications that support multiple windows support cascading. Typically, users press the Shift-F5 hot-key combination to access cascading.

CD-ROM. A read-only disk system using compact disk technology. Current standards in CD-ROM technology allow over 650Mb of data on a single CD. Computer CDs are typically used for reference materials and read-only databases, as well as some games that support large amounts of graphic and/or sound files.

CDDI (copper distributed data interface). A modification to the FDDI specification that allows 100 Mb/sec data transmission over short distances on copper cable.

Chat. A Windows for Workgroups application that allows two workgroup members to converse in real time, using the keyboard and screen.

cheapernet. A slang term used to describe 10Base2 thin coaxial Ethernet networks, so named because of the relatively inexpensive cable used and the lack of additional hardware required for installation.

Clipboard. A Windows background application that uses computer memory to temporarily hold data that has been cut or copied from an application.

ClipBook Server. A Windows for Workgroups background application that services network requests for access to a workstation's ClipBook pages.

Glossary

ClipBook Viewer. A Windows for Workgroups accessory that allows multiple Clipboard pages to be stored to disk and shared with other members of the workgroup.

coaxial cable. A type of cable consisting of a solid or stranded center conductor, surrounded by an insulating sheath, a wire mesh shield, and a non-conductive outer layer. Also called *coax cable*.

common dialog dynamic-link library. A set of functions that allows Windows application developers to build applications that share a common look and feel. The common dialog dynamic-link library reduces the amount of programming required to perform common tasks, such as opening a file.

computer name. In Windows for Workgroups, the name assigned to a workstation during installation. Although commonly the same as the login name, the computer name can be whatever users choose.

concentrator. A multi-port repeater used in Ethernet 10BaseT installations.

conventional memory. The first 640K of memory in a computer. DOS applications are normally limited to accessing conventional memory only; Windows and Windows applications are not limited to using conventional memory.

CSMA/CD. A method of transmitting data on a wire in which stations wait for an idle state on the wire, and then transmit data. If two stations transmit concurrently, a collision occurs and each station will wait a random amount of time and then retransmit. This method is used by Ethernet. CSMA/CD stands for "carrier-sense multiple access with collision detection."

dedicated server. A personal computer whose sole function it to provide services, such as printing or file sharing, to a network. Generally, a dedicated server provides higher performance than a server that doubles as a workstation.

DDE. *See* dynamic data exchange.

direct memory access (DMA). A method of transferring data between the computer CPU and a device on the PC bus, such as a network adapter. Network adapters that use DMA cannot share their DMA channel with any other device in the system.

dynamic data exchange (DDE). A method of real-time data sharing between multiple Windows applications. For example, a DDE link between a Microsoft Word document and an Excel spreadsheet would automatically update the information in the Word document when the linked Excel spreadsheet was updated.

early token release. An extension to the standard for token-ring networks that allows multiple tokens to exist on the ring. This provides higher network throughput.

e-mail. *See* electronic mail.

electronic mail (e-mail). A messaging system that allows network users to pass messages and files back and forth.

embedded object. A data file embedded in another application's data file using a process called OLE (*see* object linking and embedding). The data file and its associated application can be accessed by double-clicking on the icon that represents the embedded object.

enhanced mode. A Windows operating mode that requires an 80386 or higher CPU. Enhanced mode supports multiple DOS and Windows applications running concurrently.

expanded memory. Memory above the first 640K of memory in a PC. Expanded memory is normally extended memory that has been converted for use as expanded memory through hardware, software, or a combination of both. Expanded memory is available only to certain DOS applications that support the Lotus-Intel-Microsoft (LIM) specification.

extended memory. Memory above the first 640K of memory in a PC. Windows for Workgroups and Windows applications use extended memory.

Glossary

FDDI (fiber distributed data interface). A network topology that supports 100 Mb/sec data transmission using fiber-optic cable media.

fiber-optic inter-repeater link. *See* FIORL.

File Manager. An application available in Windows for Workgroups that provides both file management functions and, on the LAN, the ability to advertise network file services and connect to file services.

file server. A computer that gives network users access to a common set of directories for application and data sharing.

file sharing. The ability of multiple users to access the same file(s) concurrently. File sharing requires management by the application to prevent the corruption of data.

FIORL (fiber-optic inter-repeater link). A repeater that connects networks by means of fiber-optic cable.

free system resources. Memory reserved by Windows for managing the desktop environment. Regardless of the amount of memory in a workstation, the pool of memory reserved for system resources is fixed, and Windows may report "out of memory" errors if the system resource pool drops too low.

gigabyte (Gb). A unit of data storage capacity. One Gb equals 1,073,741,824 bytes.

granularity. A Windows for Workgroups invisible grid on the desktop that controls the space between icons. The Control Panel allows you to set the spacing of this grid.

graphics mode. In PIF settings for DOS applications, selecting graphics mode informs Windows that the application requires access to graphics video addresses, as opposed to text-only applications.

GUI (graphical user interface). Windows and OS/2 are examples of graphical user interfaces.

HIMEM.SYS. An extended memory manager that maps memory addresses to applications. Windows requires HIMEM.SYS (or a third-party extended memory manager) to operate.

IEEE (Institute of Electrical and Electronic Engineers). The group that establishes standards for LAN communications.

IPX (internetwork packet exchange). The communications protocol used by workstations on a NetWare network.

inactive window. Any window on the desktop that is in the background.

interrupt line. A circuit used by an I/O device to activate a task, thereby suspending other active tasks. Normally, only one device can be assigned to an interrupt line.

linear bus. A cabling topology where devices are connected at different points along a single cable.

local bus. A wiring topology in which stations are connected in daisy-chain fashion with a terminator at each end of the cable.

logon. A process that establishes the user's connection with the network. In Windows for Workgroups, the logon process also advertises the user's presence to other members of the workgroup.

Mb/sec. A transmission speed measured in one million bits per second.

MCI device. A device that conforms to the media control interface (MCI) standard, a standard developed for multimedia devices and files. An MCI device can access a variety of input and output devices and files concurrently.

Media Player. A Windows accessory that conforms to the MCI standard and allows simultaneous access to multimedia files and hardware.

MSAU (multi-station access unit). A token-ring device used to connect multiple stations into a single ring.

multimedia. The ability to combine graphics, video, and sound

Glossary

into a single application, such as video-conferencing.

NetBEUI. An enhanced version of the NetBIOS communications protocol. Windows for Workgroups uses NetBEUI for workgroup communications.

NetBIOS. A low-level network communications protocol developed by IBM and Microsoft.

NetWare. A network operating system developed and sold by the Novell Corporation. NetWare accounts for an estimated 60 percent of the current network installed base.

NetWatcher. A Windows for Workgroups application that allows you to monitor network connections or disconnect network connections from your local workstation.

network interface card (NIC). A workstation adapter installed in a PC that provides connectivity to the network.

object. Data from one application that is inserted into a data file created by another application via object linking and embedding (OLE).

object linking and embedding (OLE). A Windows background function that allows data from multiple applications to be shared. OLE supports data hot links between applications, such that updates in the source application appear in the data file in the linked application as well.

Object Packager. A Windows OLE application that allows you to insert an object in a data file.

OLE. *See* object linking and embedding.

passive hub. An ArcNet hub used to split the active signal. Passive hubs do not amplify the signal, and can only be attached to active hubs or workstations.

program information file (PIF). A settings file used by Windows to determine the system requirements for a DOS application run under Windows.

protected mode. An operating mode available to 80286 or higher systems that enables extended memory management. Protected mode refers to the CPU's ability to protect multiple tasks from interfering with each other.

queue. A temporary holding area for printer output. The queue may be a holding place in memory, or it may be maintained on the hard drive.

RAM (random access memory). Dynamic data storage that can be accessed in any order. RAM normally refers to the amount of conventional and extended memory installed in a personal computer.

ROM (read-only memory). Permanent memory built into a device. ROM memory contains executable program code that cannot be modified by normal means.

share. In Windows for Workgroups, the selection of a directory or printer for workgroup access.

shielded twisted-pair. A wire specification with two wires twisted around each other, surrounded by a foil shield.

SMARTDrive. A disk cache utility provided in Windows for Workgroups that uses system memory to store the most frequently accessed data on the local hard drive. Subsequent requests for this data can be read directly from memory, speeding up read requests significantly.

standard mode. A Windows operating mode that supports multiple Windows applications running concurrently. Standard mode only supports one active DOS application. In standard mode, all Windows and DOS background applications are suspended when a DOS application is in the foreground.

swap file. A portion of the local hard drive set aside for moving data to and from memory, as necessary. By using swap space on the disk, Windows can appear to have more memory than is actually installed on the system.

SYSTEM.INI. A file that holds Windows setup information, such as the type of monitor, keyboard, mouse, and network type.

Glossary

task list. Displays the open applications on the desktop and allows the user to jump to a specific task. The task list, a Windows pop-up screen, can be accessed by clicking the mouse cursor on the Windows wallpaper.

Terminal. A modem communications program supplied with Windows.

terminate-and-stay-resident program. *See* TSR program.

terminator. A resistor placed at the end of a bus or repeater to prevent signals from reflecting back on to the wire.

token. A combination of bits transmitted on a token-passing topology that acts as the communications packet for the network.

token-passing ring. A network design in which each station passes a token around the ring. A station can only transmit if it can attach data to the end of an unused token. Normally, only one token can exist on the ring.

tracking speed. A Control Panel setting that determines the ability of Windows to keep pace with mouse movement.

transceiver. A media converter from one Ethernet topology to another.

TrueType font. A font technology that allows fonts to be displayed on-screen exactly as they will look when printed. TrueType font sizes can be scaled to any size on both the screen and printer.

TSR (terminate-and-stay-resident) program. A program that runs as a background task under DOS. The network drivers that load prior to starting Windows are examples of TSR programs.

unshielded twisted-pair (UTP). A wire specification with two wires twisted around each other, without any additional shielding.

virtual machine. In Windows enhanced mode, refers to when Windows can create multiple 640K DOS sessions, and maintain separate DOS applications. Each application appears to run on its own separate computer.

virtual memory. In Windows enhanced mode, refers to Windows' ability to swap idle applications to disk. Virtual memory provides the appearance of additional memory in the workstation.

wallpaper. A Paintbrush image that can be used as a backdrop to the desktop.

WIN.INI. The file that stores Windows environment settings, such as output devices and wallpaper selection.

WinMeter. A Windows for Workgroups utility that graphically displays the CPU utilization of a workstation.

workgroup. Personal computers linked via a network, and logically grouped by function or department.

Index

A

A/U coaxial cable 26
About Program Manager 57
accepting requests 134
Access Type radio button 43
access levels 136
access rights 125
access to others' schedules 134
accessing a shared ClipBook page 88
accessing shared directories 76
accessories 85–95
active hubs 23, 29
adapters 178
Address command 117
ADMIN account 108
advanced memory management
    functions 160
advanced power management (APM)
    91, 206
Advanced... 163
alarm feature 129
Allow Close When Active 167
Allow Fast Paste 167
allowing others to update your
    schedule 138
Always on Top option 90–91
APM 91
Application Shortcut Keys 167
Applications Registration Editor 206

applications, third-party 101
Appts 127
archiving old messages 123
ArcNet 17, 19, 21, 23, 27–28
    basic specifications 214–215
    Plus 216
    20 Mb/sec 28
    twisted-pair 216
Attach command 117
Attached Resource Computer Network
    (ArcNet) 29
Attendees: Change... button 130
auto-detection portion of Setup 172
AUTOEXEC.BAT 37, 51, 53, 143–144,
    172, 181

B

backbone 25
Background box 163
background operation 159
background task 159
backing up data 97
backing up files 103
backup procedures 102
base input/output (I/O) address 64
base memory address 64
basic specifications for
    ArcNet 215
    10Base2 222

basic specifications for *(continued)*
   10Base5 220
   10BaseT 2190
   Token Ring 212
beacon frames 214
bell icon 128
BNC connector 26, 218
[boot] 147
[boot.description] 147
BROADCAST 66
Browse 53, 78
bus topology 25, 29
button bar 120

C

cable 175
   fault 211
   plant 18
cache memory 92
Calculator 204
cancelling print jobs 81
Cardfile 204
CD-ROM Drive 17, 78, 180
Change Logon Password 67
changing default level of access 135
Character Map 204
Chat 85, 93, 207
Check Names command 117
CHKDSK 182
client piece 107
Clipboard 86
Clipboard viewer 204
ClipBook 85–88
   accessing shared pages 88
   pages 86
   Viewer 85–86
[ClipShares] 147
Clock 204
Close Window on Exit 163
coaxial cable 18–19, 23
[colors] 145
COMBoostTime 178
COMM port 18
COMMDLG.DLL 83
common dialog dynamic link library
   (COMMDLG.DLL) 73, 83

communications buffer 178
comparative priority of a DOS
   application 164
Compose button 116
compressing mail folders 98
Comptible Networks screen 65
Computer name 49
computer virus 101
COMxBuffer= 178
concentrators 25, 220
CONFIG.SYS 37, 51, 53, 143–144,
   172, 181
Connect Network Drive... command 79
connecting to Network Drives 77
Control Panel 60, 81, 204
Control Panel's 386 Enhanced
   dialog box 165
CONTROL.INI 142
controlling viral infections 101
conventional memory 160
conversation boxes 94
Copy command 86
CPU priority 159
CPU requirements 11
create a shared folder 120
creating a Workgroup Postoffice 110
CSMA/CD 28
CUSTOM installation 35
custom PIF file 154
customizing Windows for each
   workstation 58
Cut command 86

D

DataPoint Corporation 27, 29
[DDEShares] 147
dedicated server 10, 71
_DEFAULT.PIF 157
default level of access 135
degradation, performance 80
Delete 78
Delete Directory 78
deleted mail folder 115
deleting files 209
designing the physical network 21–31
[desktop] 145

Index

Detect Idle Time box 165
[devices] 145
Dial command 93
dialing into the network 56
Directly Modifies 169
directories, shared 99, 150
directory 57
Disconnect 94
Disconnect Network Drive... 78
disconnect a user 92
Disk command 41
disk compression programs 71
disk sharing 99
disk space 12
Display Usage 163
display driver files 190
distance limits, cabling 22
DLE 86
DLL 73
DMA 17
DOS 14
    applications 71, 119, 160
        comparative priority of 164
        under Windows 153–155
    client access 45
    communications programs in a
        windowed DOS session 178
    executable file 157
    Mail 45, 49, 107
    prompt 71
    requirements 14
    DOS screen updates 163
DOSPRMPT.PIF 157
dot-matrix printers 82
Dr. WATSON 182
Dr. Watson diagnostic utility 205
[drivers] 147
driver files 187
dual twisted-pair cabling 24
dynamic data exchange (DLE) 86
dynamic link library (DLL) 73, 187

E

e-mail gateways 45
EditLevel 152
EGA-compatible 13
8415/A 13
80386/80486 advanced memory
    management functions 160
EISA 17
electronic mail 45
[embedding] 145
emmexclude= 173
EMS Memory 181
    Locked 165
    settings 162
Emulate Text Mode box 166
Enable Sharing 61
Enhanced Mode PIF Settings 164
enhanced mode 11, 34, 39, 57, 69, 155,
    160, 173, 174
ET 4000 adapters 13
EtherExpress 17, 21, 29
Ethernet 17, 19, 21, 25–27
    cable specifications 217
    fast 27
    Thick 26
    thin 217
Excel 4.0 84
Exclusive box 163
exclusive operation 159
Execution boxes 163
Exit option 126
Export 122
export folders 114
EXPORT.MMF 122
EXPRESS installation 35
extended length standards for
    10Base2 223
extended memory 160
[extensions] 145
external transceiver 218

F

fast Ethernet 27
FasTips 183
fault-domain 214
fax gateways 45
Fiber Optic 216
fiber distributed data interface (FDDI) 25
File Copy 78
File Manager 40–41, 73, 76, 78, 207

File Open command 83
File Save As command 83
file services 98
files for enhanced mode operation
    203–204
files for standard mode operation 202
Flash envelope 124
folders within folders 120
font files 187, 196–199
[fonts] 145
Fonts option 158–159
[FontSubstitutes] 145
foreground task 159
full-screen 159

G

GDI.EXE 188
General Protection fault 181–182
Genius mouse 13
grabber files 210
graphic screens 94
graphical interface 13, 169

H

hard disk requirements 12
hardware device conflict 173
hardware, network 14
Hearts 85
[Hearts] 145
Hearts game 205
Hercules-compatible 13
Hewlett-Packard mouse 13
High Graphics 161
HIMEM 14
hub 22–23

I

I/O port address 175
IBM's Premise Wiring 212
icons for DOS or Windows applications
    209
IEEE 30, 214
    802.5 211
    specifications for 802.3 219
Import command 122–123
import folders 114

Inbox 115
incremental backups 104
INI files 141
initialization (INI) files 141
installation of
    CUSTOM 35
    EXPRESS 35
    Windows for Workgroups 33
    Windows from the network 54
    Workgroup Connection 46
Institute of Electrical and Electronic
    Engineers (IEEE) 30
insufficient memory 177
Intel EtherExpress 17, 29
internal crossover 219
international support files 199
interrupt 17, 175
interrupt level 64
[intl] 145
invite button 129
IPX/SPX 37
ISA 17

J

joystick ports 178

K

key icon 128
[keyboard] 147
keyboard drivers 189
KRNL286.EXE 188
KRNL386.EXE 188

L

LAN Manager 37, 49, 65
LAN, wiring 9
LASTDRIVE parameter 38, 53
LASTDRIVE=Z 53
limiting Program Manager functions 148
Linear Bus 216
local bus 26
local copy 138
local printing 82
Lock Application Memory 166, 179
Log On at Startup 65
log of tape backups 103

Index

Logitech DOS driver 176
Logitech mice 13
Logon
    button 65
    settings screen 65
    screen 39
loop-back mode 211
lost passwords 59, 67
Lotus 1-2-3 155
Low Graphics 161

M

[Mail] 145
mail
    command 78
    engine 125
    program, DOS-based 45
    server 70
    administration 97
    gateway 114
    server 69, 108
    system 83
    3.x extension 108
mail-server piece 107
Main program group 40–41
maintaining shared folders 98
Make Directory 78
master directory 34
master Windows directory 40
master Windows server 56
Math coprocessor 18
MAU 23, 30
MCA 17
[mci extenstions] 145
[mci] 147
Media Player 205
media access unit (MAU) 23
memory management 11
Memory Requirements 12, 162, 169
merging off-line and network schedules 138–139
merging schedules 135
Messages enabled 66
metafiles 82
mice ports 178
Microsoft
    Bulletin Board 183
    diagnostic utility 205
    Mail 107, 205
    mouse driver 176
    mouse 13
    Resource Kits 183
MineSweeper game 208
Minimize command 123
modems 17
Monitor Ports 166
monitors 13
Mouse Systems mouse 13
mouse 17, 176
    driver files 190
    requirements 13
[MRU_Files] 145
[MRU_Printers] 145
MS-DOS 5.0 165, 177
MS-DOS driver files 200
MSAU 19
MSCDEX 180
msipx command 38
MSMail 35
MSMAIL.INI 109, 114, 142, 179
multimedia driver files 195
multistation access unit (MSAU) 19
multitasking 169–170
    environment 153
    options box 164
    options settings 165

N

Named Pipes 50
NAUN 214
NDDE 88
NDIS network adapter card drivers 201
NET command 52
NET START 39
NET.EXE 50, 53
    configuration 55
    popup menu 54
NETBEUI 30, 180
NETBIOS 10, 36–37, 95
NetWare 17, 37, 49, 54, 65, 84, 95
    Users 180
    server support by UNC 75

NetWatcher 85, 92, 104, 206
[network] 145, 147
network
    adapter 14, 27
    adapter drivers 14–16
    administrator 10, 97, 100, 105
    backup and recovery 102
    button 83
    cabling 22
    copy 138
    DDE 92
    dialing in 56
    driver files 194–195
    drivers 99
    Drives, connecting to 77
    Drives, disconnecting from 78
    dynamic data exchange (NDDE) 88
    Dynamic Data Interchange 206
    functions 99
    hardware 14
    icon 60
    interface adapters 48
    menu system 149
    outages 21
    peer-to-peer 45
    printers 81–82
    queues 82
    Settings screen 62
    warnings 66
    topology 21
Network... button 117
netx command 38
New Folder... 120
New Mail 124
next active upstream neighbor (NAUN) 214
No Save Screen box 169
No Screen Exchange 169
NoClose 151
NoFileMenu 151
[NonWindowsApp] 147
NoRun 151
NoSaveSettings 151
Notepad 206
Novell 65

NWPOPUP 66
NWShare handles 66

O

Object Packager
object linking and embedding (OLE) 86
off-line 125–126
OLE 86
operating modes,
    enhanced 11
    standard 11
    Windows 10
operating systems, peer-to-peer 10
optimizing server performance 57–72
Optional Parameters 161
outbox 115

P

Paint application 86
Paintbrush 206
passive hubs 23, 29, 216
[Password Lists] 59, 147
passwords 40, 52
    file 40, 59
    lost 59, 67
    restrictions 78
    synchronized 59
    table 52
Paste function 86
PCAnywhere 56
peer environment 101
peer network 61
peer-to-peer networks 45
peer-to-peer operating system 10
Performance Priority 61–62, 71
performance 99
performance degradation 80
permanent swap file 69–70
personal schedule 134
physical networks 21–31
PIF 154
    Editor 155, 206
    files 155
Planner 127
[ports] 145
post office 107, 109

Index

Postoffice Manager... option 113
PostScript-capable printer 80
Preven Program Switch box 169
preventing viral infections 101
Print Manager 40, 71, 73, 80, 82, 206
    Options menu 81
    time-out 176
Print Screen key 86
print jobs
    cancelling 81
    status of 80
print queue 81
print server 57
printer
    connections screen 54
    driver 81
    driver files 191–194
    program 81
    setup 143
    setup command 83
    sharing on the network 80
[PrinterPorts] 146
printers
    dot-matrix 82
    networked 81–82
    PostScript-capable 80
    sharing 54
printing
    local 82
    options 66
    priority 82
prioritizing tasks 132
priority button 119
private
    appointments 129
    folders 116
    meetings 137
PROGMAN.INI 141–142, 148
PROGMAN.INI, sharing groups 150
program information file (PIF) 154
Program Manager 206
Program Manager, limiting functions 148
[programs] 145
PROTOCOL.INI 64–65, 142
PS/2 mouse 13

Q
QEMM 14
QEMM386 177

R
RAM 17
Re-share at startup box 43
read-access 130
read-only
    access 77, 100
    network directory 99
    restrictions 78
Reconnect at startup box 54
Recorder 206
Redirector 50
remote connections 92
remote servers 175
Rename 78
Request Meeting... button 131
requests, accepting 134
requirements
    CPU 11
    DOS 14
    hard disk 12
    memory 12
    mouse 13
    software licensing 100
    video 13
Reserve Shortcut Keys 167
Reshare at Startup command 79
responses to meeting requests 132
Restore drives 66
restoring data 97
[restrictions] 150–151
Retain Video Memory 161, 166
return receipt 119
RG-58 26
ring topology 25
ring-in ports 23
ring-out ports 23
running DOS and Windows apps
    concurrently 155

S
save sent messages 119
SCHDPLUS.INI 142

Schedule+ 35, 107, 125–140, 207
    extension 108
    Planner 130
Scheduling 69
Scheduling Appointments 126–127
screen saver 70
security mechanisms 98
selecting a LAN architecture 27
SEND 66
Send Documents Directly box 82
Send Meeting Messages Only to my
    Assistant option 137
sending and receiving meeting
    requests 135
Sent mail folder 115
Separator Pages 71, 81
server 103
server performance
    improving 70
    optimizing 57–72
server-centric 72
servername 74
servers, dedicated 10
Set Access Privileges... command 135
Settings option 158
SETUP command 35, 55
SETUP Workgroup Connection 46
Setup 81, 171
    button 64
    Files 208
SETUP/A 34
SETUP/N 172
shadow RAM 175
shadow ROM 175
Share
    As... command 41, 76, 79
    Directory dialog box 76
    Item now button 86
    Name field 42–43
share applications 98
shared
    directories 99, 150
    directories, accessing 76
    folders 113, 116
    resource 98
shared-memory address 175

SHARED.INI 142
sharename 74
sharing
    groups with PROGMAN.INI 150
    network devices 69
    printers 54
    schedules 131
Shell library 207
shielded twisted pair cable 18–19
shortcut keys 116
Show Printers option 54
Show Queue 54
shrink-wrapped software 102
Sign-Out option 126
smart icons 114
SMARTDrive 174
SMARTDrive disk-cache software 207
SmartDrive 71
SmartDrive cache 72
software licensing 97
    requirements 100
    restrictions 98–99
Solitaire game 207
Sound chime 124
Sound Recorder 207
sound cards 178
[sounds] 146
[spooler] 146
[standard] 147
Standard Mode PIF settings 168
standard mode 11, 154, 173
star topology 22–23, 25, 29, 211
star-cluster 214
Start Applicaton on Connect box 87
Start-up Directory 161
starting Windows 57
status of print jobs 80
STEALTH mode 177
Stop Sharing... command 78
store and forward design 107
Super VGA 13
suspend DOS programs 69
swap 12
swap files 12–13, 69, 210
SWAPDISK= entry 71
swapping to disk 69

Index

synchronized passwords 59
sysedit 143
SYSINI.WRI 148, 152
System Integrity 181
System performance meter 208
system files 102
system name 36
SYSTEM.INI 59, 71, 141–148, 152, 173

T

T-connectors 26
tape backup across the network 104
tape drives 103
tape rotation scheme 103–104
Task List dialog box 155
task list 131
Tasks 127
tasks, prioritizing 132
TDD/TT 183
telephone icon 93
telephone wiring 23
TEMP=variable 176
temporary swap files 69, 71, 210
10Base2 28, 31, 217, 221
    basic specifications 222
    extended length standards 223
10Base5 28, 31, 217, 220
    basic specifications 220
10BaseT 19, 25, 28, 31, 217–218
    basic specifications 219
tentative appointments 129
Terminal communications program 207
Terminate button 159
terminate and stay resident (TSR) 171
Thick Ethernet 26
thin Ethernet 217
Thinnet cable 19, 26
third-party applications 101
third-party memory managers 14
[386Enh] 147
TIGA 13
time-out, Print Manager 176
Token Ring 17, 19, 21, 23–24, 30
    basic specifications 212
    cable specifications 211

4 Mb/sec 27
16 Mb/sec 27
Token-Express 17
token-passing 29
topology 31
tracking workgroup resources 134, 137
transceiver, external 218
Transmission Retry 176
[TrueType] 146
TrueType fonts 181, 198
TSRs 171, 181
twisted-pair, ArcNet 216

U

UNC 73, 179
    directory name 78
    name 78–79
    NetWare server support 75
uninterruptible power supplies 105
universal naming convention (UNC) 73, 179
unshielded twisted pair cable 18–19, 23, 25, 211
update drivers 46
upper memory 14
usage count 101
User name 49
USER.EXE 188
Uses High Memory Area 165
using Windows for Workgroups 73
using Workgroup Connection 45

V

vector font files 198
VGA 13
    color monitor 13
    driver 13, 71
Video
    Display 172
    Memory buttons 161
    Mode 169
    hardware 13
    modes 154
    processor 71
    requirements 13
    7 13

viral infections, preventing and
    controlling 101
Virtual Memory 69
virtual machine 160
VirtualHDirq= 174
virus-detection software 102

W

WGPO 110
WGPO\CAL directory 139
WIN command 38
WIN.COM 188
WIN.INI 141–148
WIN/3 12
WIN/S 12, 173
Windows
    help 208
    INI files 141
    installation utility 205
    operating modes 10
    Resource Kit 183
    Setup 33, 46, 143
    shortcut keys 185–186
    System Editor 207
    Task Manager 207
    3.0 print drivers 181
    Tool Helper library 207
    Tutorial 208
    Write 208
[Windows] 146
[WindowsHelp] 146

Windows for Workgroups
    accessories 85–95
    installation 33
    Resource Kit 183
    Starter Kit 29
    starting 38
    using 73–84
WINFILE.INI 142
WININI.WRI 148, 152
WinMeter 85, 89–90
wiring 9
Word 2.0 84
Word application 86
Workgroup Connection 33, 43, 55, 104
    installing 46
    SETUP 46
    using 45
workgroup name 36, 49
working off-line 125–126

X

XGA-compatible 13
XMS memory 160, 181
    locked 165
    settings 162

Tell us what you think and we'll send you a free M&T Books catalog

It is our goal at M&T Books to produce the best technical books available. But you can help us make our books even better by letting us know what you think about this particular title. Please take a moment to fill out this card and mail it to us. Your opinion is appreciated.

Tell us about yourself

Name_____
Company_____
Address_____
City_____
State/Zip_____

Title of this book?
_____

Where did you purchase this book?
☐ Bookstore
☐ Catalog
☐ Direct Mail
☐ Magazine Ad
☐ Postcard Pack
☐ Other

Why did you choose this book?
☐ Recommended
☐ Read book review
☐ Read ad/catalog copy
☐ Responded to a special offer
☐ M&T Books' reputation
☐ Price
☐ Nice Cover

How would you rate the overall content of this book?
☐ Excellent
☐ Good
☐ Fair
☐ Poor

Why?
_____
_____

What chapters did you find valuable?
_____
_____
_____

What did you find least useful?
_____
_____
_____

What topic(s) would you add to future editions of this book?
_____
_____
_____

What other titles would you like to see M&T Books publish?
_____
_____

Which format do you prefer for the optional disk?
☐ 5.25"   ☐ 3.5"

Any other comments?
_____
_____
_____

☐ Check here for M&T Books Catalog

M&T BOOKS

**NO POSTAGE
NECESSARY
IF MAILED
IN THE
UNITED STATES**

BUSINESS REPLY MAIL
FIRST CLASS MAIL PERMIT 2660 SAN MATEO, CA

POSTAGE WILL BE PAID BY ADDRESSEE

M&T BOOKS
411 Borel Avenue, Suite 100
San Mateo, CA 94402-9885

— PLEASE FOLD ALONG LINE AND STAPLE OR TAPE CLOSED —